OSWALD**COOPER** FREEMAN "JERRY" **CRAW** LOUIS**DANZIGER** LUC(AS)de**GROOT**

RUDOLFde**HARAK** W.A.**DWIGGINS** ELLIS**SITZKY** ROBERT**ESTIENNE**

DAVE**FAREY** LOUISE**FILI** TOBIAS**FRERE-JONES** ADRIAN**FRUTIGER**

ABRAM**GAMES** CLAUDE**GARAMOND** ERIC**GILL** MILTON**GLASER**

FREDERIC W.**GOUDY** CHAUNCEY H.**GRIFFITH** APRIL**GREIMAN** JOHANN**GUTENBERG**

	GREEK SOURCE	MEANING
Photography	"phos" = light	*light drawing*
Topography	"topos" = place	*place drawing*
Stenography	"stenos" = narrow	*constricted writing*
Iconography	"ikon" = image	*pictorial representation*
Biography	"bios" = life	*life writing*
Lithography	"lithos" = stone	*stone drawing*
Typography	"typos" = letters	*type drawing*

Thinking in Type

The Practical Philosophy of Typography

Alex W. White

◀☐ A spread from an early
20th century type book.
For some, this is a fasci-
nating display and gets
the blood circulating as
powerfully as looking at
the selection in the cases
at an ice cream shop.

ALLWORTH PRESS
NEW YORK

12   11   10   09   08   7   6   5   4   3

"Language is not an abstract construction of the learned...but is something arising out of the work, needs, ties, joys, affections, and tastes, of long generations of humanity. Its base is broad and low, close to the ground." *Walt Whitman, Slang in America*

Published by Allworth Press
An imprint of Allworth Communications
10 East 23rd Street, New York, NY 10010

Book design, typography, and composition by
Alexander W. White, New York, NY

Library of Congress Cataloging-in-Publication Data
White, Alex (Alex W.)
Thinking in type : the practical philosophy of typography/
    Alex W. White.
      p. cm.
      Includes bibliographical references and index.
ISBN 1-58115-384-8 (pbk.)

1. Type and type-founding.
2. Graphic design (Typography)
3. Type and type-founding History 20th century.
4. Graphic design (Typography) History 20th century.
I. Title.
   Z250.W565 2005
   686.2'21DC22
   2004026955

Printed in the United States

Thinking in Type
The Practical Philosophy of Typography

Contents

66 If you think you are capable of living without writing, do not write." *Rainer Maria Rilke* To which I add, "The same goes for designing."

Preface

We have seen the evolution of type from being professionally prepared and proofread to just another responsibility among many of the modern design professional. I wrote *How to Spec Type* in 1985 when type was beginning its transition from a product a designer bought from a provider to a responsibility of the designer himself, made on the computer in the process of designing. From 1450 through the early years of the 19th century, the printer was the typesetter and, quite often, the type designer as well. From the early 1800s to the early 1900s, the printer bought type from a foundry, a specialist who frequently developed his own technology for setting the characters. He thereby cornered the market on his particular typefaces, so if a printer eventually wanted an additional size of type in a family, there was only one place to get it.

As the 20th century progressed, offset lithography was introduced which allowed a printing plate to be made from a photographic negative. Some printers found they enjoyed and were skilled at the organization of materials in readiness for reproduction. They evolved into graphic designers, a term that was invented in 1922 by William Addison Dwiggins.* These new designers began

66 Quantum potes tantum aude" or "Whatever your talents, use them to their fullest." *Beatrice Warde's headstone, Surrey, England.*

* Dwiggins (1880-1956) designed 280 books for Alfred A. Knopf, illustrated some, wrote extensively on design, and developed typefaces, seventeen of which were released by Linotype. Dwiggins said, *"I like to design type. Like to jiggle type around and see what comes out. Like to design ornaments. Like paper. Like ink on paper. Like bright colors. Handicapped by clock."*

Thanks to Jenson, Griffo, Arrighi, Garamond, Caslon, Baskerville, Goudy, Tschichold, Dwiggins, Preissig, and Menhart, whose work has inspired me to see beauty and define type's workability for myself. ▷ Carol Wahler and my fellow board members of The Type Directors Club, for the opportunity to deepen my understanding of type and typography by their association, and for access to their extraordinary type library. ▷ Tad Crawford, for encouraging this book's existence. ▷ Sneaux, Rosinha, and Isabela for making the office a much nicer place each day. ▷ P-BOB. ▷ And Lilian, always Lilian.

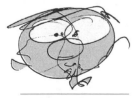

This book is dedicated to Emil, Karla, and Honzíček, whose legacy is men and manuscripts.

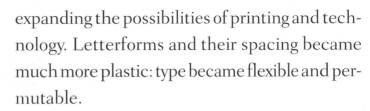

expanding the possibilities of printing and technology. Letterforms and their spacing became much more plastic: type became flexible and permutable.

In the mid-1980s, the computer became a companion in designers' offices. Throughout the 1990s, the definition of designer expanded to add the responsibilities of typesetter, proofreader, and photo retoucher. The computer has not yet proved to be *our* labor-saving device.

Typography cannot be faked. It is either clear, interpretive of the content, and appropriate to its message, or it is a random treatment that only superficially looks daring and current.

I am not aware of there ever having been a *Typography Tips and Tricks* column in a design magazine. I am certain there is no Photoshop filter for instant typographic excellence. Typography can only be mastered one hard lesson at a time. It is not for every designer because it requires a particular perspective and a gift for details. But there are a double handful of common sense guidelines that will immediately improve anyone's use of type. I have tried to put them all in this book. *Alex W. White*

NEW YORK CITY

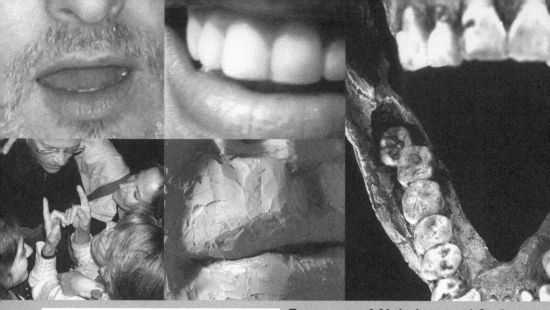

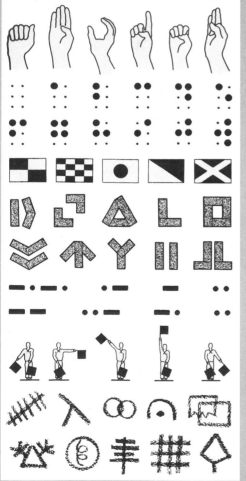

Taxonomy of Alphabets and Scripts

Alphabets	Scripts	Genera of Scripts	Families of Scripts
Czech			
Dinka			
English			
German			
Hawaiian			
Icelandic			
Irish			
Kazakh	Neoroman		
Latin			
Malay		Romanoid	
Navajo			
Serbo-Croatian			
Spanish			
Swedish			
Turkish			
Latin	Paleoroman		
German	Fraktur		
Irish	Gaelic		Hellenic
Buryat			
Chuvash			
Kazakh			
Russian			
Serbo-Croatian	Neocyrillic	Cyrilloid	
Udmurt			
Ukrainian			
Yakut			
Old Church Slavic	Paleo-cyrillic		
Modern Greek	Neohellenic	Hellenoid	
Coptic	Coptic		
Hindi-Urdu			
Marathi			
Nepali	Devanagari		
Panjabi			
Assamese		Devanagaroid	
Bengali	Bengali		
Gujarati	Kaithi		
Oriya	Oriya		
Panjabi	Gurmukhi		
Tibetan	Tibetan		Brahmic
Kannada	Kannada	Telugoid	
Telugu	Telugu		
Tamil	Tamil	Tamiloid	
Malayalam	Malayalam	Keraloid	
Burmese			
Mon	Burmese	Burmoid	
Shan			
Lao	Siamese	Saimoid	
Thai			
Armenian	Armenian	Armenoid	
Georgian	Khutsuri	Paleokart-veloid	Mesropic
Georgian	Mkhedruli	Neokart-veloid	
Amharic	Ethiopic		
Ge'ez			
Cherokee	Sequoyah		
Korean	Hangul		
Cree	Evans		
Eskimo			
Hebrew			
Karaim	Hebrew		
Yiddish			
Arabic			
Hindi-Urdu			
Kazakh			
Panjabi	Naskhi	Araboid	
Pashto			
Persian			
Turkish			

Introduction

“The art of typography which produces (books) renders countless vital services to society… The duty of typography is to be the agent and general interpreter of wisdom and truth. In short, it portrays the human spirit.” PIERRE SIMON FOURNIER (LE JEUNE), 1764

SPOKEN LANGUAGE Humans have been on earth for about 500,000 years. The first written language dates from around 3,500BC and the alphabet from about 1,500BC. Before writing, people kept information in their heads. Writing evolved in many places more or less at once, each civilization taking and expanding on what they learned through trading and travel. Writing is an act of composition, regardless of whether the thoughts are recorded as writing. Human development includes much writing before the invention of any written language: our ancestors relied on memorization. Writing makes it possible to pass information across space and time: I wrote this in New York City in 2004. You are reading it someplace and sometime else.

WRITTEN LANGUAGE & READING Language existed first as spoken systems. Afterwards, they were given their graphic representations. The variety and beauty of letterforms can be appreciated separate of their linguistic meaning, that is, for their own sake. But the essential, inescapable function of writing is to transmit information. Any letter by itself is a mark taken out of context. Letters must be seen in groups – words and sentences, as members of their families. We read by recognizing word shapes. Consequently, it becomes a significant disadvantage to set lengthy type in all caps (or, for that matter, to deny children reading as a daily exercise because they do not develop a familiarity with word shapes). If we designers always put the reader first, type will be accessible.

ALPHABET	CHARACTERS
Arabic	28
Etruscan	17
Greek, Early	21
Greek, Classical	20
Hebrew, Old	19
Latin, Early	20
Phoenician	19
Roman	26

A selection of alphabets show how quantities of sounds are captured as symbols. Galileo (1564–1642) said, “What loftiness of mind was that of man who thought of a way to communicate to whatever other person, though separated by the longest of intervals of space and time, to speak with those as yet unborn. All through various groupings of twenty simple letters on paper.”

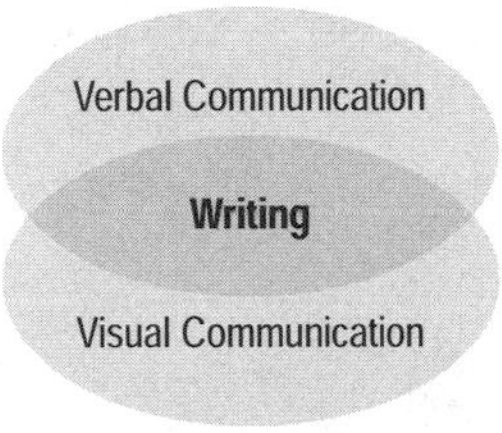

Writing is where spoken language and visual language meet. It is natural that writing look like spoken language frozen in time and place. This may, in fact, be all the guide you need as a typographer.

“I believe that reading, (is) that fruitful miracle of communication in the midst of solitude.” *Marcel Proust, On Reading*

له هلمّ اهب لك نبلا فمضي معه فتدم من قتله ووهب له نبلا فلما

ها تأبل شرا اخبرها فقالت انه والله شيطان من الشياطين والله ما

有 柯 常 他 山 來 走 見 狂 祀
來 做 不 說 西 的 那 我 、 好
全 、 什 你 反 〇 一 有 咱

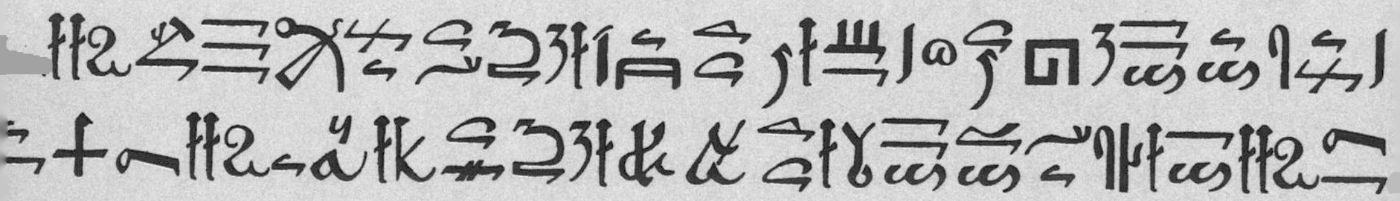

τους ὥστε καὶ τοὺς Λακεδαιμονίους πρόσθεν οὐ δεχόμενοι εἰς τὸ
οἱ Φλειάσιοι, φοβούμενοι μὴ τοὺς φάσκοντας ἐπὶ λακωνισμῷ φεύγ
οιεν, τότε οὕτω κατεπλάγησαν τοὺς ἐκ Κορίνθου ὥστε μετεπέμψα

לוֹת הַכֹּל · לְבַדּוֹ יִמְלֹךְ נוֹרָא : וְהוּא הָיָה · וְהוּא הֹוֶה · וְהוּא
בְּתִפְאָרָה : וְהוּא אֶחָד וְאֵין שֵׁנִי · לְהַמְשִׁיל לוֹ לְהַחְבִּירָה : בְּ

のくり笑とか派せ恐とに風力で多のz
菊獨人 。仗刺仗ととらら的於と量ヽく作え
五步物又l激りするくりてヽよヽの物て

гдежзиійклмнопрстуфхцчшщъыьѣэюяѳѵаѕ
ВГДЕЖЗИІЙКЛМНОПРСТУФХЦЧШЩЪЫ

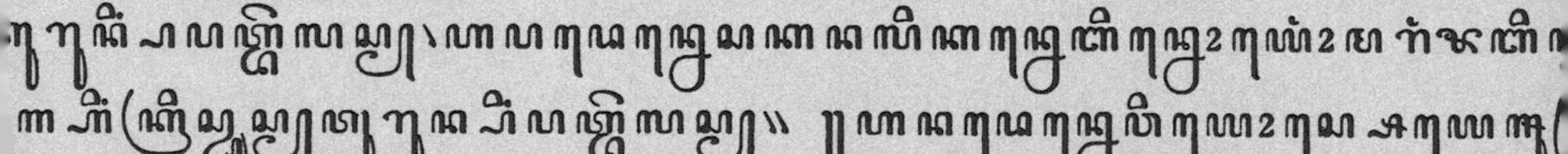

ظلم و بیداد این طایفه کار بر اهالی جزیره بقسمی تنک شد که چار ناچ
ایف شمالی آلمان آنگل و سکسن و جوت پناه برده استمداد نمودند که ش
ایت و کمک آنان از شرّ وحشیان مزبوره جانی بسلامت بدر برند این

ون اولدی سر نوشتی دل بی تحملك چیقمز درونمزده‌کی سودای سنبلك
هی سورك کم دل سلیم قادرمیدر که نظم ایده بوبله در نظیم اواسه

◁ World type: Arabic, Chinese, Egyptian hieroglyphics, Egyptian hieratic script, Greek, Hebrew with vowels (indicated by dots), Japanese, Javanese, Persian, Russian, and Turkish. Reading directions have included back and forth (*boustrophedon*), spiraled, left to right, vertical, and right to left.

TYPE HISTORY & RULES Writing systems evolved from symbol systems. Cave paintings, for example, are symbols. When man needed to record complex abstract ideas, symbols were no longer adequate. Languages that combined stylized symbols into new meanings began to emerge. The Roman alphabet, for example, is a collection of abstract symbols that no longer have meaning on their own, but work only in combination.

Movable type was invented in 1450AD. Display type was invented around 1500, when the quantity of printed material began to accumulate and identifying content quickly became more important. Metal type was in use until the 1960s. Phototype was in use in 1950 and digital type was introduced to common use in 1985. Letterforms and the technology that made them are closely related. Whether by stick, brush, chisel, wood block, metal plate, film negative, or a string of 1s and 0s, letterforms reflect the time in which they were made. Typography parallels developments in the arts, politics, literature, and science and technology. Since 1450, mankind's knowledge has expanded exponentially and written language has been part of virtually every activity.

△ Chinese (opposite, second from top) had been printed from woodblocks since the 9th century. But Gutenberg propelled world knowledge and culture by inventing *movable, reusable* type (above). This is his 1450 *Gotische Schrift* ("Gothic Script") shown at actual size.

Until the 1400s, writing as a thought container and as a visual form were generally done by the same person. Then the printer took over the role of reproduction. Authors began to care less and less about the form of their manuscripts since a printer would inherit it and convert it. Many printers were highly cultured, but as decades and centuries passed, they became more technicians and less writers. Yet the task of printers and today's designers remains the same as ever: to present information as visibly, as efficiently, and as memorably as possible.

□ The ballpoint pen made handwriting more fluid and changed the way we write and make letters. The dotted paths in this diagram show where a fountain pen would have difficulty completing the line.

The history of type's use is crucial to understanding how to use type in contemporary terms. That is why a good part of this book is devoted to the development of writing and type. By studying the pages in section 4 of this book, you will gain insight in how the marks we have came to be, how they have evolved, and how we have used them as type for the past 550 years. Confidence to break the rules is fun, creative, and serves readers.

⌂ Type can be decorative and communicative: Don Dyer's photo, Eric Gill's sketch; the author's inking for a book cover.

TYPOGRAPHY Typography is not mere typesetting. It is processing visual language to enhance its strength and clarity. Spoken language has a few components that add to the message: *Metacommunication* is about communication itself: "This is important…" *Paralinguistics* is the study of rhythm, pitch, tone, and other subtler qualities of spoken language. *Kinesics* is the study of gesture: pounding on a table while speaking may indicate anger. Visual language has equivalent considerations. By altering size, weight, spacing, position, and typeface, all sorts of messages are sent along with the content itself. That is *typography*.

Writing and designing are unified in a shared editorial technique: gather pieces, ideas, fragments, and edit repeatedly, combining, throwing out, until the result is clean and clear. Design is an evolutionary process in which an idea is refined from the general to the specific until the result satisfies the initial objectives.

A letter is an object. This puzzle, from a Mensa quiz, illustrates the point: *An eagle and an elephant have two. A tiger, a moose, a bear, a turtle, and a snake have one. Humans don't have any. What are we talking about?* Puzzles aside, is either the letter or the alphabet the main purpose of typography – or of this book? No, visual beauty and improved communication are.

Today's typographic designer, working in an environment in which there is simply far too much to see and too much to hear, must act as an editor to *reduce* as well as *clarify* messages for readers. This requires critical understanding, which grows from having read the material to be designed and visually editing it for the reader's greatest benefit. It is not enough to be a visual artist, when *information* is what we designers process.

Browsers respond to information that has a clear type progression. The natural order a browser will follow is picture-caption-headline-deck [decision point to enter the text] and then, maybe, if the story seems interesting, the first paragraph of text. A balance must be achieved between visual similarity (to unify various bits of type) and contrast (to make hierarchy clear). Too much similarity and type will look dull and skipable. Too much

☐ Typographic hierarchy leads readers through kinds of information.

❝ Typography is the mirroring of speech. Spoken language is transient. As soon as our tones die away, so does language. Through writing, language attains a temporal and a spiritual dimension. Writing can be preserved indefinitely." *Otl Aicher*

```
      C  D  F
      G  J  L
      N  Q  R         Latin
      S  U  V
      W  Y  Z
Γ Δ   A  B  E   N Ξ Π
Z H   I  K  M O  Σ Υ   Greek
Θ Λ   P  T  X   Φ Ψ Ω
      Б  Г  Д
      Ж  З  И
      Л  П  С         Cyrillic
      У  Ф  Ц
      Ч  Ш  Щ
      Ъ  Ы  Ь
      Э  Ю  Я
```

☐ Taxonomy of alphabets and scripts shows rough similarities of a selection of the world's languages.

❝ The difference between art and design (is small) if you agree that art is a representation of an individual's inner spirit." *Steven Heller*

contrast and a page will look noisy and repellant. The design process should start with elements alike, then introduce the fewest contrasts necessary to make distinctions between *kinds* of information. Starting a design with various contrasts at the outset encourages *dis*similarity. It is easier to see lack of contrast than to recognize when you have too much, and it is much easier to know where to add contrast than where to reduce it.

Connectedness makes a story come alive. Crew teams that row those skinny boats are chosen for specific strengths and must pull together for maximum speed and efficiency. Anything less than perfect teamwork results in the boat going very slowly. Similarly, words and pictures must be chosen for specific purposes and must pull together to make the value of the story as interesting and as clear as possible.

Typography is the skill that separates designers from dilettanti. ▷ Great typography is found midway between monotony and self-indulgence. It separates the thoughtful from the merely expressive. ▷ Visuals get you to look, but type delivers message and meaning, tone of voice and feeling, hierarchy and importance, explanation and clarity. ▷ It takes years to develop sophisticated typographic sensitivity. The process causes each of us to leave a trail of thousands of tiny errors in judgment. ▷ The level of attention to typographic detail increases with the post mortem of every project. ▷ Typographic mastery appears only to others; the typographer is almost never satisfied with his or her own work. ▷ Type is infinitely alluring. It would be depressing to dedicate yourself to something that can be perfected too quickly.

There are about 5,000 languages in the world. About 100 of these are considered significant. Not surprisingly, English and all languages that use the Latin (Roman) alphabet are in the small minority. This book almost exclusively addresses typographic work with the Latin alphabet. It is what I know. But the principles that apply to the Latin alphabet are, with some modification, applicable to many other writing systems.

Section 1

Type and design

What is type and where is it found?

" *If in finding a solution the typographer can produce a piece of work that has a quality of absolute correctness in the way it does its job, an aesthetic appeal which will induce the ordinary reader to read and arouse a sense of covetousness in the sophisticate, it may be called a piece of inspired typography.*" ALAN DODSON

◀□ Type takes many forms. It bombards us and surrounds us, so type must be made easy to absorb.

FOR A DESIGN TO WORK EFFECTIVELY, the type must be an integral part of the composition. If the type is altered or removed, the piece should fall apart. It doesn't matter if it's a poster, a cover, an advertisement, or corporate identity. Type strategy includes crafting a size and weight sequence for the headlines, subheads, captions, and text so each is distinctive and all work as one to make a distinctive and appealing design.

Typography is, according to the dictionary, "the art or process of printing with type." The root words that make up *typography* are *typo* (type) and *graphy* (drawing), so it literally means *drawing with type*. My definition is: *Applying type in an eloquent way to reveal the content clearly and memorably with the least resistance from the reader.*

Type and sound

Type is one part of a learned language system that works through both hearing and sight: *Phonemes* are sounds we join together. English has about 40 phonemes, but we have only 26 letters. There are some sounds that are not represented, so letter combinations like *ee, ch, sh, th, ng,* and *oi,* are necessary. *Glyphs* are written symbols that represent sounds. We have two styles of glyphs for every letter: capitals and lowercase. There are, in

A B C

abcde

abcdfe

abcdef

Quousque ta ndem abute-

Quousque tand

em abutere Ca-

DOU

Quous
tilina,
diu no
ludet?
frenata
A B C

GR

Quousq
patienti
furor ift
fefe effr
te noctu

nihil urbi
confenfus
tiffimus ha
ra vultufq
A B C D

Quousque t
quamdiu n
finem fefe
turnum pra
timor popu
hil hic mu
rum ora vu

fentis? con
teneri conj

□ Each character has several glyphs which may not look alike. Each must be learned.

◁ c1500BC Cuneiform writing in clay, shown actual size. The background shows a type sample sheet printed in Glasgow in 1783.

d	l	ſh	œ	ʒ	o	m	c
v	p	æ	ɛ	f	w	u	ꞷ
ɹ	ie	h	k	aʊ	ŋ	ʃh	ω
g	y	oʊ	ʧh	ɑ	ʈh	j	wh

□ A phonetic alphabet designed in four typefaces. It has one character for each of the 44 sounds used in English.

CERIST FOUL OF SEÏFFARDINT PI
CHERISHED GOAL OF SAFEGUARDING PE
ZEÏ PÜL ZEÏR EFFORTS END FAÏ
THEY POOL THEIR EFFORTS AND FIGHT
REZOLUTLI END EKTIVLI FOR P
RESOLUTELY AND ACTIVELY FOR PE

□ An alphabet of glyphs, marks with a direct relationship with their sounds, proposed by S. B. Telingater in 1968.

addition, a variety of shapes for each letter within these two categories. And most phonemes can be written in multiple ways. For example, *ie, y, uy, igh, eye, i,* and *ui* all represent the same phoneme in *lie, cry, buy, high, eye, slide,* and *guide.*

Correlating spoken and written language was the great legacy of the Phoenicians, an ancient trading civilization in the Middle East. In the thousands of years since the Phoenecians developed their characters, many evolutionary steps have produced the letters we now take for granted: lowercase letters grew out of medieval scribes needing faster writing processes; word spaces and punctuation helped clarify meaning; and sans serif types developed in response to social and intellectual changes in the 19th century. A teaching alphabet that represents the 44 phonetic sounds has been developed to make learning to read easier. The alphabet may have some success in schools, but its use is hampered by our lack of familiarity with the additional symbols. Shown at left are sample characters in four typefaces: Baskerville, Helvetica, Century Schoolbook, and Melior.

The very essence of typography is translating the equivalencies of spoken language into printable form. *Verbal* emphasis becomes an equivalent *visual* emphasis. The integrity of the type's form causes a visual message to be read with more or less ease. This typographic process of giving appropriate form to language is called *frozen sound*: sounds are frozen into letters; groups of sounds are frozen into words; and groups of words are frozen into phrases and sentences.

Interpreting verbal language allows the reader to "listen to type." What do we mean by "listening to type"? Imagine listening to a book recorded on tape. The reader's voice changes with the story, helping the listener hear various characters and emotions. A story told on paper should do the same thing. The "characters" typographers work with are categories of type: headlines, subheads, captions, text, and so forth. These typographic characters are our players and must be matched for both individual clarity *and* overall unity.

Sumerian 4000BC	Cuneiform evolution 3500BC	3000BC	Ugaritic 1300BC	Phoenician 1300BC	Greek 700BC	Roman 50BC	Minuscules 800	Blackletter 1200	Serif 1757	Sans serif 1850

NON-ALPHABETIC | **ALPHABETIC**

Type as form

The letters we use are the product of 5,000 years of written evolution. At about the time of the first human communities – and the time of the first farming – the people living in what is now Iraq and Syria began to make marks that recorded their herds and harvests. At first, the marks were very representational. The mark for a cow looked like a cow. As speed and need imposed themselves, the marks became more and more abstract, until they couldn't be understood without having learned their meanings. A separation between spoken and written languages continued until the Phœnician's developed a system that used far fewer symbols, each symbol representing a specific sound. In their trading on the Mediterranean, the Phœnicians passed their system on to the Greeks, who made changes as their spoken language required. The Greeks passed it on to the Romans, who made further changes, and we use the Roman (or Latin) system with only a couple of minor changes.

Writing developed around 3,000BC. *Alphabetic writing*, where each sound is represented by a symbol, developed around 1,600BC. Of the two, alphabetic writing is the greater development because it simplified language and made it accessible to all.

Typographers use elements and traditions inherited through generations of writing, printing, and reading. Many typographic rules were adopted from handwriting as printable type forms were developed in the 1400s and 1500s. Historically, typography was handled by the printer who cut his own typefaces, designed the page, and reproduced the design on paper. In the 20th century, typography and printing separated. Around 1950, typographers and typesetters became outside vendors who set type to the specifications of the designer or art director, which evolved into a new responsibility. Computers, forcing a new working methodology, have nearly obliterated the typography specialist since all type decisions are made within a page design program. Designers are widely expected to be masters of an art form that takes many years to learn.

Spabefgomty Spabefgomty Spabefgomty Spabefgo
Spabefgomty SPABEFGOMTY Spabefgomty Spabefgo
abefgomty Spabefgomty **Spabefgomty** Spabefg
abefgomty Spabefgomty *Spabefgomty* Spabefgo
abefgomty Spabefgomty SPABEFGOMTY Spabefgo

Aoccdrnig to rscheearch at an Elingsh uinervtisy, it deosn't mttaer in waht oerdr the lteters in a wrod are. The olny iprmoatnt tihng is taht frist and lsat ltteres are in the rghit pacle. The rset can be a mses and you can siltl raed it wouthit a pobrelm. Tihs is bcuseae we dno't raed ervey lteetr individually, but as parts of familiar wrod shapes.

The order of letters affects meaning, as in this 1997 logo. Predictably, clothing bearing the French Connection United Kingdom logo leads f.c.u.k.'s sales. An internet pass-along illustrates that letter order may not be as important as we've thought.

Typographic order is manipulated in Stephen G. Perrin's 1976 "Complete Do-It-Yourself Declaration of Independence Kit," which includes the correct characters and punctuation to produce your own document.

" Between the two extremes of unrelieved monotony and typographical pyrotechnics there is an area where the typographic designer can contribute to the pleasure of reading and the understanding of what is being read." *Carl Dair*

" Perfect typography is certainly the most elusive of all arts. Sculpture in stone alone comes near it in obstinacy." *Jan Tschichold, Homage to the Book, 1968*

Designers can today choose from the greatest variety of letterforms in the history of written language. That many of these types are so quirky as to be illegible is a mathematical certainty. That many are inappropriate for a given message is also numerically obvious. It is among the designer's responsibilities to be aware of the types available and to choose those that communicate clearly and with the correct tone for every message.

Type has rhythm. A speaker who drones at a single speed is causing listeners extra work to dig out the content; presuming they care enough to make the effort. By comparison, a speaker who alters her rhythm of delivery, by pausing before beginning a new idea, for example, makes the content clearer by grouping information into sensible clusters. Such pauses in rhythm are expressed typographically by altering a single element unexpectedly and by breaking the ends of lines of display type at logical places, rather than whenever a line happens to be filled with letterforms. If the line is broken arbitrarily or in the wrong place, reading and comprehension is slowed down. If natural line breaks don't work visually, changing typefaces may be necessary.

Comic books are particularly good at showing the meaning of words (left). That the words being shown are *Ka-Boom, Kkshhkkkkk, Smash,* and so forth doesn't detract from the excellent relationship of words and the way they are shown to make their meaning felt. It is more difficult to do this with words that have more complex meanings. Children's books sometimes enlarge type a little to represent a shout, and make it smaller to represent a whisper. This rates as relatively lively typography.

Poor typography results from misunderstanding the importance of the "not-letterforms" and concentrating only on the letters themselves. "Not-letterforms," or the space surrounding letters, is seen between characters, words, lines, and between blocks and columns of type. It is the contrast of the letter form to its surrounding space that makes type either less or more legible. Legibility is central to typography because type is, above all else, meant to be read.

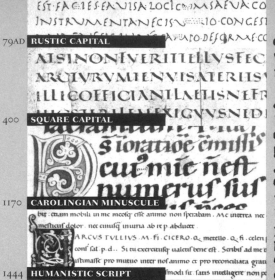

Consistent spacing makes reading easier because the reader is unaware of inconsistencies in rhythm, which is to reading what static is to the radio. The measure of a good typeface is whether every letter combination is spaced for optical equivalency so no dark spots appear where letters are too close. Even spacing produces even typographic "color," or gray tone.

It is important to understand the distinction between type and script. Script, or handwriting, was the only "type" that existed until Johannes Gutenberg perfected the technique of casting identical letters out of metal that could be reused on a printing press in 1450. Script was developed by several civilizations simultaneously in what is now the Middle East and Far East. Writing has changed as the materials used have evolved from sticks in clay to reed pens to sticks on wax tablets to quill pens to steel pens to ball-point pens to porous-tip pens to sticks on touch-sensitive screens. Handwriting has always been affected by its use: a casual, hurried hand for personal notes or an elegant, carefully modulated hand for official documents. In Latin script, the one the Western world uses, script capital letterforms reached their point of perfection with the Roman inscription on Trajan's Column in c114AD. Lowercase, or minuscule, letters didn't fully evolve until about the ninth century AD, as a result of speedier writing and improvements in both writing surface material and pens.

Today, we have two styles of type that emulate handwriting: italics and scripts. Italic types evolved in Venice in 1500, when the region's angled handwriting style was used as inspiration. Script types were introduced shortly after, but fell out of use until Robert Granjon's *Civilité* in 1557. The first English script type was made in 1672. Script typefaces have always been true to their handwritten roots. Italics are distinct from script types in that they are designed to complement a roman, or upright, typeface with which it shares design characteristics. Some digital italic and script types have extensive collections of alternate characters, generally gathered in "expert sets," that make typesetting look more like handwriting.

The Characteristics of Letters

Name	a = "aye," *aleph* (*bull*) in Semitic and Hebrew, *alpha* in Greek
Sound	a = "ay," "aah," "ah," "uh," "aw," and silent
Place in alphabet	a = first, before b, c, d, etcetera
Rules for use	change in sound when ordered with other letters, etcetera
Shape(s)	♉ ⚹ ᚨ A A Λ λ ʌ ɑ ɑ ɑ ɑ ɑ ɑ ɑ ɑ ɑ ɑ ɑ ɑ ɑ ɑ ɑ ɑ

The Characteristics of Type

Family	a = Akzidenz Grotesk Regular, a = Fairfield Medium
Style	a = roman, *a = italic*
Case	a = lowercase/minuscule, A = UPPERCASE/MAJUSCULE
Weight	light, regular, **medium, bold, extra bold**
Size	a = 6pt, a = 12pt, a = 24pt, a = 48pt
Position	above below
Color	**black,** gray, white
Treatment	textured, **shadowed**, sideways

□ Hermann Zapf drew a variety of forms of each letter in 1944 studies for a calligraphic type.

□ Type can be abstracted to its essentials and still be readable. Spanish artist Joan Míro used lettering in many of his paintings. This is a 1936 cover for *Transition* magazine. Richard Kegler and Michael Want digitized his characters into a typeface in 1993.

ZIS
SECHUAN

□ Merging two existing glyphs as a letterform experiment requires, first, identifying the minimal characteristics of each letter and, second, preserving them in balance. These student letter combinations are in Caslon, Univers, and Bodoni.

The characteristics of type

An alphabet – there are many, of which Latin is the most familiar to us – is made of glyphs. According to linguist Earl M. Herrick, each written letter has five characteristics:

▶ It has a name.

▶ It has a specific spoken pronunciation.

▶ It has a place in the alphabetical order of its language.

▶ It is subject to rules for its use. In Polish, for example, the sequence of letters *szcz* is permissable. In English, that sequence is not, unless used in a word of Polish assimilation.

▶ It has a certain basic shape or, often, a few basic shapes. The letter *A*, for example, may be shown as A, *A*, a, or *a*. The letter's shape is an abstraction that Eric Gill referred to when he said, "A capital *A* does not cease to be a capital *A* because it is sloped backwards or forwards, because it is made thicker or thinner, or because serifs are added or omitted."

To this list, we may add that type glyphs have additional characteristics:

▶ It is a member of a family

▶ It has a style

▶ It has a case

▶ It has weight

▶ It has size

▶ It has a position

▶ It has a color

▶ It has a treatment, or the lack of a treatment

Utility in type is closely related to the generic. There is beauty and opportunity in taking generic style and exaggerating it to create something new. For example, Helvetica, the most popular and generic sans serif face, is nostalgic and evokes a time – the 1950s and 1960s – when there was less clutter and noise of competing messages. Helvetica doesn't avoid complexity, but ensures complexity doesn't exist for its own sake. Because of readers' familiarity, it needs a design treatment in display settings to become visible.

□ Type has been used in art throughout the centuries, as in *The Death of Saint Dominic*. The saint's words are upside down – indicating death is already here. But type itself became the focal point in art in the 20th century. Shown at left are samples by Filippo Tommaso Marinetti (*Letter from the Front*, 1917. Marinetti called his poster-poem a *tavole parolibere*, or "free-word table." By making it very difficult to read the poem, he wanted readers to participate in creating an experience for themselves.); Réne Magritte (*Les traces vivantes* [The Living Traces], 1927. The tree trunk has "naked woman" on it in French, perhaps because a tree is suggestive of the image of a woman.); Ferdinand Léger (from *La fin du monde* [The End of the World]. The composition says in French, "accelerated movie" and "slowed-down movie."); Paul Klee (*Vorhaben* "Intention," 1938. Klee used pictographs and alphabets throughout the 1930s.); Alan Kaprow (*Words*, 1962. "I am involved with the city atmosphere of billboards… in scrawled pavements… in pitchmen in Times Square."); Jasper Johns (*0-9*, 1960); Roy Lichtenstein (*We Rose Up Slowly*, 1964); Maurice LeMaitre (*Untitled*, 1974); Paul Eric Berger (*Mathematics #62*, 1977); Jenny Holzer (*Laments*, 1989); and César Galicia (*Sketch*, 1996).

Elegant typography

What is *elegance in typography*? It is all necessary information with no uneccessary complexity. It is the distillation of content to its essence. It is, in other words, *expressive clarity*.

Designers want to challenge the reader, to provoke them and to entertain them. We also want to design on the edge – or at least to tip our hats at the edge and acknowledge the design era in which we practice. We want to serve the profession and the art of typography. But how? The way to create expressive typography is to predigest the copy, understand the message, and show off its meaning and its importance to the reader. This cannot be separated from the editing process. Know what the thrust *ought* to be, then make that point crystal clear through design choices. Contrast type style, size, weight, position, color, or treatment to show hierarchy and give enough information for the reader to decide whether to become involved with the text, where the story really is.

Complexity will not get a message across because, though it may be interesting to look at, the message won't be legible. Simplicity alone will not get a message across because, though it may be easy to read, its importance won't be recognized. Only expressiveness combined with lack of complexity will make the message both interesting and legible.

Choosing a typeface that enhances the content is certainly important. Words are symbols of emotions and ideas that manipulate the reader. But choosing the right typeface is not as important as using a neutral typeface well. Dutch designer Piet Zwart (1885–1977) said, "Pretentious [letter forms] oppose the utilitarian task of typography. The more uninteresting a letter is in itself the more useful it is in typography." By using fancy letters, the danger is that typography will begin and end with choosing the typeface. That is not typography, but fashion. The most forward-looking design is generally the first to look dated. On the other hand, traditional, conservative design looks timeless, but it is highly derivative. How can these two ends be balanced?

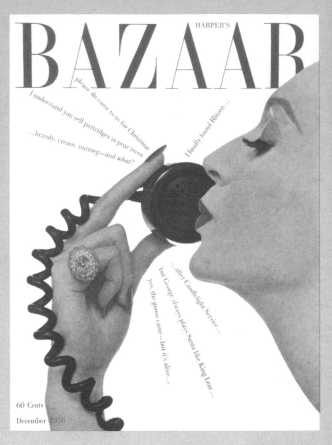

This 24-point headline is set as if it was just large text. Default settings have been left intact.

This improved 24-point headline is set as if every interspace was meaningful. It is darker and more visible.

◁ *"BAZAAR"* is clearly display type: it is big and it is meant to be seen first on this 1958 cover by Henry Wolf. The radiating type, though text size, is also display type since it is meant to attract attention. Size alone is not a determinant for text or display type. Intention is.

▯ Text and display may work together to convey a single idea, as in this 1960s ad for Y&R Advertising.

◁ An idea may be expressed many ways depending on how the primary type is handled. These studies were done by an unknown Czech designer.

◁ Spacing is more visible in display type. Think of display type not as type setting, but as *shape management* in which each character is a discrete shape. Digital font spacing is generally optimized for text sizes, so default settings must be overridden.

Text and display

Text is generally thought of as the small, gray type that contains the bulk of a message. Display is the big type that is supposed to stop the browser rushing to turn the page. Once upon a time in the history of printing, there was so little printed matter in existence, display type was unneccessary. Those who could read would read whatever they got their eyes on. Labelling was relatively insignificant. As more books became available, naming their contents – from book covers to headings – became a benefit. The earliest display type was simply bigger text. The industrial revolution in the 1800s brought an avalanche of display faces to help make advertising messages more visible. In today's hyperactive information and media environment, readers require us to state immediately and convincingly what our message is, or to be ignored entirely.

Display type has traditionally been defined as *type over 18 points in size*. Typographic treatments in the past half century have changed the definition to *any type whose purpose is to be seen first*. It is therefore properly called *primary type*, regardless of size.

The purpose of primary display type is to lure the reader to secondary type, so keep primary type short and provocative. Establish a tone, a typographic attitude in the display type, where reduced legibility is best tolerated by readers. The secondary type, which may be a subhead or a caption, provides sufficient information for the browser to decide whether to engage with the first paragraph of text. Once in the text, nothing should be done to repel the hard-won reader: this is not the place to graphically amuse or entertain.

Type, like the spoken voice, can be powerfully bold or elegantly understated. It can shout or gracefully inform. It can be stuffy or informal, universal or parochial, traditional or state of the art, highly complex or primitive. But unless the reader grasps something of value, his conversion from a looker to a reader will not occur. Put interesting information where it can be found. Break the type into palatable chunks and recognize that captions are the first type many readers cover.

Allen Industrial Supply

Buzzeo Roof Shingles

Certina Watches

Damas Optometry

Beth Hair Salon

London Film Production Fair

Getraer Gauge

Texas Hospice

Imasco Ltd

John Heyer Paper Ltd

Kahn & Co Carpet

Living Aids Ltd

Mitch's Lawn Care

Nautech Yacht Equipment

Occulenti Contact Lenses

Chicago Pharmacal

Quality Electric

Dr DF Rush, Chiropractor

Sudbury Transit

Teen Forum

Ursula Flower Shop

Vail Blinds

Willis Painting

Xpedx Freight

York Centre

Zemkie Copywriting

The language of type

How is type designed? *29* · Looking at type *31* · Parts of letters *47* · Type classification *49*

> " *Type is a medium of philosophical enjoyment. It is interesting to discover typographic rules containing inconsistencies in logic, which are in use only because of tradition. It is also interesting to ponder the origin of these errors, the practical reasons for their perpetuation, and to suggest remedies."* BRADBURY THOMPSON

◀ Letterforms can be abstracted to convey additional information, as this alphabet of logotypes shows.

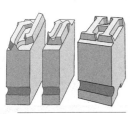

☐ Type has been made of metal since 1450. These characters, when printed, would read **Hnh**.

" Choose a typeface that works with the sound you want to make."*Anonymous*

◀ Type has color and texture, as this dark, rough example by J.V. Videní shows. It may also be light and organic, as this 2003 illustration by Laruen Redniss shows, or type may be even and gritty as in this C1930 quilt by Lena Moore.

" Perfect typography must be unorthodox typography. It may mean using wrong fonts, cutting hyphens in half, using smaller punctuation marks, in fact, doing anything that is needed to improve the appearance of typography. There should be no rule except to make type pleasing to the eye."*Aaron Burns*

THE RIGHTNESS OF A TYPE is determined by what it is *used for*. Advertising must be visually competitive, so it needs faces that are slightly "different." Text, by having been reached as a result of persuasive display type, has already won its readers, so using a "different" typeface would only impede absorption by drawing attention to itself. Low resolution type, on-screen display for example, benefits from certain type characteristics: relatively uniform stroke weight, open letterspacing, and, when serifed, short, thick serifs. Some types have been designed specifically for such uses.

Type attracts readers. Type arouses emotions. Like color, some types are cold and some are warm. Each type has a feel created by the relationship of the thick and thin strokes, the proportion of width to height, the way corners meet, and a myriad of other stylistic traits. But regardless of tone, type must be legible and, at least in text settings, must add clarity.

Type treatments have an attribute of rightness or wrongness, determined by the message, the medium, and the audience. What works splendidly for one situation may not work at all for another. But putting the reader's needs first is always a right decision. In discussing the design of forms, Erik Spiekermann

Quare multarum quoq; genti
ipſo benedicédas oés gentes h
aperte prædictum eſt:cuius ill
ſed fide cóſecutus eſt:qui poſ
filium:quem primum omniu
cæteris qui ab eo naſcerétur tr
eorum futuræ ſignum:uel ut
tinétes maiores ſuos imitari co

Quare multarum quoq; ge
ipso benedicédas oés gente
aperte prædictum est:cuiu
sed fide cósecutus est:qui
filium:quem primum omn
cæteris qui ab eo nascerétu
eorum futuræ signum:uel
tinétes maiores suos imitar

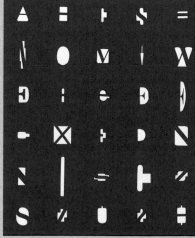

◁ Nicolas Jenson's 1470 roman (*far left*) and a 1999 digital interpretation show many small æsthetic judgments that must be made in a typeface revival.

❝ Why worship typographic tradition? We pay our debt to the past when we preserve craft laws and principles that the old typographers handed down. But progress demands that we add some achievement of our own to the heritage." *Anonymous, c.1932*

ᴀɴᴛɪQᴜᴇʀɪᴀ ᴛʀɪʙᴇᴄᴀ

◻ Right readingness is manipulated in this logo for a shop in New York.

◁ Type's *color* can be used to guide the reader from primary to tertiary information. Dark to light is most logical (*far left*).

mouka
mouka

◁ Type is both the shape of the letters themselves and the spaces around and within the letters. Emil Ruder made a study of negative space within characters using a variety of typefaces.

says: "Design forms for the user. If you want to get something from somebody, why not make it easy for them to give it to you?… Define every requirement. Design top left to bottom right. Put the most important questions first. Things that belong together get placed together. Leave enough space for the responses. Make the form look like it came from your company. If your forms look good, your company looks good. And if your forms look good, they work."

Where did type come from? It evolved from handwriting, which was invented in the Middle East and evolved over the past 5,000 years. Since its invention, printers and designers have experimented with type. While fashions change, certain standards and rules have emerged. Today type comes from several sources: fonts that are found on or are added to your computer; letters you find and scan in; letters and alphabets you design yourself in programs like Illustrator, Font Lab, and Fontographer; and letters you draw or write yourself then scan in and place as tiffs.

Design can be split into two broad categories: editorial and advertising (*opposite*). There are ten applications of editorial type, eight of which are indicated in the example: ① headlines, ② subheads/decks, ③ captions, ④ breakouts, ⑤ text, ⑥ department headings, ⑦ bylines and bios, and ⑧ folios and footlines. The remaining two, coverlines and contents, do not appear on typical interior pages so are not included in the illustration. Because advertising is simpler in message and presentation, there are fewer type applications needed: ① headlines, ② subheads, ③ captions, ④ logos and taglines, and ⑤ text.

Type has "color," that is, it is relatively light or dark gray. Darker type generally attracts attention and so is used at larger sizes. Readers are most comfortable with medium, normal, or book weights, so these are best for text settings. Though more legible than bold type at text sizes, light type is less legible as it gets smaller.

Design is the arrangement of shapes, both figure and ground. Letterforms are also shapes: the figures and the space surrounding and within them, called "counters." Type's color can be

ABCDEFGHIJKLMNOPQRSTUVWXY

abcdefghijklmnopqrstuvwxyz

0123456789

0123456789

ABCDEFGHIJKLMNOPQRSTUVWXYZ

0123456789 X 0123456789

.,.;-¿?¡!/".."|•'[{()}]

¼ ½ ⅛ ¾ ⅝ ⅔

åçéîñøüÅÇÉÎ

ff fi fl ffl æ Æ Œ

©®™ &$¢£†‡§¶

Bold MEDIUM SMALL CAPITALS ***Black Italic*** Roman **Black** Medium *Italic*

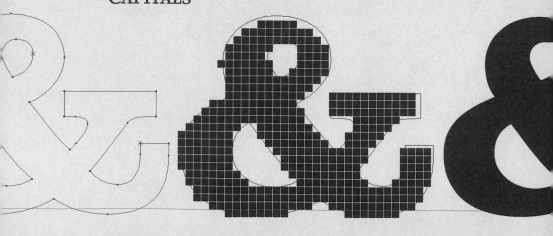

profoundly affected by adjusting the intercharacter and inter-line spacing attributes used.

Letterforms have a dual role: they are both message containers and shapes. While readers read type, they do not "see" it. If typographic design registers in the reader's mind at all, it is – or should be – only in the subconscious. Designers, by contrast, must both read and see type.

How is type designed?

Will Burtin, in the Foreword to Ben Rosen's 1963 *Type and Typography: The Designer's Type Book*, says "Each typeface is a piece of history, like a chip in a mosaic that depicts the development of human communication. Each typeface is also a visual record of the person who created it – his skill as a designer, his philosophy as an artist, his feeling for…the details of each letter and the resulting impressions of an alphabet or a text line."

A typeface is a design of a collection of characters. Until the advent of phototype in the 1960s, a font was a collection of related metal letters in a single size. The scalability of phototype made a font a collection of related characters without regard to typeset size. A digital font is the software that describes related scalable characters. The design of the letters themselves is not copyright protected in the United States, but the exact outline description is. Making changes to an outline description file requires permission from the foundry who made it. You may, however, print characters, scan, and outline them, and make alterations to these new "character descriptions." And you may embed fonts in PDF and EPS files for viewing and printing by others. Please respect type designers' work as you would expect others to respect your work. Don't steal fonts.

It may well be true that rules are made to be broken, but you can't break typographic rules until you know what they are. Originality comes from knowing what has come before: an understanding of type history and current practice leads to variety and innovation.

Spacebetweenwordsc
scribesbeganaddingsp
makelineseven,whose
fection.Scribesalsodev
which made words fit
berg revolutionized le
movable, reusable typ
came essential. He use
could be cut to exa
Eventually, the space
widths that were pro
being used. The goal

ABCDEFGHIJK
LMNOPQRSTU
VWXY&Z12345
abcdefghijklm
nopqrstuvwxyz
FF Bodoni Classic

ABCDEFGHIJK
LMNOPQRSTU
VWXY&Z12345
abcdefghijklm
nopqrstuvwxyz
ITC Bodoni Seventy-Two Book

ABCDEFGHIJK
LMNOPQRSTU
VWXY&Z12345
abcdefghijklm
nopqrstuvwxyz
Lanston Bodoni

ABCDEFGHI
LMNOPQRS
VWXY&Z123
abcdefghijk
nopqrstuvwx
Monotype Bodoni

ABCDEFGHIJK
LMNOPQRSTU
VWXY&Z12345
abcdefghijklm
nopqrstuvwxyz
Bauer Bodoni

ABCDEFGHIJK
LMNOPQRSTU
VWXY&Z12345
abcdefghijklm
nopqrstuvwxyz
Berthold Bodoni Old Face

ABCDEFGHIJK
LMNOPQRSTU
VWXY&Z12345
abcdefghijklm
nopqrstuvwxyz
Berthold Bodoni Antiqua

ABCDEFGHI
LMNOPQRS
VWXY&Z123
abcdefghijk
nopqrstuvwx
WTC Our Bodoni

	XXX Condensed	XX Condensed	X Condensed	Condensed	Regular	Extended
Roman	R	R	R	R	R	R
Antique	R	R	R	R	R	R
Gothic	R	R	R	R	R	R

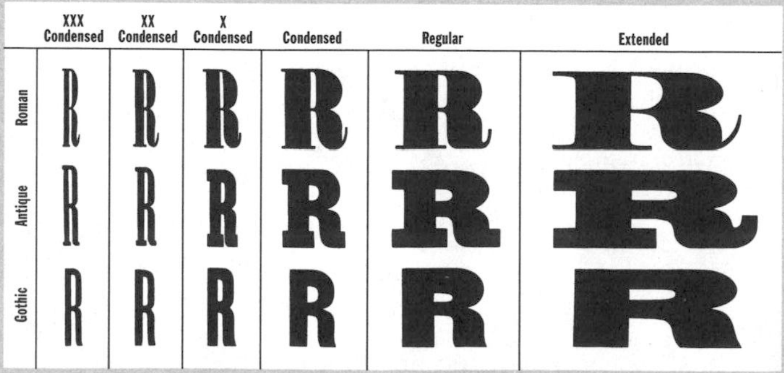

Looking at type

More than ever before in human history, we take type for granted. The computer has made type and its arrangement a daily practice for nearly everyone. The mystery of type well used is diluted by day-to-day familiarity. But when type was a new invention, when typographic evolution were afoot, nothing about type was taken for granted. Even Latin typeforms were invented (*opposite*) by copying the handwriting in northern Italy. Each printer had to make his own type – there were no type foundries yet – so each had his own style. By seeing one another's work, printers developed type designs rapidly, though each font required months of non-paying work to complete.

Ideally, typographers transform an author's copy into palatable, easy-to-read text. A typographer adds value to the content by interpreting it for maximum absorption. In reality, we see quite a bit of type that does nothing to make the content easier to read. Why? What are the rules of legibility that are being broken or, worse still, ignored?

Typography isn't typesetting. Typesetting, traditionally a craft by specialists, has, in the digital evolution, often come to mean allowing the computer's default settings to dictate final outcomes. Typography, on the other hand, is knowing how to set defaults for optimal spacing and legibility while recognizing the moments when breaking the defaults is exactly the right decision.

Using type well requires an understanding of the following:

Legibility A measure of a type's ability to be read under normal reading conditions. It is a result of assessing the inherent legibility of a typeface and applying optimal spacing attributes.

Readability A measure of the type's ability to attract and hold a reader's interest. Increasing readability often causes a reduction in legibility, so care must be taken, particularly in text settings, where legibility is more important than in display type.

Shapes of letters Our modern Latin letters – as well as modern Arabic – evolved in different directions from the Phoenician alphabet, as shown in the chart compiled by linguist

◀ Though it is counterintuitive, 90% of typography is about manipulating the emptiness that surrounds each letter, word, and line. Optimal typographic white space doesn't draw attention to itself. The first four lines are set without wordspacing. The middle four lines are set with normal wordspacing and the last four lines are set with 200% normal wordspacing. Notice how difficult reading is when wordspacing exceeds what we are accustomed to and how the linespacing, which remains consistent throughout, appears to change as the wordspacing opens up.

ACEH
ILMO

⌂ Ten interpretations of the same source design, Bodoni's type of 1800, organized by color. *Bauer* is the least accurate, while *FF* and *ITC* are equally true to the original (*above*).

◀ Type was cut in a *series* beginning in the 1830s and by the 1880s, a series usually included at least the six variations, as shown in the three families here: Roman (serifed), Antique (slab serifed), and Gothic (sans scrif).

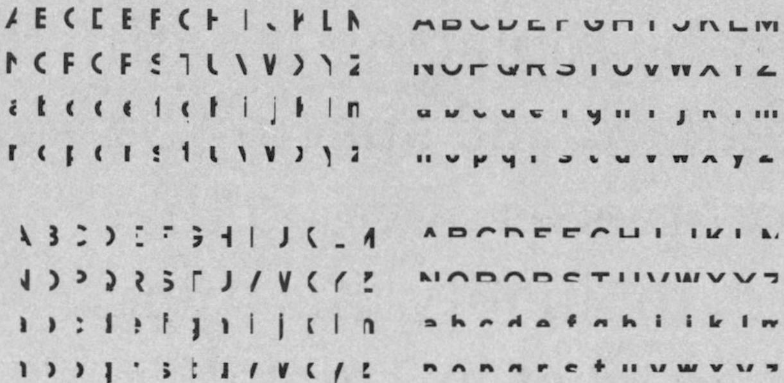

Modern Latin	A B C D E F H I K L M N O P Q R S T Z
Early Latin	A B ⊏ D E F H Ƨ K L M N O P Ɋ Ƨ T Z
Early Greek	Λ Λ Γ Δ Ξ ꓱ � B ꓘ ꓘ Λ ꓶ ꓕ O Π Φ Ρ Σ Τ Z
Phoenician	K ꓘ Λ Δ Ξ Y B ꓕ ꓴ ꓶ ꓶ ꓶ ꓶ O ꓕ Φ ꓩ W ꓕ I
Early Aramaic	ꓘ ꓴ ꓥ ꓵ ꓥ ꓘ ꓵ ꓶ ꓶ ꓶ ꓶ O J ꓕ ꓩ ꓶ
Early Arabic	ꓶ ꓶ ꓶ ꓙ ꓴ ꓶ ꓴ ꓶ ꓶ ꓶ ꓶ ꓶ ꓶ ꓶ ꓶ ꓶ

Safengomby
Optima

Safengomby
Dead History

Safengomby
Poppl-Laudatio

Safengomby
Rotis SemiSerif

Safengomby
Syndor

Safengomby
Rotis SansSerif 55

Safengomby
Rotis SemiSans 55

Safengomby
Rotis SemiSerif 55

Safengomby
Rotis Serif 55

OVIOIIOII
IIIIVOIIIAI
IIOOIIVIII
VIAIIOAVIO

□ There are three letter shapes in our alphabet: vertical, round, and diagonal. These shapes often do not fit together evenly, causing spacing problems that must be fixed.

◁ Semi-serif faces fill the gap between serif and sans serif faces. Sometimes a semisans can be mistaken for a serif face whose serifs have been chopped off (*far left*). *Rotis*, among a few others, is a semisans by virtue of being midway in a family that extends from a sans serif to a serif version, giving the designer a set of four typographic voices that relate closely to each other (*near left*).

◁ Type cases were placed above each other. The *upper case* held capitals, or *majuscules*, and the *lower case* held numerals and non-capital letters, or *minuscules*. The California Job Case (*right*) became the standard storage system because it fit all characters in a single tray.

Thomas Milo (*opposite*). Our alphabet – only capital letters, minuscules weren't developed until about 750AD – passed through the Greeks and Romans and had characters added or deleted to meet the needs of its changing users. The Romans perfected the alphabet's forms on the Trajan Column in 114AD (*opposite*, actual size letter). Letters were drawn with a broad reed pen or painted with a square-ended brush on stone, then chiseled, slightly accentuating the ends. ▷ Latin letters can be grouped into four categories based on their shapes: vertical (il, EFHILT); curved (acegos, COQS); a combination of vertical and curved (bdfhjmnpqrtu, BDGJPRU); and diagonal, or oblique (kvwxyz, AKMNWXYZ). Letters within each group are more likely to be mistaken for each other. Tops are more identifiable than bottoms (*opposite*). And right edges are more identifiable than left edges.

Shapes of words & All-caps/lowercase We do not read by looking at individual letters. We read by recognizing word shapes, which is a combination of the external shape and internal structure of the empty areas. Familiar letterforms create familiar word shapes, speeding the reading process. ALL-CAPS WORD SHAPES ARE MORE ALIKE, WHICH SERIOUSLY SLOWS READERS. *LIKE ITALICS, ALL CAPS SHOULD BE USED IN TEXT SPARINGLY, ONLY TO CREATE EMPHASIS.* **IN DISPLAY TYPE, ALL CAPS INCREASES VISIBILITY AND WORKS WELL IN SHORT HEADLINES.** ALL CAPS TAKES UP TO 35 PERCENT MORE SPACE THAN LOWERCASE OF THE SAME SIZE. USE LINING FIGURES, WHICH LOOK LIKE CAPITAL LETTERS (1234567890) IN ALL-CAPS SETTINGS SO NUMBERS DON'T DRAW UNNECESSARY ATTENTION TO THEMSELVES.

Type size is measured in points in the United States (72 to the inch) and measured in millimeters in the rest of the world. Text sizes range from 8 to 12 points, depending on x-height. Type size is closely related to line length: reading is affected by having more than about 50 characters per line. A design should be adjusted to balance type size and line length to achieve that number of

This is Wilke Roman set so there are an average of seventy characters per line, including word spaces. This setting, which is 10-point type, forces the reader to traverse a column that is too wide. The easiest way to determine optimal type size for a given column width is to try setting a specific type and counting characters. If setting more than the optimal number of characters per line cannot be avoided, add a few points of linespacing. This will give readers a comfortable return path to the beginning of the next line.

This is Wilke Roman set so there are an average of fifty characters per line, including word spaces. This is an ideal setting for reading comfort. The column width necessary for this ideal setting calls for 14-point type.

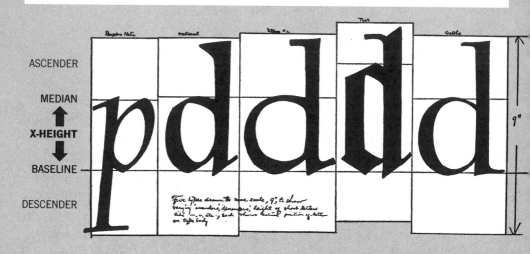

ASCENDER

MEDIAN

X-HEIGHT

BASELINE

DESCENDER

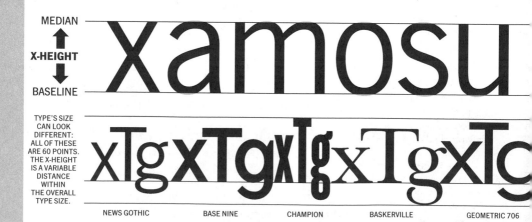

MEDIAN

X-HEIGHT

BASELINE

TYPE'S SIZE CAN LOOK DIFFERENT: ALL OF THESE ARE 60 POINTS. THE X-HEIGHT IS A VARIABLE DISTANCE WITHIN THE OVERALL TYPE SIZE.

NEWS GOTHIC   BASE NINE   CHAMPION   BASKERVILLE   GEOMETRIC 706

◁ Relative x-height is shown in this 1940 study by Frederic Goudy. Letters from five of his typefaces are drawn to the same scale. The overall heights are equivalent and indicate the type's "body," or the size of the metal block on which it would have been cast.

the federals~15000 confederates
Killed≡Wounded:25000 Prisoners
Destruction of Richmond by Fire
THE EASTER MONDAY VOLUNTEER
REVIEW: Preparations≡Brighton
From our Special Correspondent
≡Epidemic≡Russia≡Special Letter
Good Friday ≡ Brother Ignatius

▢ A lack of descenders allows lines of lowercase type to be set tighter on the Daily Telegraph's 1865 "news bill."

Cactus
Roman

▢ *Cactus Roman* might be called a "super-serif" because its spikes are essentially serifs placed rhythmically over the entire body of each letter.

characters per line. If there are more than 60 characters per line, linespacing must be added. ▷ Use size contrast to make the most important words most visible. Ordinarily, this means making display type larger than text. More creatively, small display type can whisper with significance if all the other type is uniformly large. ▷ If text is too small, it can't – and almost certainly won't – be read. Large text looks like yelling and forces the reader to read lines in sections rather than as a whole. ▷ When setting small type, use medium weight and a face with a large x-height. Use a slightly condensed face – saving width – and increase the point size to make copy fit and maximize legibility. Or do your readers a real favor and cut some copy to make the remaining text larger, more openly spaced, and much more legible.

X-height The *perceived* size of type is determined by its x-height, the distance from the baseline to the top of the lowercase letters' median (*opposite*). It is called the x-height because an ordinary lowercase *x* has neither ascender nor descender. Other lowercase letters that lack ascenders and descenders, like *a, m, o, s,* and *u,* have rounded tops and bottoms of the letters that slightly exceed the baseline or median. ▷ X-height is not a unit of measurement, but a distance within the overall size of the type, which is measured from the tops of the ascenders to bottoms of the descenders. All 60-point types, for example, are equivalent in overall size, but their appearance can very greatly because the x-height occupies different proportions of that distance. ▷ A large x-height makes type look larger, because more of the overall area is occupied by lowercase letterform. A large x-height imposes proportionally short ascenders and descenders. Types with large x-heights require additional linespacing to compensate for their lack of built-in negative space.

Serif/sans serif Types that have small lines at the ends of major strokes have serifs, types without are sans serif. Serifs aid reading across lines but they force too much space between letters in display type. That is why serifs are often preferred for text and sans serif types are preferred for display. ▷ Serifs help direct eyes horizontally. Because they poke out beyond the edges of

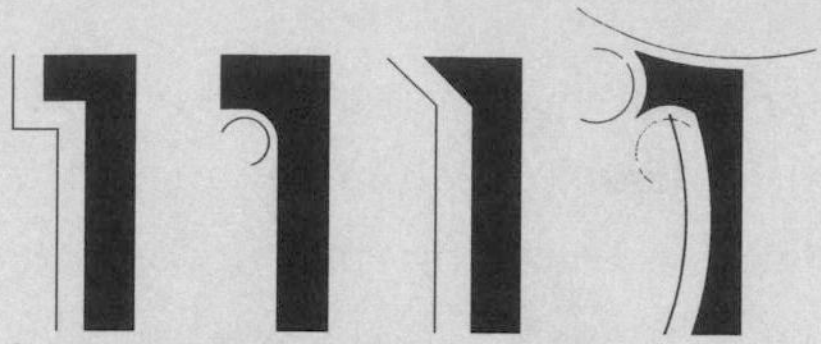

Strokes necessary to make serifs and brackets

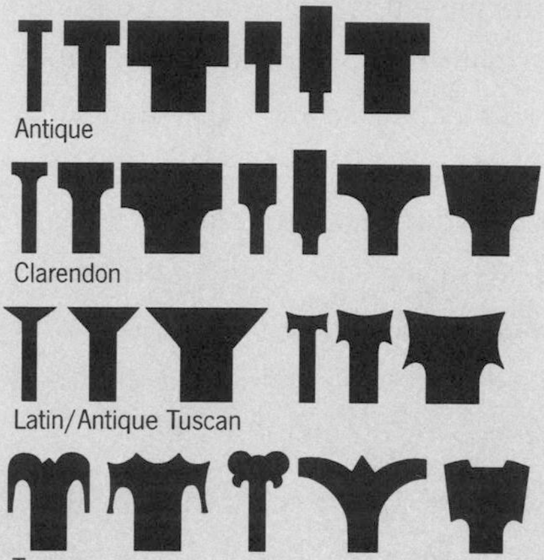

Antique

Clarendon

Latin/Antique Tuscan

Tuscan

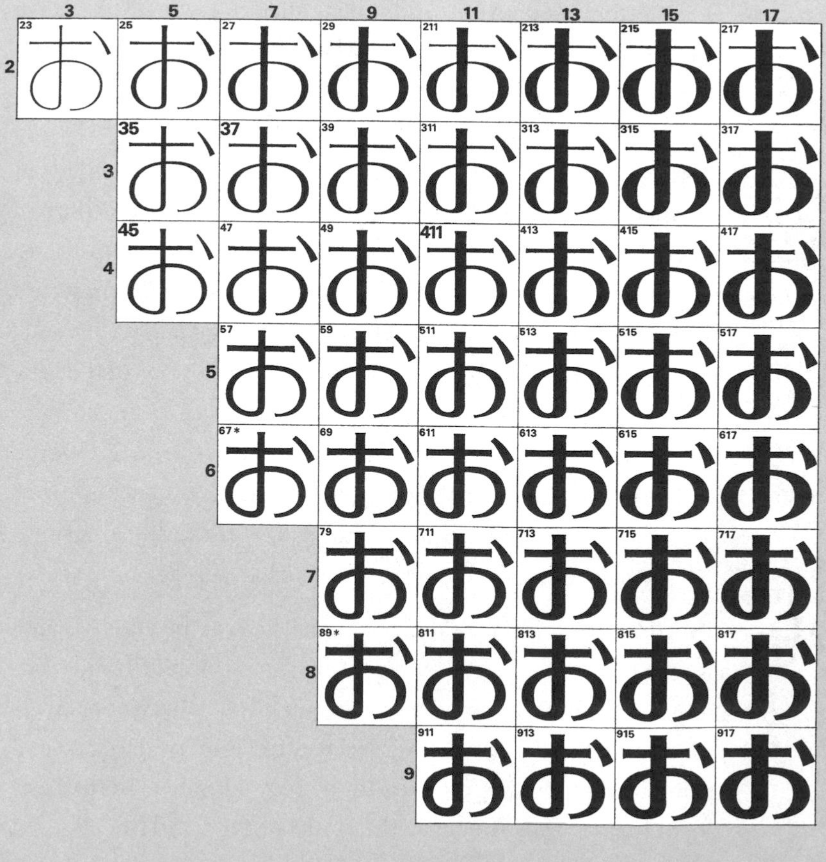

Two logos that don't just *have* serifs, they *use* them. Woody Pirtle uses six different serifs attached to a simple, bold armature. The ᴇ is made entirely of serifs.

IENT-TIOUS
CIAL-SIVE
TIAL-TIENT
CIES-SCENT
SCENCE-SCIO
US-ICK

Serifs are exaggerated to their fullest in this very dark 1895 display face.

Weight is shown in this 1971 chart for the development of *Typos*, a large family of Japanese typefaces (*far left*). The versions are arranged in increasing horizontal stroke widths from top to bottom and in increasing vertical stroke widths from left to right in 100ths of the square unit in which each is shown. Equivalent weight flexibility can now be achieved through a single Multiple Master font.

"If the 'tone of voice' of a typeface does not count, then nothing counts that distinguishes man from the other animals."
Beatrice Warde

characters, they force a certain amount of space between characters. Sans serif can be just as readable as serif faces if you open the letterspacing a bit and add extra linespacing to compensate for the lack of horizontal direction. ▷ Were serifs an aesthetic refinement by Roman carvers, or were they only products of the tools in use at the time? There are no Roman writing manuals in existence, so we must guess. In the time of Christ, letterers used reed pens and brushes for smaller works and chisels for monumental works. They painted letters on stone before chiseling them out. The diagram in the upper right corner of the opposite page shows the constituent strokes painted to make several letters. The brush itself caused the strokes to end in serifs. So serifs were both a result of the tools in use *and* an aesthetic decision.

Weight Type's weight is described as hairline, book, medium, bold, and black and is determined by the ratio of each character's negative space to its strokes: larger counter spaces are found on light faces, and small counter spaces are found on bold faces, as shown in Shashi Rawal's 1963 series of *S* studies (*opposite*). ▷ Medium weight is most readable: type that is too light doesn't stand out from the paper, type that is too bold has counters that fill in and are indistinguishable. ▷ Type with extreme contrast between its thinnest and thickest strokes makes poor reading because of "dazzle." ▷ Regardless of typeface used, reversing type out of a background makes it look smaller and thinner. Compensate by making it a little bigger and bolder, until the optical discrepancy becomes invisible.

Italics are used to emphasize or differentiate short passages, like quotes, titles, and foreign terms, from roman text settings. They are most effective when used sparingly. If used too much they make text looks frenetic and their meaning as *special information* becomes unclear. Italics, which are not as easy to read as roman, slow readers to the point of abandonment. Italics are also lighter than their roman equivalents, so are a bit harder to discern from their background. ▷ Some designers believe that italics, with their a diagonal stress, suggest action and speed and have inherent dynamic qualities. That is more an aesthetic per-

Roman	Italic	Reverse Italic
Manifest	*MENTA*	*Adams*
Wells 1828	Wells 1828	Wells 1828
Sound 18	*Pourtc*	Chesters
Page 1859	Nesbitt 1838	Cooley 1859
Opera ITALIA	*Thunder*	Blank6
Vanderburgh, Wells & Co. 1877	Wells & Webb 1840	Page 1879

ribus hris annotandas
rium · quod partim p:
partim usu proprio : et

☐ 160 years of italic type development: Cursive script (handwriting), Italian c1500.

se, suaq; confirmet: nec ulli
desipere fateatur. sed sicut
alijs tollitur omnibus . Ni
sunt , qui eam stultitiæ aa

☐ First italic type by Aldus Manutius, Venice 1501.

N ulla uia est. tamen ire
I nuiaque audaci propero
V os per inaccessas rupes

◄ ☐ Ludovico degli Arrighi's second italic type, Rome 1527

Fert Fatum parteis in
Fato Romani post
Prælia, debellatum O
Roma caputĝ fuit M

☐ First italic type with oblique capital letters, Basel 1525.

Christianiß. Regis pru
tum editis suis in sacras
tum euulgandu viroru
monumetis de Republi

☐ Claude Garamont's italic type, Paris 1545.

Æadem, is admone
Amstelodamo, non mo
Missuma Gubernati
urbe Protinus abscer

☐ Christopher van Dyck's italic type, Amsterdam 1660.

POETRY IS WHAT MILTON SAW WHEN DON MAR-QUIS HE WENT BLIND

HEADLINE TREATMENT

RELATE HEADLINE to text by repeating the design treatment on the initial caps. Good craftsmanship calls for alignment of the initial's baseline with the one of the text baselines. It is usual to have it agree with the third or fourth text baseline INITIAL CAP TREATMENT

Even typographic color trumps any other rule of typography. These FULL CAPITALS and lining figures stand out too much in an ordinary 5,896-character* paragraph.

Simply reducing the size of capital letters to emulate small caps is inadequate. These REDUCED CAPITALS and shrunken lining figures look too light in a 5,896-character* paragraph.

It is necessary to use letters that are correctly weighted. Authentic SMALL CAPITALS and old style figures have the same color as their surrounding 5,896* lowercase letters.

*This number is just an excuse for showing figures in the illustration.

◁ Wood samples illustrate the three basic type styles: *roman*, *italic*, and *reverse italic*, sometimes called *backslope* or *contra-italic*. The last has never been a common style because, even in brief display settings, it is difficult to read. Wood type can be found at flea markets, like these from an open-air market in Manhattan.

◻ Italics – and reverse italics – are used to illustrate speed in Zero's (Hans Schleger) 1950 British modernist poster for a gasoline company.

Small letters

defgh

large letters

defgh

◻ Capitalization is one way to emphasize the beginning of a sentence, a new thought, and a proper name. Bradbury Thompson suggested a few alternatives in 1945, basing his ideas on the simplicity of the idealistic *monalphabet*, using only lowercase letters. • use a bullet before each sentence. u̲nderline the initial letter. **s**et the first character in bold. ℰnlarged lowercase letters can substitute for capitals.

ception than a factual one, but the idea that italic type is *fast* or *racy* is almost always used as a graphic crutch. Italics were invented as a way to emulate regional handwriting in 1501 and to fit more type in the same space. In the modern era, motion can be indicated in a more creative and convincing way. ▷ Most readers want to be unaware of letters. They find a lot of italics "fancy" and disturbing.

Capitalization has evolved into a systemic way of signalling kinds of content. Until the late 1700s, capitalization was a freeform way of indicating emphasis. Elisha Coles, an English printer, wrote in 1674, "Whatsoever words the Author laies any kind of stress of force upon, these he either writes in a different character, or else prefixes a Capital before them, or both." Today, capitalizing the first letter of a word indicates a proper name or the beginning of a sentence.

Initial capitals are used to indicate the starting point of text or to break text into manageable chunks. They must be base-aligned with one baseline of text, usually the third or fourth. The first line of text must be spaced closely to the initial, especially important with initial letters that are open on the top right corner like *A* and *L*. The first few words of text may be set in all caps as a transition.

Small caps and old style figures are used in lowercase text so typographic color is maintained. Small caps are a bit bigger than the x-height and visually weighted with lowercase characters. Regular capital letters would be too dark and assertive. Using real small caps is much better than simply reducing the size of regular caps, which look too light (*opposite*). Small caps are available in *expert fonts*. Old style figures (1234567890) are sometimes called "lowercase numbers." Use old style figures in text and use lining figures (1234567890) with all-caps and in tables and charts.

Alternate characters Typefaces may include second versions of a few letters, like **A** and **Ꜳ** *or* **T** and **Ꞇ**. Some types include "biform" alternate characters, which may be large lowercase letters that replace caps, or small caps that replace lowercase letters.

UU BB CC DD EE FF GG HH II
JJ KK LL MN NN OO PP QQ RR
SS TT UU VV WW XX YY ZZ

a a b c d d e e f g h i j k l m n o p q r r ſ ſs t u v
r y zz ch ſch ck ff fi fl ſt ffi ſa ſe ſo ſr ſu ſä ſö ſü ſſi
ſt ſſi tz ſa ſe ſo ſp ſu ſä ſö ſü es llt

a b c d e f g che e gh k i l m n o p q r s t u z v ʒ x y th ph h.
A B C D E F G CH E GH K I L M N O P Q R ω S T E U Z. X Y TH PH H.
a be c di e ffe gu che e ghi kia i elle ji imme umne o pi gu rre ω sse tt ſe u zia vu ʒitta. ieſe ſyω the ph baca

a e i o u v.   oi au ui uc ei ia ii ie io iu iu oi uo.

ab ac ad af ag al am an ap ar as at.   ba cha da ſa gha la ja ma na pa ra ſſa ta ſa za va ça.
ib ic id if ig il im in ip ir is it.   bi ca che di ft gt ghe le je me ne pi re ſe te ſe ze ve çe.
cb ec ed ef eg el em en ep er es et.   be ce che de fe ge ghe le je me ne pe re ſe te ſe ze ve çe.
ib ic id if ig il im in ip ir is it.   ſi ci chi di fi gi ghi ki li ji mi ni pi ri ſi ti ſi zi vi çi.
ob oc od of og ol om on op or os ot.   bo cho do ſo gho lo jo mo no po ro ſo to ſo zo vo ço.
ub uc ud uf ug ul um un up ur us ut.   na cha du ſo gha lu ja mu nu pu ru ſu tu ſu zu vu çu.
bra chra dre fre ghre pre tri vri bro chro frω grω pru tru ſbe ſcu ſd-u ſſa igt ſkia ſla ſma ſno ſpe ſprun ſta ſtrin ſvo.

O Padre noſtro, che ne i cieli ſtai,
Laudato sia 'l tuo nome, e'l tuo valore:
Vigna ver noi la pace del tuo Regno.
In terra fatto sia la tuo volere;
Come si fa ne la celeste corte.
Dà hoggi a noi la cottidiena manna.
E cosi come il mal, che haven soffirto,
Perdoniamo a ciascun, e tu perdona
Quel, che haven fatto contra i tuoi precetti.
Non ci tentar con l'antico aversario,
Ma fa, che siamo liberi dal male.
Amin.

A ve Maria di molte grazie piena,
Con teco sia l'altissimo Signore.
Tu fra le Donne benedetta sii;
E benedetto il frutto del tuo ventre
Ieſu. O Madre de l'eterno Sire,
Porgi i tuoi dulci prieghi inanzi a lui
Per noi, che siamo erranti, e peccatori.
Amen.

C hi dirà queste in genocki devoto,
Col vostro votto virra furiente,
E col cappello giu del suo capella,
Speri, chel voto suo non sarà voto.

Some faces have complete sets of alternate characters that feature longer (or shorter) ascenders and descenders.

Ligatures Gutenberg's printing emulated local manuscript writing, which featured carefully justified lines. He crafted 290 letters, abbreviations, and ligatures to make even lines. Printers found so many characters impractical when they made their own fonts and rapidly reduced their total characters until today's ligatures, which are found in *expert sets*, include just ff, fi, fl, ffi, and ffl. Using joined letters resolves intercharacter spacing problems and add distinction to a design. The ct and st ligatures are also relatively common in text faces. Less common ligatures include the AA, Æ, LA, Œ, ꟹ, ꝛ, and TT combinations, for use in all-caps display settings, and fj, gi, it, ky, sp, and tty. *Logotypes* are preset words like *And*, *For*, *of*, and *The*.

Fractions Pre made combinations most used: ⅛, ¼, ⅓, ⅜, ½, ⅝, ⅔, ¾, and ⅞. Other fractions can be made from superior and inferior characters.

Titling capitals Designed with altered proportions – usually lighter weight – and refined serifs, titling caps are to be used at display sizes.

Swash characters Characters with ornamental flourishes. There are three categories: swash letters that begin or end words; "demonstrative" swash letters that relate well to neighboring characters; and fancy caps that are ornamental alternate characters. Swash caps should never be used in all-caps settings for two reasons: they are based on calligraphic lettering (which would never use them this way), and they are meant to be appreciated only a few at a time.

Superior letters A selection of 12 characters used in French and Spanish to abbreviate words: abdeilmnorst.

Hyphenation is the practical necessity of breaking words into syllables at the end of lines of type. It should only be used in text settings, never in display (with the lone exception when the idea of "breaking" is the point of the headline itself). There are two

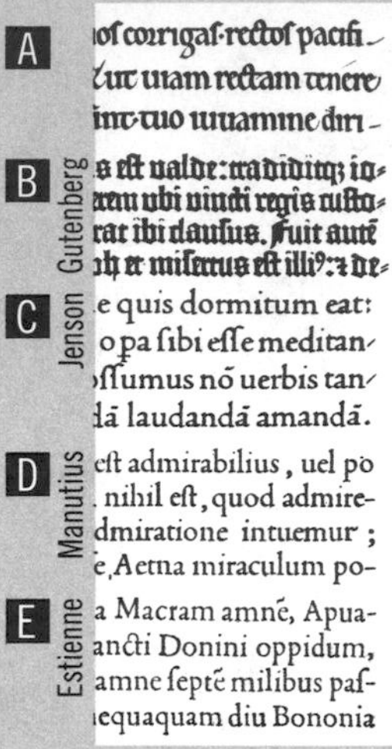

ˇ	subscript		Greeks	c600BC	written
⌣	subscript		Romans	c200BC	written
-	subscript		Carolingian minuscule	c800	written
⸌	character		Carolingian minuscule	c900	written
-	character A	Anglo-Saxon	c1100	written
=	character		Gothic	c1300	written
⸝	character B	Gothic	c1450	type
⸝	character C	Latin	c1470	type
-	character D	Latin	c1495	type
-	character E	European standard	c1549	type

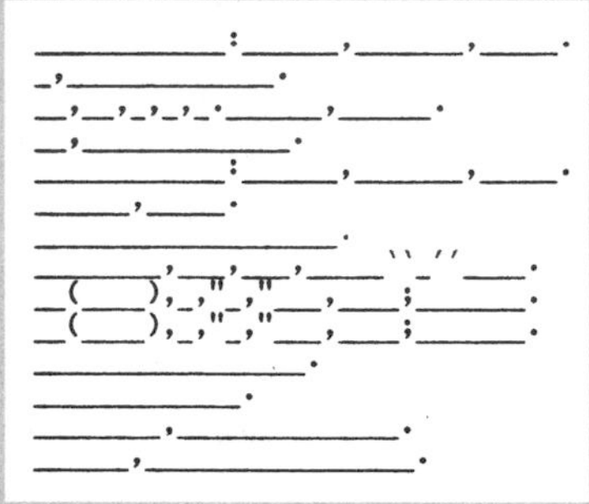

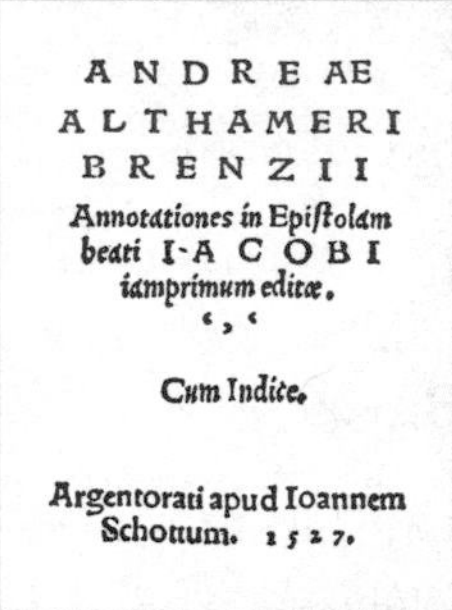

Side labels: Gutenberg, Jenson, Manutius, Estienne

ANDREAE
ALTHAMERI
BRENZII
Annotationes in Epistolam
beati I·A·COBI
iamprimum editæ.
Cum Indice.
Argentorati apud Ioannem
Schottum. 1527.

**Change.
For a dollar.
The NY Lottery**

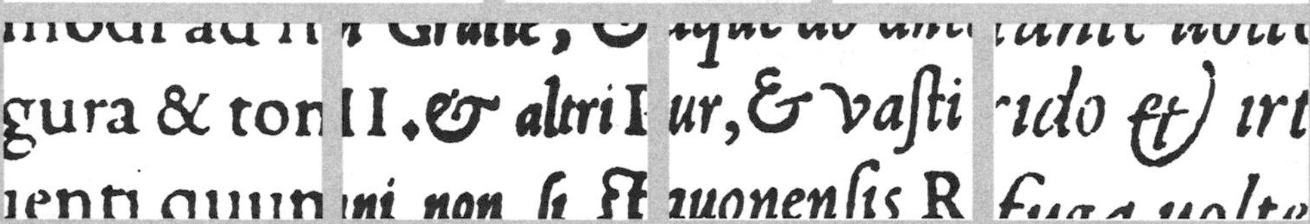

Nicolas Jenson 1470
Antonio Blado 1532
Robert Estienne 1549
Gabriel Giolito 1556
Aldus Manutius 1495 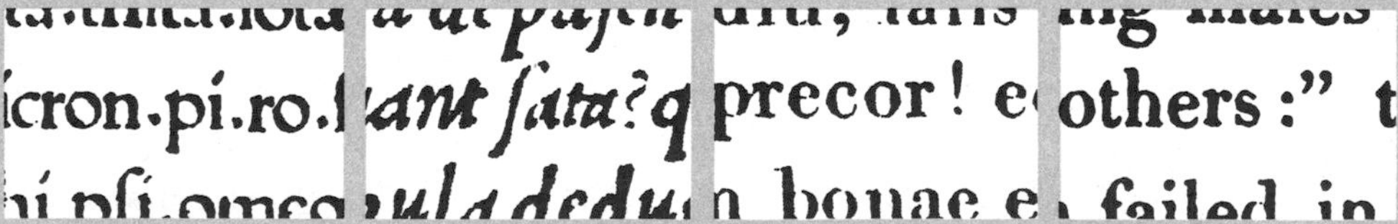
Aldus Manutius 1501
Giambatista Bodoni 1791
Edward Walker 1826

Hyphens center on the x-height. Adjust them for all caps by moving them up to the optical center of the caps.

HYPHENS CENTER ON THE X-HEIGHT. ADJUST THEM FOR ALL CAPS BY MOVING THEM UP TO THE OPTICAL CENTER OF THE CAPS.

x-height. Ad‡   X‡HEIGHT. AD-

CAP LINE
MEDIAN
BASELINE

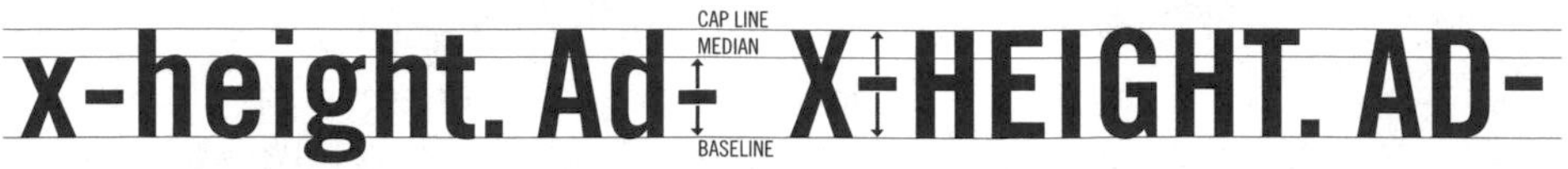

Hyphenate Hyphen-ate

kinds of hyphenation: "hard rag," a rougher edge caused by a large hyphenation zone setting that more liberally allows words to be pulled to the next line without hyphenation, and "soft rag," a smoother, more pleasing edge, caused by a small hyphenation zone setting that breaks words more frequently. An ideal ragged edge should look like a torn sheet of paper. Best of all is the "saw-tooth" edge, which has alternating long and short lines. ▷ A *hyphen* is the shortest horizontal bar. It indicates a broken word at the end of a line of text. The next longer bar is an *en-dash*, which is the width of half the point size of the type. It is a separator between numbers and compound words. The longest bar is an *em-dash*, which is the width of the point size of the type. It is used for breaks in dialogue. Depending on the font, some en- and em-dashes are too long and create noticably light spots on the page. Substitute the hyphen to preserve even type color, which takes precedence over using the "correct" mark.

Punctuation There are two kinds of punctuation: *elocutionary,* the earliest marks that indicate pauses for reading aloud; and *syntactic,* much more recent marks that indicate thought groupings. ▷ Among the first to use a punctuation system was Aristophanes of Byzantium in 260BC, who had marks to indicate three different lengths of spoken pauses. Greek and Roman authors each used his own variety of dots and virgules – a slash (/), from *virgula,* "rod" – and his own placements to indicate word separations, pauses, and ends of sentences. In general though, a·dot·separated·words.a·dot·at·the·baseline·indicated·a·pause like·a·modern·comma.and·a·raised·dot·at·the·cap·height indicated·a·stop·like·a·modern·period˙ Standards for punctuation began only with the development of printing. ▷ Shakespeare's punctuation is meant to guide spoken delivery: his system uses a comma for a short pause, a semicolon for a longer pause, a colon for an even longer pause, and a period for a full stop – which Shakespeare would sometimes put in the middle of a sentence. ▷ Hyphens, parentheses, and brackets center on the lowercase x-height. When used with all caps, they must have their baselines adjusted to center on the cap height.

Numerals develop quickly after the zero is invented in India:

c250BC India *Nana ghat*

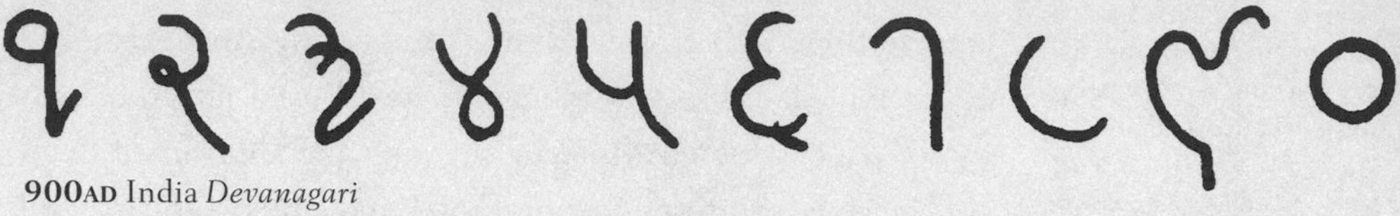

900AD India *Devanagari*

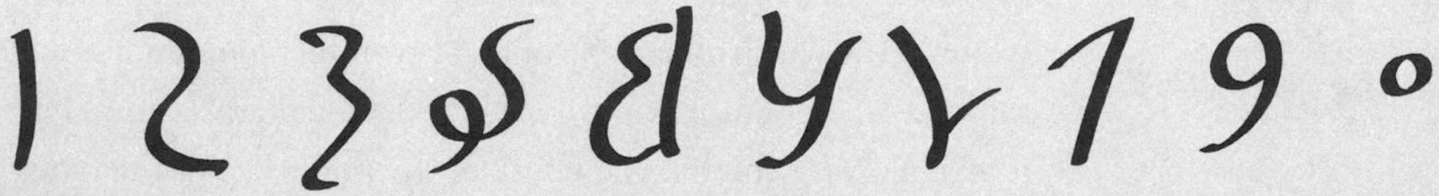

950 Eastern Arabic

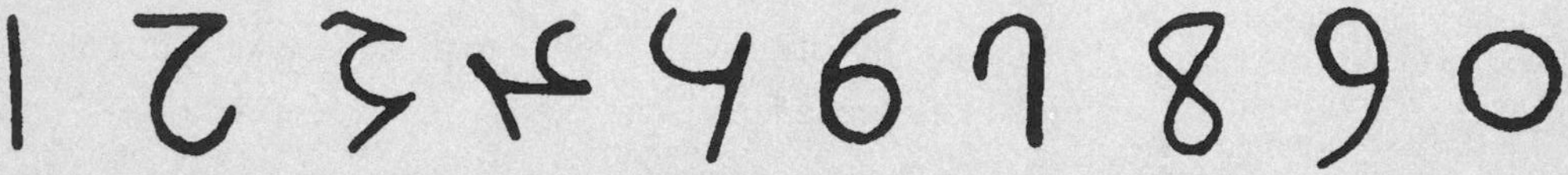

976 Spain *Ghobar*

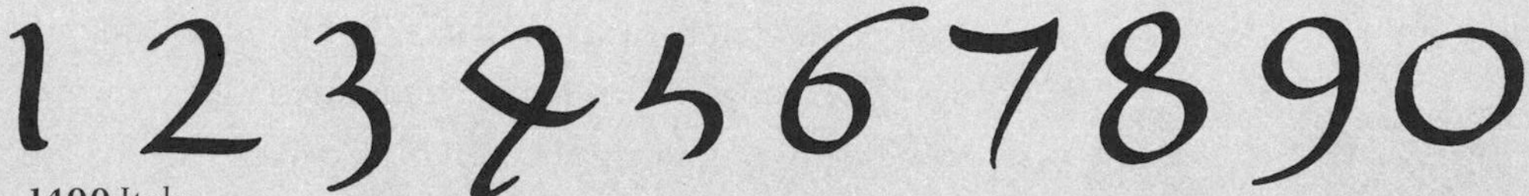

1400 Italy

1545 Paris *Garamont*

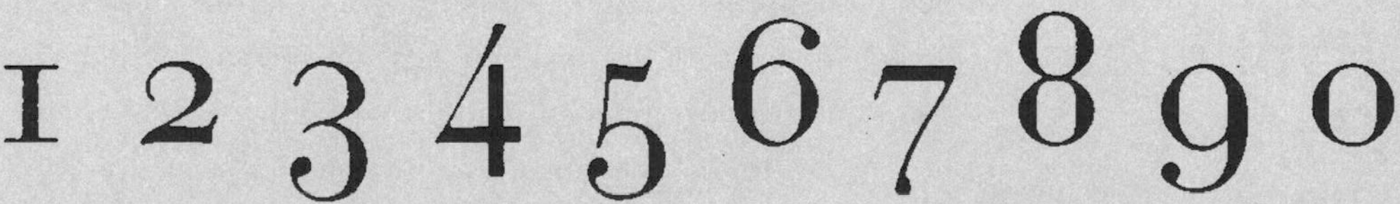

1794 Berlin *Unger Fraktur*

1908 New York *News Gothic*

1	𒁹	8	𒐜	100	𒐏
2	𒐻	9	𒐝	200	𒐏
3	𒐼	10	𒌋	300	𒐏
4	𒐽	11	𒌋𒁹	400	𒐏
5	𒐾	12	𒌋𒐻	600	𒐏
6	𒐿	20	𒌋𒌋	800	𒐏
7	𒑀	40	𒑶	1000	𒐏

0 1 2 3 4 5 6 7 8 9

⌂ Cuneiform numerals are very early marks in clay. Machines that could read numerals were developed in the late 1950s. Anton Stankowski developed abstracted numerals for machine reading (*lower line*) c1960. He left only the necessary vertical lines of each figure.

Fnagle®
Fnagle®
Comive™
Comive™

⌂ Register® and Trademarks™ should be sized to blend into the color of type. They look best when set smaller than the text's point size (*bottom examples*). Sans serif symbols read better at small sizes.

Quote marks There is a big difference between inch (") and foot (') marks, which are a leftover from the typewriter, and real quote marks. Quote marks should look like 6s and 9s: " ▓▓▓ " and ' ▓▓▓ .' Quote marks have evolved since their first use in Paris as sideways Vs in 1557. English printers replaced them with inverted commas before a quote and apostrophes, which had been invented in the early 1600s, at the end of a quote.

Numerals Numbers came before written language. The numbers 1, 2, 3, 4, 5, 6, 7, 8, and 9 were developed by the Hindus in India in about 250BC. They added the 0 in about 400AD. The name of these numbers, *arabic numerals*, was attached when Arabs brought the Hindu system to Europe through trading in Spain. In addition to the numbers themselves, Hindus also invented the placement of ones in the far right column, tens in the next column, hundreds in the third column, and so on. ▷ Roman numerals evolved around 30BC from the Etruscans and Greeks, and used letters to represent numbers: *I* for one, *V* for five, *X* for ten, *L* for fifty, *C* for hundred, and *M* for thousand. Though elegant to look at, the Roman system is not as easy to use in mathematical figuring as the Hindu system. That is why we see Roman numerals used on buildings and watch faces but not on spread sheets. ▷ Our capital letters evolved from the Romans while our numerals evolved from Arabic figures based on Indian characters. These are two sources of character shapes. Numerals don't look like they belong in the same style. To avoid dark spots in text settings, use old style figures ("lowercase numbers") with lowercase type which have ascenders and descenders. Use lining figures ("capital numerals") with all caps. Old style figures are available in "expert fonts." Lining figures developed only in the 1800s, with the increase in all caps advertising headlines. ▷ Superior and inferior figures are used to make fractions while maintaining even type color. To make proper fractions in most programs, in *Define styles*, set *Super/subscript size* at 60 percent and the *Superscript position* at 28 percent and the *Subscript position* at 0 percent.

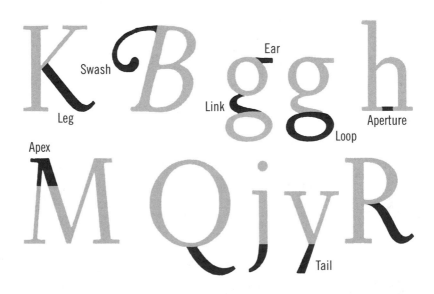

▢ Ascenders are exaggerated in this logo for a British purveyor of men's quality goods.

❝ Even with all the beauty and ingenuity of a well-designed typeface, a single letterform is still the lowest common denominator. When we experience disappointment with letters, let's not be afraid to do what comes naturally: let's draw." *Gerard Huerta (1952–)*

❝ Geometry can produce legible letters, but art makes them beautiful. Art begins where geometry ends, and imparts a character transcending mere measurement." *Paul Standard*

NATURAL HISTORY

▢ This magazine flag deconstructs its letters into their constituent strokes for an unusual and memorable personality.

Parts of letters

In the course of an informed conversation about type, using names of letter parts helps get a point across much better and reveals more knowledge – and therefore greater expertise and a better-informed opinion – than your boss or client. There are twenty-five letter parts that need to be known, and of those, eight are a bit esoteric. These eight have been indented and are shown in the lower illustration on the opposite page.

Aperture Narrow opening at end of an open counter.

Apex Point where two diagonal strokes meet.

Arm Horizontal stroke that is free on one or both ends.

Ascender Part of lowercase letter that extends above the mean line.

Bar Horizontal stroke that is attached at both ends.

Bowl Curved stroke that encloses a counter.

Counter Fully or partially closed space.

Descender Part of some lowercase letters that extends below the baseline.

Ear Small stroke that projects from the upper bowl of some lowercase gs.

Hairline The thin strokes of a serif typeface.

Junction Point where two strokes meet.

Leg Bottom diagonal on *k* and *K*.

Link Stroke connecting top and bottom bowls of *g*.

Loop The lower bowl of a two-story *g*.

Serif A small line that crosses the ends of main strokes.

Shoulder Curved stroke coming from a stem.

Spine Main curved stroke of *s* and *S*.

Stem Primary vertical or diagonal stroke.

Story Single-level lowercase g and *a*; dual-level lowercase g and a.

Stress Direction of thickening in a curved stroke.

Stroke A primary line, whether straight or curved.

Swash A flourish that replaces a serif.

Tail The descender of *Q*, *j*, or *y*; the short stroke on *R*.

Terminal The end of a stroke that lacks a serif.

X-height The height of lowercase letters that lack ascenders and descenders.

ABCDEFGHIJKabcdefghijklm
ABCDEFGHIJKabcdefghijklmr
ABCDEFGHIJKabcdefghijklm

ABCDEFGHIJKabcdefghijklm
ABCDEFGHIJKabcdefghijklm
ABCDEFGHIJKabcdefghijkl

ABCDEFGHIJKabcdefghijklr
ABCDEFGHIJKabcdefghijklmnc
ABCDEFGHIJKabcdefghijklmn

ABCDEFGHIJKabcdefghijklm
ABCDEFGHIJKabcdefghijkln
ABCDEFGHIJKabcdefghijklm

ABCDEFGHIJKabcdefghijkl
ABCDEFGHIJKabcdefghijklm
ABCDEFGHIJKabcdefghijklm

Type classification

The first types were replicas of local manuscript models in current use. In northern Europe, this was blackletter. In southern Europe, this was Chancery Italic. It is much lighter and more legible, so it became a bigger player in the evolution of type design. These early Italian types are known as Old Style, and many are still in use today with only minor refinements, principally to make their shapes more consistent.

Any type classification system is subject to argument and exception. The one I use is simple – simple being preferrable to complex in almost everything – and has eight categories, some broken into subcategories that are very useful to know. Remember, however, that type design is an art and, like all art, some faces fit in more than one category at a time. Even something as simple as serif/sans serif can't be definitively determined on many faces where that very distinction is meant to be blurred. So, too, category names describe type characteristics, not precise historical dating.

1. Serif Type with cross-lines at the ends of strokes. There are four categories of serif types: Old Style (1450s–1600s), Transitional (1700s), Modern (late 1700s), and Slab Serif (1800s).
Serif Old Style The first types designed were based on Roman capitals for majuscules and humanist bookhand for minuscules. They are designed and used best for text setting. *Garamond* is the basis of nearly 1,000 fonts, including third generation digital interpretations of phototype interpretations of metal type interpretations. Robert Slimbach's 1989 *Adobe Garamond* is perhaps the most accurate representation of Claude Garamond's original early 1600s design, though *Stempel Garamond* (1924), *Garamond 3* (1936, from Morris Fuller Benton's 1917 American Type Founders designs), and Jan Tschichold's *Sabon* (1967) are fine examples. Garamond has relatively bold serifs because of coarse paper, which had to be dampened before printing to accept an impression, and the wooden press, which could not be adjusted to lighten the impression.

ABCDEFGHIJKabcdefghijkl
ABCDEFGHIJKabcdefghijklm

ABCDEFGHIJKabcdefghijkl
ABCDEFGHIJKabcdefghijklmn

ABCDEFGHIJKabcdefghijk
ABCDEFGHIJKabcdefghijkl

ABCDEFGHIJKabcdefgh
ABCDEFGHIJKabcdefghij

ABCDEFGHIJKabcdefghi
ABCDEFGHIJKabcdefghijl
ABCDEFGHIJKabcdefghijkl

ABCDEFGHIJKabcdefghij
ABCDEFGHIJKabcdefghijklmn
ABCDEFGHIJKabcdefghijklm

VENETIAN OLD STYLE Based on the handwriting of Italian scribes, it first appeared in about 1470. It is characterized by axes angled to the left, bracketed serifs, an angled cross stroke on the lowercase *e*, and low stroke contrast (thins aren't very thin because printing at the time wasn't able to handle such delicacy).

ALDINE OLD STYLE are types designed in the style of Aldus Manutius's 1490 characters. They have greater stroke contrast and the cross stroke on the lowercase "e" is horizontal. DUTCH OLD STYLE or GERALDE evolved from a blending of German blackletter and Aldine Old Style, so they have darker color, larger x-height, and greater stroke weight contrast.

Transitional serif Types that show the evolution from Dutch Old Style to Modern in the mid-1700s, and show chartacteristics of both: more accentuation between thick and thin strokes, flat serifs, and very slightly inclined axes on curves. Designed and used best for text setting. No longer based solely on handwritten examples, these were the first type refinements of letters as shapes in their own right. John Baskerville (1706–1775) was an English master calligrapher who became one of the most influential type designers in history. His types were lighter than Old Style, and the curved emphasis was more vertical. Baskerville also reinvented the way paper was made, using heated plates to smooth the surface (equivalent to today's *wove* surface), and developed a darker ink. His type refinements were not well received: Benjamin Franklin wrote Baskerville that a friend reported "Baskerville eyepain" was caused by the "thin and narrow strokes of your letters."

Modern serif First faces designed based not on a handwritten model but on the idealized shape of letters themselves. They first appeared in the late 1700s. Firmin Didot and Giambattista Bodoni were the primary evolutionists. Modern faces are the result of several technical advancements of the period. Copperplate engraving allowed much greater detail and paper quality continued to improve in smoothness. Modern types have a more

ABCDEFGHIJKabcdefghijklm
ABCDEFGHIJKabcdefghijklmn
ABCDEFGHIJKabcdefghijklm

ABCDEFGHIJKabcdefghijklm
ABCDEFGHIJKabcdefghijklmno
ABCDEFGHIJKabcdefghijklm

ABCDEFGHIJKabcdefghijklmn
ABCDEFGHIJKabcdefghijklmn
ABCDEFGHIJKabcdefghijklmn

ABCDEFGHIJK&abcchctdeffghijklmnopq
ABCDEFGHIJKabcdefghijklmno
ABCDEFGHIJKabcdefghijklmnopqrstu
ABCDEFGHIJKabcdefghijklmn
ABCDEFGHIJKabcdefghijklmn
ABCDEFGHIJKabcdefghijklmnopqrst
ABCDEFGHIJKabcdefghijklmn

mechanical appearance – constructed rather than drawn – and they have extremely high stroke contrast, vertical axes, and horizontal, unbracketed serifs. They are particularly well-suited for display and can be difficult to read in continuous text.

DIDONES were created during the 18th century.

TWENTIETH CENTURY MODERNS are more stylized and have even greater stroke contrast.

Slab serif The Industrial Revolution in the mid-1800s introduced mass production and advertising. Posters encouraged very bold, highly visible types. First called "Egyptians" after the popularity of archaeological discoveries taking place at the time, slab serifs are extremely effective for display use. All slab serif types are distinguished by relatively consistent stroke weight and serifs that are as thick – or thicker – as the vertical strokes. The search for even bolder, more visible faces in the late 1800s lead to types without serifs so letters can be more tightly packed together. These came to be known as grotesques or sans serifs.

NINETEENTH CENTURIES were the first slab serif faces.

CLARENDONS have bracketed serifs, or curves where the serif meets the character's strokes.

UNBRACKETEDS have serifs that meet the strokes without curves.

NEO CLARENDONS Twentieth century refinements of earlier slab serifs with increased usefulness for text.

2. Sans serif means *without* in French. Sans serif types, therefore, are types that have no serifs. The earliest sans serif letterforms were written 2,000 years ago, but William Caslon IV tried to market the first sans serif type in 1816. Vincent Figgins, calling the type "Sans surryph," and William Thorowgood, calling it "Grotesque," tried their versions in England in 1832. The term "Gothic" was applied to these new types in America. Jan Tschichold and the Bauhaus and de Stijl movements spread the use of sans serif types in the 1920s. There are three categories of sans serifs: Grotesque and New Grotesque, Geometric, and Humanist. All have relatively little stroke contrast and are highly legible as display and, with added spacing, successful as text.

ABCDEFGHIJK ABCDEFGHI
ABCDEFGHIJKabcdefghijkln
ABCDEFGHIJKLMNOPQI

ABCDEFGHIJKabcdefghij
UBCDEFGHIJKabcdefghijklmn
UBCDEFGHIJKabcdefgh

ABCDEFGHIJKabcdefg
ABCDEFGHIJKabcdef

ABCDEFGHIJKabcdefgh
ABCDEFGHIJKLMNO

Sans serif Grotesques and **New Grotesques** First released sans serifs. New Grotesques are more recent – generally Swiss – designs that are refinements of earlier grotesques. Erik Spiekermann says: "Univers, the classic European face, is the first family with mathematical weights: 21 weights from very light to very heavy and legible under nearly every condition."

Sans serif Geometrics Bauhaus-inspired simplicity, mono-weight strokes, and near-geometric perfection make these harder to read than grotesques.

Sans serif Humanists are based on Roman proportions, look somewhat hand drawn, and blend features of both serif and sans serif. They have the greatest stroke contrast of the sans serifs.

3. Script Script faces, more so than italics, resemble handwriting. Scripts can be arranged by chronology, style (ranging from formal to casual), or even by intended use. The best may be a system based on similarity to actual handwriting: **Italian miniscule** (*Poetica*), **English interpretations of Italian letterforms** (*Optilord Swash*), **Brush scripts** (*Pelican*), **Broad pen scripts** (*Post Antiqua*), **Monoline scripts** (*Memimas*), and the catchall category of **Combination scripts** (*Roman Script D*).

4. Glyphic Based on stone carving, rather than pen drawing. Characters have low stroke contrast and are best used as all-caps, which is the way source carvings were rendered.

5. Blackletter Northern European scripts at the time of Gutenberg's movable type. Also called Gothic and Old English.

6. Monospaced Types in which all letters and numerals occupy the same width, useful for tabular and columnar arrangements.

7. Decorative All the types that don't fit in the other categories. Because their letterforms are either elaborate or abstract, decorative types are rarely useful for text settings. Many decorative faces lack lowercase characters and full punctuation.

8. Symbol, ornament, and dingbats Illustrations and symbols whose complexity is limited only by the number of bezier points in their outline descriptions.

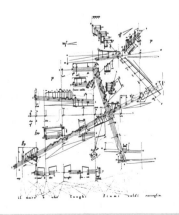

Space and type

> *By every measure as significant as the words to be printed, for typographers, the empty spaces on the page are active shapes that contribute to the expression of the whole. We refer to this as 'unity' — in all creative fields, the essential quality of design."* KARL-AUGUST HANKE

◁ Lack of space results in a stuffed message. This can be used to advantage, when the message itself is stifling (*far left*, by Charles S. Anderson), or to disadvantage, by making reading impossible.

◁ Equal letter, word, and linespacing turns reading into deciphering, as in *The Puzzle Gravestone*, Samuel Bean's 1865 commemoration of his wife. Reading direction can be vertical, horizontal, or diagonal, and from left to right, right to left, downwards or upwards.

◁ Poster by John Bark. *In typography, meaning is a condition of the position of an event in space. Position – order in space – matters. When concern for position is relaxed, visible language becomes loose in the joints." Peter Burnhill*

▢ Ground can exist behind (*left*) or in front of a figure (*middle*). Ground is sometimes ambiguous and exists in both places simultaneously (*right*).

THE BEST SPACE IS INVISIBLE. It supports the message with subtlety and grace. In every instance when we notice space, there is too much or too little of it. Either way, our attention has been drawn away from the message to the form in which the message is being delivered. That's bad for communication.

In typography, as in all design, space is there to make the foreground – the type, the design elements, the message – look good. Without attending to space, the filled-in areas will look misaligned, packed too tightly, and times, flying apart for lack of proximity. Typography is 10 percent letter management and 90 percent space management.

Space is a vital aspect of musical notation since pauses are as important as notes played. The history of music shows a variety of approaches (*far left, top to bottom*): *neume notation* c900 with its arcs indicating general rises and falls in pitch; *tablature* c1500 that shows a lute's strings and letters to indicate fret fingerwork; *the staff* c1600 that requires a clef sign to indicate musical range for the notes; an experimental 50-line staff from 1952 as a statement of the absurd; and *partitioning*, in which the page is divided into sections that use space flexibly (this 1972 example by Bussotti uses angled staves to describe acceleration).

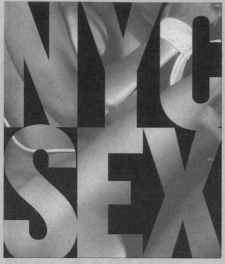

plataanit
monique
lange

OTAVA

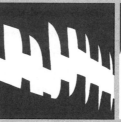

"The graphic signs called letters are so completely blended with the stream of written thought that their presence is as unperceived as the ticking of a clock in the measurement of time... But to be con-

"The graphic signs called letters are so completely blended with the stream of written thought that their presence is as unperceived as the ticking of a clock in the measurement of time... But to be con-

"The graphic signs called letters are so completely blended with the stream of written thought that their presence is as unperceived as the ticking of a clock in the measurement of time... But to be con-

"The graphic signs called letters are so completely blended with the stream of written thought that their presence is as unperceived as the ticking of a clock in the measurement of time... But to be con-

"The graphic signs called letters are so completely blended with the stream of written thought that their presence is as unperceived as the ticking of a clock in the measurement of time... But to be con-

"The graphic signs called letters are so completely blended with the stream of written thought that their presence is as unperceived as the ticking of a clock in the measurement of time... But to be con-

"The graphic signs called letters are so completely blended with the stream of written thought that their presence is as unperceived as the ticking of a clock in the measurement of time... But to be con-

"The graphic signs called letters are so completely blended with the stream of written thought that their presence is as unperceived as the ticking of a clock in the measurement

"The graphic signs called

letters are so completely

blended with the stream

of written thought that

their presence is as unperceived as the ticking of

Not letterforms

The spaces surrounding and within letters are as significant as the letters themselves. In fact, the shapes around the letters *define* the letters. Managing the spaces between and around letters makes type more or less legible.

Charles A. Bigelow wrote in 1977, "[Type] is a figure-ground synthesis in which the letterforms are the figure, the salient element, and the counterforms and spaces are the ground, the unnoticed element… Although the empty space of the ground has resisted precise analysis, it is nevertheless intuitively understood by all good practitioners of the lettering arts… The question (to) ask appears simple, 'What is good letterspacing?'" In answer, Bigelow describes a complex system requiring a photoelectric reader sensitive to value. But the goal he defines is twofold: that each letter should appear to be exactly in the center between its neighbors, and that the overall setting have consistent color.

Consistent color is achieved by managing spacing attributes (*opposite*). Excepting the top row, none of the *letterforms* have been altered in these studies. The only changes are to the *spaces* between and around them.

Change the type weight The top row is set 9-point solid Avenir Light, Roman, and Heavy.

Change the letterspacing The three paragraphs in the middle row are set 9-point solid Avenir Light. The spacing attributes have been adjusted in the left paragraph to tight letterspacing and open word spacing; the middle paragraph attributes are normal; and the right paragraph has open letterspacing and tight word spacing.

Change the linespacing The three paragraphs in the bottom row are set 9-point Avenir Light. The left paragraph is set solid, that is, with no additional linespacing; the middle paragraph is set on 12 points of linespacing, that is, with 3 points of additional linespacing, and the right paragraph is set on 15 points of linespacing, that is, with 6 points of additional linespacing.

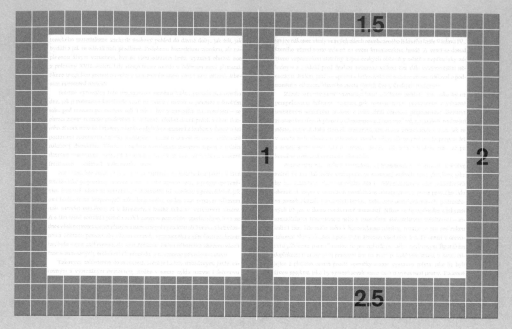

It is easy to make copy look crowded inside a box, which is why this ugly treatment is often seen. As with other design relationships, proportion is critical. The appearance of the correct space between text and box is dependent on the type's size and the linespacing used. Here the linespacing is greater than the space between the type and box, so the relationship between type and box is emphasized over the more important relationship of type to type.

For greatest legibility, the type to type relationship must be emphasized over the relationship of type to its surroundings. The linespacing used in this paragraph is less than the space between the type and the edges of the box. White space is properly used as a *connector* of type to itself and as a *separator* of type from its surroundings.

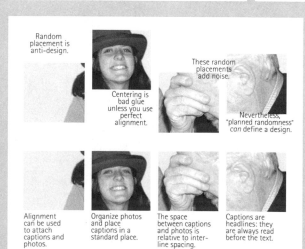

Random placement is anti-design.

Centering is bad glue unless you use perfect alignment.

These random placements add noise.

Nevertheless, "planned randomness" *can* define a design.

Alignment can be used to attach captions and photos.

Organize photos and place captions in a standard place.

The space between captions and photos is relative to inter-line spacing.

Captions are headlines: they are always read before the text.

⬚ Missing characters are the focal point – and the message – in this headline from a corporate ad.

⬚ The edges of letter-forms must be optically aligned at display sizes.

◁ Alignment can dissociate or join elements, as these captions and images show (*far left*). And it can be used for drama: the vertical edge of flush left type contrasts with dynamic imagery in Anton Stankowski's 1953 poster promoting "airways and runways."

Background Margins are the first space readers see and create a reader's initial openness to the page. Margins must be in proportion to the page and the type-filled area. Tradition dictates that the inside margin be the smallest, the head margin the next smallest, the outer margin the second largest, and the foot margin the largest (*opposite*). ▷ Don't put copy in front of a color unless it is very light – equivalent to about a 10 percent tint – and don't put type in front of an image. It negates the pictures value *and* it makes the copy much harder to read. ▷ Uncoated paper makes type easier to read because there is little reflection, but makes pictures look a bit fuzzy because ink absorbs into the fibers. Coated paper makes type harder to read because it is shiny, but it makes pictures look great because the ink is held out on the surface and the dots retain their crisp edges.

Alignment/Optical alignment is essential for display type where larger letterforms make mere mechanical alignment more apparent. Characters have a variety of shapes, and, when set using normal defaults, they don't look even. Rounded characters (*bcdeopqsBCDGOPQRS2356890*) and characters that end in a diagonal (*kvwxyzAKLVWXYZ47*) or horizontal (*jrtEFJT*) stroke must poke out a bit beyond a mechanically correct edge so they appear to be correctly aligned. Mechanical alignment is done by the computer and only considers the left- and right-most edges of characters. Punctuation and serifs may be ignored for optical alignment. ▷ "Hung punctuation," first used by Gutenberg to emulate scribes' practice, is placed outside the measure for an optically even appearance. All visually small characters like the comma, period, hyphen, apostrophe, or quote mark, should be placed outside the measure to avoid an optical indention. Larger punctuation marks like the colon, semi-colon, question and exclamation marks, parentheses, brackets, and slashes appear to occupy the same space as letters, so they may be held within the measure. Some page makeup programs can now hang punctuation automatically, but optical correctness remains the measure by which quality typography is judged.

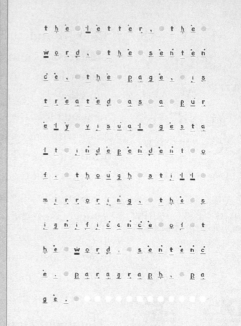

Tracking is macro spacing
No track

Tracking is macro spacing
Very tight

Tracking is macro spacing
Tight

Tracking is macro spacing
Normal

Tracking is macro spacing
Loose

Tracking is macro spacing
Very Loose

Letterspacing is seen in proportion to word spacing. This paragraph is set with too much letterspacing, given its amount of word spacing. This causes the words to merge into line groupings and slows reading

Letterspacing is seen in proportion to word spacing. This paragraph is set with too little letterspacing given the amount of word spacing. This causes the lines of type to break into individual word groupings. Letterspacing is seen in propor-

This last paragraph is set with the right letterspacing, given the word spacing used. Each word retains its integrity as a discreet entity, yet the line's integrity is also maintained, making reading effortless. This

Letterspacing

The essence of letterspacing is to make the letters appear equidistant from one another. Readers should never be aware of type's spacing unless the purposeful tightening or loosening of spacing, which indicates an increase or decrease of reading speed, is an illustration of itself. Both text and display are affected by spacing. It is more important for display type to be properly spaced, however, because bad spacing is more noticeable at large type sizes.

Good letterspacing can be defined very simply as *invisible spacing*. Neither too tight nor too open, it should not draw attention to itself. Good letterspacing creates even type color: there should be enough space to separate letterforms without weakening the word units.

Letterspacing is perceived as tight or loose in relation to word spacing and should be tighter at display sizes than at text sizes so the letters create a darker, more visible word shape. Condensed types should be more tightly letterspaced than normal or expanded types. Small type should be more openly letterspaced so individual characters are more easily identifiable.

Letterforms can generally be separated into four shapes: those that end vertically on both sides (hilmnuEHIMNRU), those that end with a hanging stroke on one or both sides (fjrtFJLP TY1), those that end in angles on one or both edges (kvwxyz AKVWXZ47), and those that end in curves on one or both edges (abcdegopqsBCDGOQS2356890). Letterspacing is the craft of fitting these shapes together so they look right.

There are two ways to adjust letterspacing: *tracking* and *kerning*. *Tracking* refers to adjusting the spacing of all type in a word or paragraph. Default tracking characteristics can be customized in the Preferences panel of all page makeup programs: one change that is often useful is reducing global word spacing in relation to character spacing. *Kerning* refers to adjusting the space between a specific pair of letterforms. Tracking is *macro* space adjustment. Kerning is *micro* space adjustment.

◀☐ Experimental letterspacing appeared as early as 1503 by Thomas Anshelm in his *De laudibus sanctae crucis*. Type was set with equal letter and line spacing. Printed in black and red on bright yellow, this was a difficult piece to prepare. A modern equivalent is by Bob Aufuldish that makes use of a horizontal and vertical grid. Both are meant to be seen rather than read effortlessly.

"Writing is not a series of strokes, but space, divided into characteristic shapes by strokes." *Gerrit Noordzij*

ADP FedEx DELL CIT

☐ Spacing is often used in logos, where few elements must create a carefully crafted, memorable impression.

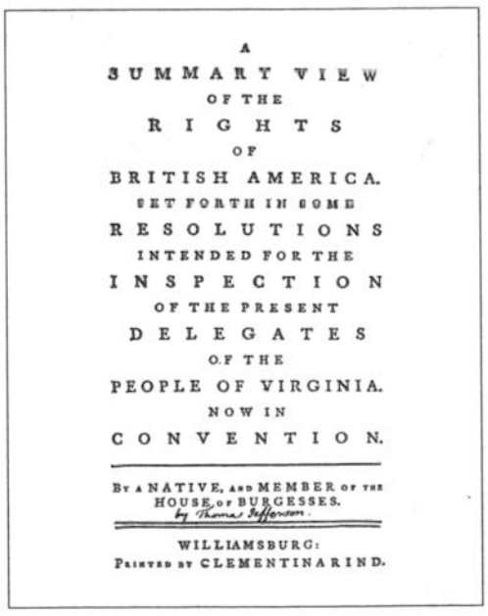

A SUMMARY VIEW OF THE RIGHTS OF BRITISH AMERICA. SET FORTH IN SOME RESOLUTIONS INTENDED FOR THE INSPECTION OF THE PRESENT DELEGATES OF THE PEOPLE OF VIRGINIA. NOW IN CONVENTION.

BY A NATIVE, AND MEMBER OF THE HOUSE OF BURGESSES.

by Thomas Jefferson.

WILLIAMSBURG: PRINTED BY CLEMENTINA RIND.

☐ Letterspaced caps are used in Thomas Jefferson's *Summary View*, a 1773 document encouraging separation from England.

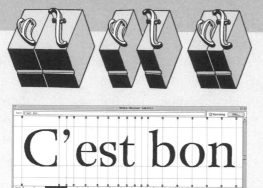

A"	ay	Fa	Ku	OX	RO	**TA**	U.	WA	xa	y.	'
A'	by	Fe	Ky	OY	RT	TC	U,	WC	xc	y,	,1
AC	CO	Fo	ka	oc	RV	TG	**VA**	WO	xe	'A	1.
AG	CT	Fr	ke	oo	RY	**TO**	VO	W.	xo	'.	1,
AO	CY	Fu	ko	ov	r'	TS	VY	W,	**YA**	',	10
AQ	Co	f'	**L"**	ow	r.	TV	**V.**	Wa	YG	.'	11
AT	Ce	fa	**L'**	ox	r,	TW	**V,**	We	**YG**	,'	14
AV	DA	fe	LA	oy	ra	TY	V:	Wi	YS	'A	16
AW	DV	ff	LC	**PA**	rc	**T.**	V;	Wo	**Y.**	'd	17
AY	DW	fi	LG	PO	rd	**T,**	**Va**	Wr	**Y,**	'o	31
Ac	DY	fl	LO	**P.**	re	T:	**Ve**	Wu	**Y:**	'r	41
Ad	e'	fo	LS	**P,**	ro	T;	**Vi**	Wy	Y;	's	51
Ae	ev	fs	**LT**	Pa	rw	**Ta**	**Vo**	wa	**Ya**	't	61
Aq	ew	ft	**LV**	Pe	rx	**Tc**	Vr	wc	**Ye**	'v	74
Au	ex	ij	**LW**	Po	ry	**Ti**	**Vu**	we	**Yo**	'w	76
Av	ey	KC	**LY**	Pr	SA	**To**	Vy	wo	**Yu**	'y	7.
Aw	**FA**	KG	**Ly**	py	ST	**Tr**	v.	w.	ya	"A	7,
Ay	FG	KO	OA	Qu	SY	**Ts**	v,	w,	yc	."	7:
a'	FO	Ka	OT	RA	s'	**Tu**	va	XC	ye	.'	81
av	**F.**	Ke	OV	RC	st	**Tw**	ve	XO	yo	.1	91
aw	**F,**	Ko	OW	RG	sy	**Ty**	vo	Xy	ys	,"	01

❝ Bad spacing is bad spacing in any era."
Aaron Burns (1922–1991)

Avelãs
Avelãs
Avelãs
Avelãs

Kerning is the space adjustment between a pair of characters. Their closeness should resemble that of their neighbors and thus become invisible.

Consistency and context are the keys to kerning. If the surrounding type is relatively open, kerning makes ill-fitting pairs more open. If the surrounding type is relatively tight, kerning matches the neighbor's tightness.

Before movable type was invented, scribes wrote and spaced characters by eye as they went. Gutenberg's first fonts included dozens of paired characters to emulate the written hand. Metal type did not allow even letterspacing for a physical reason: the metal blocks that held the letters had to abut. Characters that needed to be closer together would be cut and filed to allow the metal bodies to be placed closer together (*top left*). Phototypesetting made the process much easier and faster and introduced a new era in very tight letterspacing which today looks like an out-of-date style.

Page makeup programs automatically kern awkward letter pairs, a process that is more reliable at text sizes – where minor inconsistencies are acceptable – than at larger display settings, where inconsistent letterspacing is a telltale of mediocre design. It remains the designer's responsibility to create perfectly spaced display characters.

To check kerning, flip a design upside down so the positive shapes (the letterforms) and the negative shapes (the spaces between the characters) lose their meaning and just become shapes. Inconsistencies will become much more identifiable. Or imagine water being poured between each character pair. A well-kerned word would require an equivalent amount of water filling each intercharacter space.

Fonts that are advertised as having hundreds or thousands of kerning pairs are inelegantly prepared. A well-designed font, one in which the spacing attributes have been thoughtfully perfected, should not need more than about one hundred kerning pairs.

FRESH MADESUSHI

Justifying type re-
quires forcing space
between words. Nar-
row columns have too
few word spaces, so
this becomes visible.

J. B. Lenoir
B. B. King
J. A. T. P. Blues

This is six-point The Sans
Semi Light Plain set justified
across a measure of six
picas. The word spacing is
greater than the linespacing,
so vertical "rivers" of white
appear. This is one telltale
sign of poor typography.

Using the space bar   to
align columns is a   poor
solution: spacing   increments are limited   to
the type size in use.   So
true alignment is un- likely.

Flush left type has
even word spacing.
Narrow columns will
have leftover space
at the right edge,
where it is harmless.

J.B. Lenoir
B.B. King
J.A.T.P. Blues

This is six-point The Sans
Semi Light Plain set justified
across a measure of six
picas. Here the linespacing
is greater than the word
spacing, easing reading.

Set tabs to create a   true
vertical alignment.   You
will have a sharp left edge
and you will have   fewer
adjustments if the   type
size is changed   later.

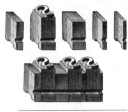

Wordspacing

Typographer's work is judged by the spaces between words as
well as between letters and lines. Using defaults does not always
provide quality text type, and rarely provides quality display type.

Ideal wordspacing, like ideal letterspacing, should be invisible.
It should be just enough to separate word thoughts. Too much
word spacing breaks a line of type into individual words (*top left,
two examples on the right*). These four experimental text settings
are from a 1978 issue of *Visible Language* magazine and emphasize (L-R) the line, the word space, the column, and the word.

Wordspacing didn't come into use until the 4th to 8th centuries. SCRIBESWEREREQUIREDTOUSEWORDSPACINGWHILECON-
VERTINGALLCAPSWRITINGLIKETHIS into the then-new minuscule
letters with majuscule initials. In medieval Europe, scribes
made facing pages symmetrical. The ultimate expression of this
was to write every line so it would perfectly fill the width of the
column. The only way to do this was to abbreviate words, which
came to be called *contractions*. With the development of movable type in the latter 1400s, such *justified* type was attained by
adjusting the spaces, rather than the words.

▶ As described on page 62, wordspacing and letterspacing are
seen relative to each other. Open goes with open, tight with tight.

▶ Grossly uneven word spacing occurs in justified type across
a narrow measure. Set as flush left type.

▶ Reduce wordspacing after small punctuation like periods and
commas. Adding a full space simply makes a hole. This is especially important in display type.

▶ Don't put two spaces after a period at the end of a sentence.
Sentence beginnings were enhanced by typing two spaces after
a period on monospace typewriters in the 20th century. Called
french spacing, it is not necessary with variable-spaced type.

▶ Vertical and diagonal rivers appear when word spacing is
greater than linespacing, particularly in justified type.

▶ Many fonts have too much wordspacing as their default. Setting the word spacing at 60 or 80 percent of "normal" is ideal.

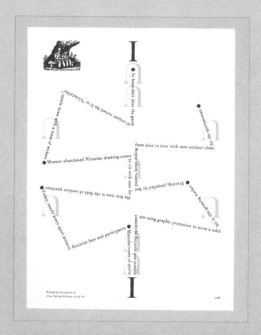

Nestled under Petrin hill, Malá Strana slopes down in a cascade of red roofs interspersed with lush gardens and vineyards. The area, with its medieval layout of alleys, passageways, steps, and culs-de-sac, is ideal for wandering. Time stands still as the Vltava casts its hypnotic spell.

```
                              Nestled
                        under Petrin hill,
Malá Strana
slopes down
in a
    cascade
          of red
                roofs
    interspersed
         with lush gardens        and
                                     vineyards.
The area, with its medieval layout
    of alleys,
passageways, steps
              and culs-de-
              sac, is ideal for wandering.   Time stands
                                               still
as the Vltava
          casts its hypnotic          spell.
```

◁ Bradbury Thompson uses type as line in his croquet illustration from a 1955 issue of Westvaco *Inspiration for Printers*. The wickets are upside down capital *U*'s. A creative birth announcement makes literary allusions using line structure – and lack of it.

◁ Lyrics' baselines are given a special treatment to reveal the feeling of the songs and their Brazilian performer, Djavan.

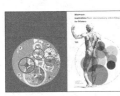

◁ Alignment on the left unifies the headline, issue number, and copyright information in Bradbury Thompson's title page for a 1945 issue of Westvaco's *Inspiration for Printers*. Student explorations using abstraction and space with flush left, flush right, and justified type.

Line spacing and line breaks

A 19th century parlor game made poems out of texts like the Bible and Charles Dickens. By breaking the text into segments and giving each phrase a poem-like position, ordinary prose seemed to become more meaningful and symbolic (*left*).

Line length We read text in "sacadic jumps," in groups of three or four words (*page 66*). Lines that are too short chop reading by interrupting these sacadic jumps. Minimum line length must be at least one such group, that is, three or four words long. Beyond four groups – twelve to sixteen words – the eye tires and reading becomes effortful. Maximum line length should not be more than about twelve words, or 50–60 characters.

Justified vs flush left Justified type is set so each line is exactly the same width. To achieve this, leftover space at the end of each line is distributed among the word spaces. It is common for word spaces to vary from one line to the next, creating uneven color and revealing poor craftsmanship, especially in narrow columns with only two or three word spaces. Extremely uneven word spacing causes rivers – wiggly vertical columns – to form. On the scale of typographic righteousness, this is a major sin. Flush left type, on the other hand, inserts even word spacing throughout a column and leaves emptiness on the right end of each line. By adjusting the hyphenation preferences, the ragged right edge can be set. The smaller the hyphenation zone, the more frequently hyphens will be used and the smoother the ragged edge. This is known as a *soft rag*. A *hard rag*, made when hyphens are disallowed or allowed only in a wide hyphenation zone, has a more uneven right edge because words that exceed the allowable maximum get dragged down to the next line in their totality, leaving a gap. ▷ Setting text centered or flush right ragged left makes reading particularly difficult because it makes it harder to find the beginning of the next line. It may be used for captions that are no more than three lines deep. ▷ "Breaking for sense" is a technique in which copy is broken into natural phrases, regardless of line length. This must typically be used in display type.

JUSTIFIED

FLUSH LEFT WITH NO HYPHENATION

FLUSH LEFT WITH HYPHENATION AT 3 PICAS, 0 POINTS

FLUSH LEFT WITH HYPHENATION AT 0 PICAS, 3 POINTS

FLUSH LEFT WITH HYPHENATION AT 0 PICAS, 3 POINTS

FIFTY
CHARS
PER
LINE

SIXTY
CHARS
PER
LINE

This is ten-point Barmeno Regular set to a measure of twenty-nine picas, the space that is available. Two points of additional linespacing have been added, equivalent to the "auto" linespacing default. When the character-per-line number exceeds sixty, reading becomes measurably more difficult. Counteract this unpleasantness by enlarging the type size or narrowing the column to get fifty to sixty characters per line, or, if the type size you are using is required, as in this example, by adding two to four points of linespacing.

This is ten-point Mrs Eaves set with no additional linespacing. Because it has a small x-height, it requires less linespacing than the Barmeno example to the right.

This is ten-point Barmeno Regular set with no additional linespacing. Because it has a large x-height, it requires more linespacing than the Mrs Eaves example to the left.

Talk to the Hoof
Post Office Box 4
Stamford, Lincs
PE9 1NA, U.K.
44 0 1780 65587
talktothehoof.com

Talk to the Hoof
Post Office Box 4
Stamford, Lincs
PE9 1NA, U.K.
44 0 1780 65587
talktothehoof.com

TWO-INCH NAIL SHOT INTO CARPENTER'S BRAIN: HARM NOT SERIOUS

TWO-INCH NAIL SHOT INTO CARPENTER'S BRAIN: HARM NOT SERIOUS

In addition to the five schemes diagrammed above, paragraphs may be indicated in all sorts of creative ways. This treatment contrasts a single normal space after each period with exaggerated space after the period that completes a paragraph. This technique is simple and elegant: it uses space in a fresh way by offering a new solution to an old problem. The only catch is that paragraphs cannot end at the coincidental end of a line of type. No paragraphs should ever end at the top of a column. The last unfilled line of text looks carelessly abandoned in a highly visible place. This treatment is particularly susceptible to mistreatment. But only a dedicated designer would attempt its use. Paragraphs may be indicated in

This treatment is based on the idea that each paragraph must be fully filled. Each column's width is adjusted to achieve a perfectly-filled rectangle shape. Initial caps must base align with, say, the fourth line of text. Paragraphs may extend as long as necessary, but they must be at least four lines deep, like the initial. Length of each paragraph matters: it wouldn't do to have two paragraphs in a row be the same width. The initial would seem to be floating unattached to the beginning of its paragraph. Such typographic craftsmanship takes time but it elevates the work to a higher level of competence and quality.

Treat paragraphs like individual captions. Each is positioned in a column or it can be hung like a flag on a pole.

One graph follows the previous by aligning on the next baseline. The easiest way to do this is to use tabs.

This treatment breaks copy into bite-size chunks, which is one of the kindest tasks a typographer can do for a reader.

Linespacing/Optical linespacing Typography is, among other things, the craft of making fine adjustments so type is as appealing and effortless to read as possible. It is balancing the letters with space. Too little linespacing, like in this paragraph, darkens an area of type and makes readers feel claustrophobic.

Too much linespacing causes the reader to become aware of individual lines. Adding space between lines of type is called *leading*, after the technologically outdated practice of placing bars of metal between set lines of type. Line spacing should be sufficient to make returns to the left edge of a column easy, but not so much that the column's integrity as a stack of lines is compromised. ▷ Longer lines, lines with more than sixty characters, require additional linespacing. ▷ Types with small x-heights need somewhat less linespacing because the ascenders and descenders ensure optical space between lines of type. ▷ Types with large x-heights need additional linespacing. ▷ *Minus linespacing*, that is, taking out linespacing so the baseline-to-baseline distance is less than the type's point size, is useful with all caps settings, where there are no descenders and it is an asset to make the type darker. ▷ Adjust linespacing when setting passages in all-caps or lining numerals to achieve optically consistent spacing.

Paragraphing Visually separating ideas while maintaining overall unity is a big part of typography. Paragraphs separate ideas by signalling that a new idea is coming. There are numerous ways of flagging a paragraph beginning. Placing space at the beginning of a section of type is only one way to paragraph. There are various other ways of accomplishing this job: you may skip a line space (or half a line space, which usually looks better – but do not also indent!); you may indent the first line (the distance is in proportion to the linespacing: greater linespacing requires deeper paragraph indents – but do not also skip a linespace!); or you may use a more imaginative system. One such method is to break copy into hierarchical significance and indent accordingly.

⬕ Linespacing in metal type was increased by inserting strips of lead between lines of type, hence the term *leading*.

◁ Line spacing becomes inconsistent (*far left*) when lining figures are set amidst a U/lc setting. Add a point or two of extra space above lines for optical evenness (*near left, fourth and fifth lines*).

◁ Paragraphing tells the reader a new idea is beginning. From left: no additional space is given – each paragraph simply begins flush left and relies on short, unfinished last lines as indicators; skipping a line space with no indent; indention of the first line with no line space; hanging indent ("outdent"); and hierarchical indention to signal importances.

⬕ Paragraphing is used as a tool as early as 1486 in this page from the *De Antiquitate Judaica* by Joannes Rubeus Vercellensis.

A▷

B▷

C▷

D▷

E▷

F▷

G▷

H▷

Type in three dimensions

Printed space is represented in two dimensions: height and width. This ad, playing on the phrase "easier to find" with a tiny "$412" by itself in the upper left corner, is a contrast of fullness and emptiness.

The third dimension, depth, can be used as an attention-getting technique, though it has to be implied in two dimensional design. There are four ways of creating the illusion of three dimensions with type. Each can be broadly interpreted:

Overlap elements Placing an object in front of another re-creates reality effectively. Image in front of type is far more convincing than type in front of image, but be sure not to obscure type so much that it can't be read. Ambiguous space is created when one or more of the elements is transparent. Ⓐ Put imagery inside letters to make them look like letter-shaped windows. Ⓑ Use solids and transparency to build a pile of letters; letters can look so real they cast shadows. ⒸScaled type is placed across the tops of five newspapers and layering is used at the risk of making illegible in a 1928 poster. Ⓓ Put imagery in front of type. Silhouetted art hides parts of letters, therefore it is seen to be in front; transparent shape placed in front of type. Ⓔ Use paper's thickness. Print on front and back of sheet (*right*); print letters, tear or damage the paper and photograph; cut a hole to actually see through to another layer; or photograph cut letters in paper.

□ These three-dimensional type visualizations are micro versions of the categories described at right.

Scale and hierarchy ⒻBig objects are perceived as nearer. Use space and size to imply depth. Switch the expected scale of objects for a fresh interpretation.

Perspective The translation of volumes and spatial relationships to two dimensions was perfected only in the 15th century. Ⓖ Craft three-dimensional letters and photograph; distort and skew letterforms; or draw three-dimensional letters.

Motion Moving objects are more real than stationary objects. Ⓗ Motion can be implied by blurring in Photoshop, by slicing an image into pieces, or by repeating an element.

❝ It is only shallow people who do not judge by appearances. The mystery of the world is the visible, not the invisible." *Oscar Wilde, in a letter*

3 73

[A]▷

[B]▷ [C]▷

[D]▷

Abstracting type with space

Type is usually placed into space, that is, type is perceived as being in front of the white background. Dynamic results from the background being brought to the foreground, in front of type. This works best in display type, where characters and words are large enough to accommodate the insults perpetrated on them. Text type, being small, is more sensitive to being tipped into illegibility, either by accident or on purpose. Besides, once the browser has been hard won into being a reader, nothing should dissuade him from *staying* a reader.

The best way to abstract figure and ground is to think of both entities as equally valid shapes. Figures impose themselves on the space in which they exist. A black letterform pushes the white space beneath it out of its way, so you might say the white space has taken all the pain. To abstract type, make the black shapes take some of the pain, too. Make the white shapes push the black shapes out of the way.

Chop pieces of letters off to allow space to come to the front and impose itself on letters. At left are student samples from an exercise I give that causes them to see space incrementally: purely in the background, alongside a figure, then fully integrated and equal partners with the figure. ⒶThe first study positions the type purely in relation to the internal structure of the imagery. This is an organic design. The type is foreground and accommodates the image. The image is background and takes no pain whatever. A grid is introduced for the next studies. ⒷBreaking the live area into 25 units (a five-by-five grid), the second study places ground alongside the image and requires the type to relate only to the grid: type and image both become figure with the intruction of a new ground. ⒸContinuing the use of the five-by-five unit grid, the third study requires that emptiness be introduced into the image. Type and image each must take pain to accommodate the grid. This forces ground, defined by the grid, to be perceived as figure. ⒹThe fourth study is experimental and asks that an additional figure/ground relationship be created. Without much left to find, the search itself is worthwhile.

PHOEBUS PALAST

ANFANGSZEITEN: 4 6¹⁵ 8³⁰
SONNTAGS: ¹⁴⁵ 4 6¹⁵ 8³⁰

IWAN
DER SCHRECKLICHE

STOP YOUR COUGH
— Like LIGHTNING!

VENOS LIGHTNING COUGH CURE

Panzerkreuzer POTEMKIN

Sex, God & Greed

TYPOGRAPHIC CONTRASTS

Size
Large : Small
Tall : Short
Wide : Narrow
Condensed : Expanded

Position
Symmetrical : Asymmetrical
Right : Left
High : Low
Isolated : Grouped
In front : Behind
Rhythmic : Random

Form
Roman : Italic
Majuscule : Minuscule
Organic : Mechanical
Abstract : Representational
Distinct : Ambiguous
2D : 3D

Color
Black : Color
Dark : Light
Bright : Muted
Warm : Cool
Neutral : Saturated

Density
Light : Bold
Thick : Thin
Opaque : Transparent
Stable : Unstable
Filled : Empty
Deep : Shallow

Direction
Vertical : Horizontal
Perpendicular : Diagonal
Forward : Backward
Clockwise : Counterclockwise
Converging : Diverging

Structure
Serif : Sans serif
Organized : Chaotic
Aligned : Freely placed

Texture
Fine : Coarse
Smooth : Rough
Shiny : Matte

Typographic unity: similarities and contrasts

❝ *A (publication) consists of five elements: the text, type, ink, paper and binding. To create a unity from these five elements so the result is not a passing product of fashion, but assumes the validity of permanent value – that should be our desire."* GIOVANNI MARDERSTEIG, The Apologia of the Officina Bodoni, 1929

DESIGN IS A SEARCH FOR UNITY. It is a continuous balancing act between sameness and emphasis. Parts must look different to express their content, or else a page will suffer from oatmeal-itis in which everything looks like a unified but unappealing bowl of grayness. At the same time, the parts of a design must be unified so they make a single, powerful impression.

Contrasting type styles that share characteristics (*left*) achieves both goals. Introducing minimal contrasts ensures maximum agreement while defining meaningful differences.

Gui Bonsiepe wrote: "Design means, among many other things, arranging elements into a whole that makes sense… In typography, order is mainly a question of relationships within groups of elements and the distribution of these elements on a page." Bonsiepe defines two kinds of order: *1) The order of the system* in which each type element (headlines, text, and captions) is part of a system. The smaller the number of these elements, the higher will be the degree of order of the whole. *2) The order of arrangement* refers to the way elements relate to each other and the frequency with which the corners of elements align.

◁ Typographic similarity unites the three elements in Jan Tschichold's 1927 poster. Limited typeface availability and adherence to an emerging design philosophy resulted in revolutionary creativity. The opposite design philosophy is shown in a patent medicine ad from 1938. Speaking of this ad at the time, Denis Butlin, a British ad copywriter, said, "The PMA typographer really comes into his own with drop cap, small sizes of Condensed Gothic mixed with Plantin 110 and, of course, the authentic white on black PMA nameplate." Alignment joins three types into a single unit in this 1967 Hans Hillman poster for *Battleship Potemkin*. Typographic contrast separates the Latin, printed in 14/16 black, from the English translation, printed in 10/12 italic red, in this excerpt from *Pro Archia Poeta*, an oration by Cicero in 62BC. Yet there is obvious similarity: the column depths are perfectly even, spacing is classically proportional, and the contrasting types are both members the Bembo type family. Designed by Bert Clarke and letterpress printed in 1967.

❝ Learn the difference between attention-getting type and information-conveying type. Design accordingly." *Anonymous*

Californian
ABCDEFGHIJKLMNOPQ
abcdefghijklmnopqrstuvw
1234567890

Franklin Gothic Condensed
ABCDEFGHIJKLMNOPQRS
abcdefghijklmnopqrstuvwx
1234567890

Clarendon
ABCDEFGHIJKLMN(
abcdefghijklmnopqrst
1234567890

ITC Quay
ABCDEFGHIJKLMNOPQRST
abcdefghijklmnopqrstuvwxy
1234567890

Loire
ABCDEFGHIJKLMNOPQ
abcdefghijklmnopqrstuvwx
1234567890

Monotype Grotesque
ABCDEFGHIJKLMNOPQ
abcdefghijklmnopqrstuv
1234567890

Menhart Manuscript
ABCDEFGHIJKLMNOP
abcdefghijklmnopqrstuvw
1234567890

News Gothic
ABCDEFGHIJKLMNOPQ
abcdefghijklmnopqrstuvw
1234567890

Nicolas Jenson
ABCDEFGHIJKLMNOPQ
abcdefghijklmnopqrstuvwxyz
1234567890

Meta Roman
ABCDEFGHIJKLMNOPQRS
abcdefghijklmnopqrstuvw
1234567890

Other preferred serif types:

Baskerville	*Caslon*	*Joanna*	*Berling*
Garamond	*Modern 20*	*Centaur*	*Caecilia*

Other preferred sans serif types:

Akzidenz Grotesk	*Frutiger*	*The Sans*	*Gill Sans*
Trade Gothic	*Univers*	*Futura*	*Officina*

◁ The reasons this design (*far left*) works are: **1. One type family** in which capitalization is used to differentiate; **2. Alignment** in which, for example, the repeated *de*'s are hung flush right and the text columns tops align with PAR; **3. Sensitive touches** like lowering opening quotes and base-aligning close quotes.

◁ The height of the all caps MAGYARUL agrees with the x-height of NEM BESZÉLEK; the counter spaces of BDV have been condensed and equally spaced apart; type weight and geometric shapes unite these three letters for a seating company logo. Pity it isn't for fish.

❝ Art is simply a right method of doing things."
Thomas Aquinas, Summa Theologiae, c1265

❝ Discipline in typography is a prime virtue. Individuality must be secured by means that are rational. Distinction needs to be won by simplicity and restraint. It is equally true that these qualities need to be infused with a certain spirit and vitality, or they degenerate into dullness and mediocrity."
Stanley Morison

What is right with your type?

Because of the constant rain of information on our heads, it is more important now than ever before that we design messages with something noticeably right about them. They must be *seen*, so the focal point must startle. Then they must be readable, so information is gotten across painlessly. If something is *readable*, it *might* be read. If it might be read, it might be *remembered*.

The *right* referred to in the breaker head above is a relative term. It can, for example, be audience-specific. Pharmaceutical advertising, long a locus of dreadful typography, got its start in the early 20th century as patent medicine advertising (PMA). Denis Butlin, a PMA copywriter, wrote in 1938, "A subconscious nostalgia seems to insist that people over forty should revere the things they knew when they were young." Therefore, "advertisements are conceived, written and typeset in a style characteristic of advertising thirty or forty years ago and strike just that chord in the aging sufferer's heart that sets his nostalgia all agog... These advertisements, to the people to whom thay are meant to appeal, *look* genuine... Hence the psychological justification for those dirty, old-fashioned advertisements that violate the chastity of your morning newspaper." That is a compelling argument for ugliness, which is a legitimate tool in the arsenal of a well-equipped and open-minded designer.

Chefs who use fresh ingredients are a step ahead of chefs who use wilted or frozen ingredients. So, too, designers who use good type have an advantage over those who use whatever is handy. The "showings" on the opposite page are all set 36/24, that is, with minus linespacing. This shows the relative size of the x-height, the distance from the baseline to the median of the lowercase letters. Each typeface is set at the same point size. Note that each showing ends on the right side at a different place in the alphabet. This reveals the type's comparative width. Every face has its own width that must be respected and considered when choosing a face. Digitally compressing or expanding letterforms is not a satisfactory solution that produces good design.

PARAPET PARAPET

PARAPET PARAPET

PARAPET High and Low Abstraction · UNDERSTANDING THE WORD

Definition & Similar Words

Definition
(n) A low protective wall built where there is a sudden dangerous drop.
For example, along the edge of a balcony, roof, or bridge.
(Late 16th century. Via French from Italian parapetto, from "parare" (to shield) + "petto" (chest) (literally from Latin "pectus".)

Related Terms
abatis, arch dam, bamboo curtain, barbed-wire entanglement, barrier, brick wall, cable, ditch, embankment fence, fortalice, fortification, gate, iron curtain, postern gate, rampart, stone wall ...

Associated Images

■ Selected for Free Exploration and Further Exploration

[A]

PARAPET High and Low Abstraction Drafts · FREE EXPLORATION

■ Selected for Further Exploration

[B]

PARAPET High and Low Abstraction Drafts · FURTHER EXPLORATION 1

Idea	Reference	Font
Parapet as battlemented protective wall		City (Bold) + Cheltenham (Bold)

Abstraction Min. — **PARAPET**
Abstraction Med. — **PARAPET**
Abstraction Max. — **PARAPET**

■ Selected for Further Exploration 2

[C]

PARAPET High and Low Abstraction Drafts · FURTHER EXPLORATION 1

Idea	Reference	Font
Parapet as fence/gate with ornamental features		Cheltenham (Bold)

Abstraction Min. — PARAPET
Abstraction Med. — PARAPET
Abstraction Max. — PARAPET

■ Selected for Further Exploration 2

[D]

PARAPET High and Low Abstraction Drafts · FURTHER EXPLORATION 2

B & W
Gray Scale
Color

[E]

REALITY
Actual object
Color video
Color photograph
Grayscale photograph
Realistic painting
Line drawing
Stick figure drawing
ABSTRACTION

Type is the one area in design education in which learning "right" thinking is critical because typography is a logical process. Sensitizing the eye and mind to perceive inherent meaning and real – rather than automatically assumed – differences takes practice and discipline.

Introductory typography exercise

This is an exercise for sophomores. It is not intended as a first experience with type, which must be work with letters and spacing in a less illustrative process. This exercise evolves through three or four critiques before the final is due.

Purpose To explore typographic abstraction, legibility, and letter-to-letter relationships by designing one source word in three ways.

The goal is to balance legibility (a quality of efficient, clear, simple reading) and readability (a quality that promotes interest, pleasure, and expression of meaning). Is it possible to make a typographic solution both functional (legible) and unconventional (readable)? Ideally, you will cross the line between legibility and readability, or creative expression. What choices do you make when abstracting type and inhibiting legibility? The study of simple to progressively complex organizations is valuable to learn the scope of what is possible.

Process, Part 1 Managing abstraction is essential to graphic designers. Like value (lightness and darkness), abstraction is a relative term: by comparison, one thing is more or less abstract than another (*left, above*). You have selected a source word from a list. It is a noun: a person, place, or thing. It can therefore be readily illustrated. A▷ Look up the definition of your word. Use a thesaurus to find equivalent words. Become an expert on your word: when and why was it coined and how has it changed in time? Compile a visual clip file of your word including images, textures, and other extreme closeups that might imply your word without showing it in its entirety.

Process, Part 2 Select a slab serif typeface that is unique in class. B▷ Begin sketching ways to integrate your word with samples from your visual clip file. Some sketches will produce more abstract ideas than others: become aware of this comparison. Categorize your sketches in order of abstraction. C▷ Select and interpret one idea as a literal (less abstract) study. Interpret another as moderately abstract. D▷ Select a third as most abstract. This last will be considered too abstract if your word and it's meaning can't be recognized. It may help to think of your word as a restaurant name or book title that illustrates itself.

You *must*...

🐾 Work exclusively in Illustrator or FreeHand.

🐾 Use the same slab serif face in each study. Set and convert to outline paths.

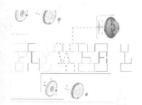

🐾 E▷ One study must be RGB and use two colors: 110r 88g 69b plus any other color except black. One study must be grayscale and not merely *have* value, but *use* value. One study must be bitmap (solid black and white only).

🐾 All studies are to be exactly 54p0 wide and centered on horizontal 51p0x66p0 heavyweight bright white sheets.

🐾 Export final studies into Photoshop and save as 600dpi RGB/grayscale/bitmap tiffs.

🐾 Provide a labelled Mac CD containing a folder of all preliminary studies; a folder of the final three studies; a folder of the three final tiff files. Put the CD with all printouts in an appropriately labelled 9"x12" envelope.

A3 B2 C3 D1 E1 F1

A2 B3 C1 D2 E1 F1

A3 B3 C2 D2 E3 F1

A2 B3 C1 D2 E1 F2

A2 B3 C3 D1 E1 F2

A3 B1 C1 D3 E2 F2

A1 B1 C2 D1 E1 F3

A2 B2 C1 D3 E3 F3

A2 B2 C2 D1 E2 F3

Advanced typography exercise

This is a more advanced exercise for juniors and seniors. It has three preliminary critiques before the final is due. Elements are assigned so students don't waste time deciding what to use: the exercise isn't about choosing material, but choosing *what to do with it* to convey a message.

Purpose To explore manners of organizing typographic elements, space, and imagery into coherent groups that express hierarchy and show clear relationship finding.

Process, Part 1 Use the 600dpi tiff image provided. Place your image in a Illustrator document so the longest dimension is 3p0 in from trim on a 66p0 x 51p0 page. Print on a bright white, heavy-weight sheet.

Process, Part 2 Design three book covers. *The single most important aspect of this exercise is to abstract the type and imagery.* All work must be done in Illustrator. Using the chart below, choose one attribute from each of the six columns and combine in a single study. Make a second study using another attribute from each column. Combine the remaining attributes from each column and combine in a third study. *No other elements may be used and no elements, including type, may be repeated.* Compositions are to be 42p0 x 55p6 vertical. Execute all preliminary studies full-size.

All studies must use the single version of the assigned font. Though using a single type-face keeps you from using *font* contrast, there are five typographic contrasts that remain available:

- Position (Col A)
- Size (Col C)
- Type treatments you may
- Value (relative darkness) (Col B)
- Base alignment   add to the font in Illustrator.

You *must*...
- ❧ Explore abstraction and legibility.
- ❧ Be prepared to defend the logic of your *precise* design relationships.
- ❧ Show how well you can *see* meaningful design relationships.
- ❧ Massive enlargement and reduction of your image is encouraged.

Format Three final prints on high-resolution, bright white heavy-weight paper. *Lightly pencil* the study's "recipe" on the back bottom right corner of each study. Prepare three 300dpi repro-size files of your final designs. Crop to exactly 42p0 x 55p6 vertical. Name files and your CD intelligently for the user. Buy an attractive and suitable 9"x12" envelope. Make a label for the outside so it relates inside to outside. Put all preliminary studies, your three finals, and your labelled CD in the envelope.

☐ Art for this exercise was selected from Dover's collection of steel engravings. They are not chosen for any intrinsic related-ness to book titles: lack of belonging *requires abstraction* to convey meaning.

---

¹ **The Masks of God**
  Joseph Campbell
² **The Custom of the Country**
  Edith Wharton
³ **Exile's Return**
  Malcolm Cowley

☐ Book titles for this exercise are selected for their *interpretability*. Novels, because of their broad content on many subjects, and their emphasis on the human condition, work well.

A Alignment	**B** Color	**C** Type size	**D** Visual emphasis	**E** System anomaly*	**F** Book title
1 Flush left	Black on white	Maximum of 18pt	Type dominant	Unification/Isolation	*Masks*
2 Centered	White on black	Minimum of 200pt	Image dominant	Direction	*Custom*
3 Flush right	B, W, and Grays	300pt difference	Emptiness dominant	Rhythm	*Exile's*
These systems create an anomaly based on relative position.	Negative space, whether white or black, must appear in both fore- and back-ground of each study.	One study must use very small type, one must use very large type, and one must use extreme size contrast.	Dominance does not mean exclusivity. Each study must contain all the elements used in the other studies, but they must be differently weighted.	Explore relative position, relative direction, and a break in rhythmic posi-tioning to create an anomaly, or focal point.	

✱ *An anomaly is an element that breaks a visual system and becomes the focal point. For an anomaly to be visible, the system must be consistent and recognizable. Therefore creating an anomaly is really a result of your ability to create a coherent system.*

LINGUA
TRIUM SÆCULORUM,
QUA
INNOVATUS EST LITERATUS ORBIS
TERRARUM,
ET
*SCIENTIA DIVINARUM RERUMQUE HUMA-
NARUM, ADSUMMUM EVECTA EST
FASTIGIUM.*
ARS ARTIUM
TYPOGRAPHIA
Togeſſt:

Weyřečný Drogßo Wěku Bazyk,
Kniha:
Metodito obnowen a Weſkeř Swěta
Mydřj y Umění gak Duchowni, tak Swětſké,
Jnamenate otwirene,
na Neywýſſßí Grad / neb Stupeň pozdwiženo /
Kunſti, nad gine Kunſti,
TYPOGRAPHIA.
Ginač:
Knjho-Tjſkárna/
Dů weſſelé
Seculárnj Třj-Sta letni Slawnoſti,
Když totiſſo po ſſtaſtné probjhlých Třych Set Let od Wynalezenj /
Ywobodné Kunſti Typographſké/
Řeče ſſ taßo Léta Páni 1440. Snaßnoſti / a Schopnoſti
Jana Kuttenbergia,
Nobile a Waſtence Kuttenberſkého /
Tiſk Jana Karla Hraby w Praze 1740.

PLaſt StrDI / a Rog WCžL
W Zatonſe ſtarIM
Gaťo negaťL Obraz tenťráťe VťáganI ∗
RInI pať ſDe W Praze
Gaťoſ̌to SLaWI e Cjſťé ZeMIe
RaLžgn VeI ∗
S WatI IangeyoMVCeI
DtrC Dobré yoWIeſtI ∗

A proto
Re/ gaťo tenťráťe/ za DľágeV /
Anobrž za paVbaV sLaDtoß WLaſtenCVM ∗
W CheáMV Pánle SWatého GiLgi přeDLoženI ∗
Od
Kuleže WogtleCßa BVtgera / W GirnáCß ADMinI-
ſtratora /
Na Den SWatého DezIDerIa /
Kterſ ſe poCžItá oCtaVa SWatého Iana ∗
S DowoIenjm Duchownj Wrchnoſti.

Wypuſſteno w Praze / w Karlě Jana Hraby / GB. Miloſti PP. Setwitu
Akademiyngj Cjſařſtß Impreſſora.

Tiſk Karla Jana Hraby w Praze.

EXVnDet VobIs gLorIoſa proſ-
perItas,
LIterIs CoMes paX & Vbertas.

Toß paſ IEſE WIaſtence neſſo / ktyſ gſ̌my Mobiteſſti Oby-
watelowe na provolagiaj ſwe woſstnoſti : ſm toßo Kunſtu Au-
thorem/ neb Naleznyſem byſ / ß poteſſnoſti Sοßu wzdywſ̌ßy.

Joanni Kuttenbergenſi, qui primus omnium literasæ
imprimendas invenit de toto orbe bene merenti Ivo
Wicigiris hoc Saxum pro monumento poſuit Anno 1508.
(ddd)   Tobě przeyum : Baterima teſ̌

Multùm Religio multùm tibi Græca Sophia
Et multùm debet lingua latina tibi
Omnes Te ſummis igitur nunc laudibus ornent
Te Duce quando Arshæc mira re...

RDyſ weſrßni zatoǔani
němotſⱼ Gratiam tui
non poſſemus. Tať/ gaťoſ̌ /
ti nemuſ̌eme / ptotoſ̌ wynjſ̌ugⱼ
na woſstnoſti byſ̌ ſ̌um Duſ̌ / ſm
borum mortuorum. Pſal. 118. Tⱼ
melioris origo,poſtarſu weſto Iⱼ
předmuſ̌teſ̌/ a na pamět wwoſbⱼt
ßanⱼ / pamětſu oßenzßdäwienⱼ...

Accipe poſteritas quo...

SHymet Potomcy I ⱒ wⱒtⱼ
Narodu / kterſⱼ priſgiti mⱒ
DDſ̌ oznamowatⱒ / a oDⱒ
ẻnyſm byſtⱒ a...

Lingua trium ſæculorum. Tiſk Jan...

№

Empresa de Tra
Fluviais de
Contribuinte N.º
QUATRO AGUAS · ILHA
Transporte - ADU
Todas as tax...
Conservar este bilhe...

The Sauna family is first shown in the book — Regular Italics with 2 ligatures

'Read naked'.
Black

THIS PINK BOOK DOESN'T
Regular

 only contain
Bold with Dingbats

sauna stories,
Bold Italics with 1 ligature

but it can also be read inside the sauna…
Bold

And it survives!
Swash Italics

Even better, some stories are getting **visible** in a sauna only,
Regular with Bold

SNEAUX PRESS
☐ Size ☐ Serif/sans ☐ Form ☐ Weight ☐ Case ☐ Width

 progress
☐ Size ☐ Serif/sans ☐ Form ☐ Weight ☐ Case ☐ Width

jeFE PRESS
☐ Size ☐ Serif/sans ☐ Form ☐ Weight ☐ Case ☐ Width

 Sneaux PRESS
☐ Size ☐ Serif/sans ☐ Form ☐ Weight ☐ Case ☐ Width

  PrOGRess
☐ Size ☐ Serif/sans ☐ Form ☐ Weight ☐ Case ☐ Width

PRESS Jefe
☐ Size ☐ Serif/sans ☐ Form ☐ Weight ☐ Case ☐ Width

Combining typefaces

Typographic difference is a tool for developing hierarchy and distinctions between kinds of information. Visually presorting content serves the reader by showing length and complexity. It is easy to make typographic changes that are random or amusing, but it is hard to make thoughtful, purposeful changes that help the message and retain design unity. Too many fonts distract the reader from the work of reading.

Daniel Berkeley Updike wrote in the 1937 second edition of his *Printing Types: Their History, Form and Use*, "The problem of choosing types wisely remains precisely what it was (when the first edition of this book was published). Indeed, the necessity for the cultivation of taste and judgment in selection is greater today than it was fifteen years ago, because of the mass of material from which to choose and the delicate differentiations of design in the types themselves. Background, tradition, research, taste, a sense of suitability and practicality must, as in the past, aid one's choice, and then each person must work out the further problem of selection for himself." It has gotten considerably more difficult in all these regards since 1937.

How to combine similar types is daunting. If contrast is needed within an area of serif type, it is better made within a single family, say, with roman and italics, than by using two serif families, where the difference may not be as visible. And even if it is, it will appear jarring and self-conscious rather than smooth and natural. Consider type families that have both serif and sans serif versions which have multiplied in recent years. You will want a family that has a regular and a bold weight; regular italics; regular and bold small caps; and lining and old style figures. In addition to these letterform contrasts, you will have size, case, spacing, and position with which to make meaningful distinctions.

Start by selecting the text face, since this is where the reader will spend the most time. When matching serif and sans serif types, look for inherent similarities: a slightly condensed serif, for example, will look better with a slightly condensed sans serif.

Combine Frutiger, a humanist sans serif, with an oldstyle serif. This is 13-point Italian Old Style, a point larger than the Frutiger for x-height equivalency. *Find and make similarities be-*

Combine Syntax, a humanist sans serif, with an oldstyle serif. This is 14-point Nicolas Jenson, three points larger than the Syntax for x-height equivalency. *Find and make similarities between dissimilar types vis-*

Combine Gill Sans, a humanist sans serif, with an oldstyle serif. This is 13-point Adobe Garamond, a point larger than the Gill Sans for x-height equivalency. *Find and make similarities between dissimilar*

Combine Avenir, a geometric sans serif, with a transitional serif. This is 12-point Baskerville, the same point size as the Avenir, matched for x-height equivalency. *Find and make similari-*

Combine Neuzit Grotesk, a geometric sans serif, with a transitional serif. This is 13-point Bell, two points larger than the Neuzit Grotesk for x-height equivalency. *Find and make similari-*

Combine Triplex, a geometric sans serif, with a transitional serif. This is 11½-point New Caledonia, a half point size smaller than the Triplex for x-height equivalency. *Find and make similari-* ties between dissimilar

Combine Griffith Gothic, a grotesque sans serif, with a modern serif. This is 13-point Bodoni, one point larger than the Griffith Gothic for x-height equivalency. *Find and make simi-*

Combine Trade Gothic, a grotesque sans serif, with a modern serif. This is 11½-point Veljovic, a point smaller than the Trade Gothic for x-height equivalency. *Find and make similarities between dis-*

Combine Univers, a grotesque sans serif, with a modern serif. This is 11-point Centennial, a point smaller than the Univers for x-height equivalency. *Find and make similarities between dis-*

Combine Clarendon, a slab serif, with a modern serif. This is 12-point Didot, the same size as the Clarendon for x-height equivalency. *Find and make similarities between dissimilar types*

Combine Cæcilia, a slab serif, with a lighter weight of itself. This is 11-point Cæcilia, the same size as the bolder Cæcilia for x-height equivalency. *Find and make* similarities between dis-

Combine Officina Serif, a slab serif, with a lighter weight of its sans serif counterpart. This is 12-point Officina Sans, the same size as the bolder Officina Serif for x-height equivalency. *Find and make similari-*

COEXISTENCE

⬕ These two logos (*above*) use type contrast for expressive interest. Mixing types, by definition, means a condition of disagreement (*opposite*). But design calls for agreement, or unity, even among dissimilar parts. Create unity by choosing types with similar shape.

⬕ Match x-heights by changing the point size of one type.

⬕ Match roundness by comparing the *b, c, d, e, o, p,* and *q.*

⬕ Match width by comparing wider letters, like the *m* and *w*, which show greatest difference.

Mixing types well to clarify content is dependent on using adedquate contrasts, but not so much contrast as to break the design's unity. Mixed types can share shape, proportion, weight, x-height, typographic color, or even the time period of the typefaces' designs. Keeping half a mind on what is *right* about a given pairing will ensure design unity, what the reader initially sees.

Size Large & small The larger type must be *visibly* larger. A point or two larger at text sizes is not enough — and is certainly useless at display sizes.

Do make type 25-33% larger, so, for example, in 10-pt text, a breaker head would be set in 12½ or 13-pt type. 36-pt display type would be enlarged to 45 to 48 points.

Structure Serif & sans serif A common contrast is sans serif for display (because it fits closer and becomes darker) and serif for the text (because it is thought to be easier to read at longer lengths).

Do match overall shapes of letters. Don't mix types with strong serif styling or sans serif types because the differences can be so slight as to be unrecognizable.

Weight Heavy & light Depending on family, skip two weights to make the bolder face look purposefully selected.

Book to medium isn't a significant boost in type weight; book to bold is.

Form CAPS & lowercase Set a phrase in all caps to make it stand out in a lowercase paragraph.

All caps are harder to read in long passages. Keep them short or they may not be read at all.

Width Regular width & condensed/ expanded Condensed and expanded types, if they are sufficiently narrower or wider than the normal versions of their type families, are outside the normal width and thus more difficult to read. Keep type brief that is set in condensed and expanded faces for emphasis.

Don't mix types with extreme contrasting widths: extreme letter shapes affect reading speed. Don't digitally compress or expand regular types: it is ugly. Use real fonts that have been drawn proportionally.

Mixing typefaces is a bit like mixing seasonings when cooking. There may be general agreement among chefs that some flavors go very well with other flavors. But the creative cook is willing to experiment and try new combinations to give her diners new eating experiences. The dictum that a designer can get away with anything *so long as it looks like it was on purpose* applies to type combinations just as it does to every other design decision.

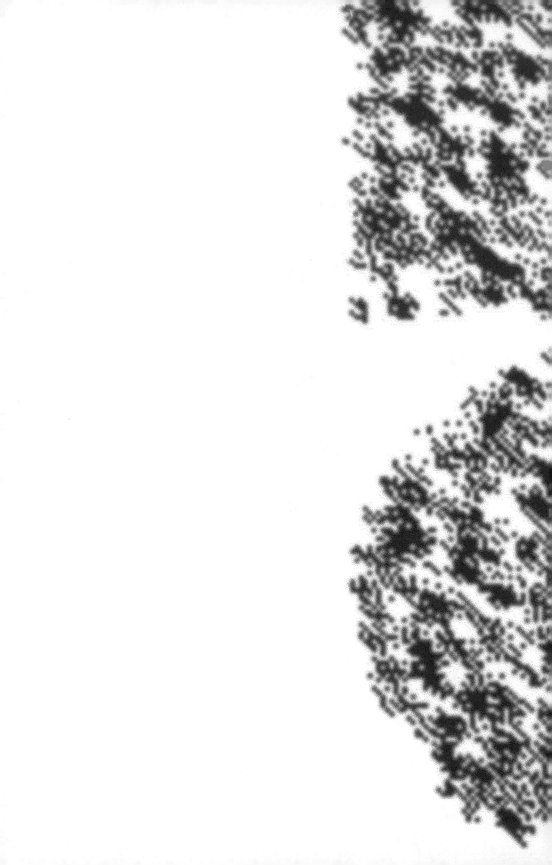

Section 2

What readers want

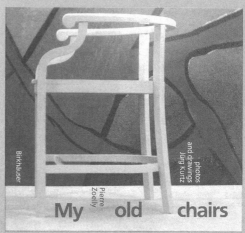

Birkhäuser
Pierre Zoelly
photos and drawings Jürg Kurtz

My old chairs

Esqui

Ben-icio Del Toro

* English translation: Benny of the Bull...

Lost without his pencil
Self-taught, his paintings were never "good enough" to frame.

ther Ernst
r father's
have had
nouc.
mplained
is love for
whom he
ingly and
is brother
n the high
inherited
his father
on." So in-
e studied

le which
oor to the
ne, across
: the cen-
ookkeeper
re was no
as precise-
the teens
hitectural
be. Some
ery happy
y memory
une, each

Two friends are walking crosstown discussing the stock market. "How does it work?" "Simple: you buy a dozen chicks, feed them, watch them grow up. Then you buy a rooster. Soon you have more chicks and a whole yardful of chickens. A terrible storm comes and your chickens drown. *Ducklings* you should have bought! That's the stock market." **This is a favorite story told**

by K
as s
imm
Olm
two–
wind
a ma
inter

82 Midhurst *Sanatorium*

What makes readers respond

Who's your audience? 93 · **Abstraction and clarity** 93 · **Hierarchy** 95 · **Information mapping** 97

◁ **Content made interesting:** boring picture of guys at a table made memorable. **Hierarchy:** one level leads to the next, to the next, to the *text.*

> **"** *To catch a mouse, makes noise like a cheese."*
> HERB LUBALIN

◁ **Headlines** make their points through abstraction. **Subheads** explain headlines.

" When it comes to handling text, I like to challenge the audience a bit, but I know enough to back off when you really want people to read it."
Michael Mabry

◁ **Imagery** stops me. **Captions** make me think the story will be interesting. **Text** is built to make reading easy.

" Today's amassment of information [makes it] harder, not easier, to extract essential knowledge. The problem is no longer one of making information available, but of facilitating understanding. That is exactly the role of today's typography: maximizing comprehension." *Zuzana Licko*

WHAT MAKES *YOU* RESPOND AS A READER? If you can codify the visual prompts that catch and keep you interested, you can distill them into good design for others. Here is what works for me:

▶ **Inherently interesting content.** This is a rare commodity. Most content arrives to the designer dull. Good designers and editors expose content by making it *interesting to the reader.*

▶ **Multilevel readership that encourages scanning.** Such hierarchy signals primary, secondary, and tertiary importances in both words and pictures.

▶ **Headlines that make me want to know more.** Primary type's job is to lead me to secondary type. The best way to do that is to tell only part of the story, the most intriguing part, and to show it in a way that reveals the story.

▶ **Subheads that complete the story.** Secondary type's job is to lead me to additional information, whether pictures and their captions or breakouts, pull quotes, or other display material. In few situations is a headline/subhead combination sufficient for me to know subconsciously whether I want to commit to the text.

▶ **Arresting pictures.** They help tell the story without my commitment of time or attention. They are cropped and sized to reveal importance. They are not the same as pretty pictures, which may stop me, but, unless they are about beauty itself, do not lead me into the story.

▶ **Intriguing captions.** Captions should do a lot more than describe what I can already see for myself. They should help me see the importance of the image and build a bridge to the text.

LEGIBILITY

BEN SHAHN CHAOTIC	IGNATIUS ORDERLY
Menhart D ORGANIC	Preissig Ant. GEOMETRIC
Benda Romana CASUAL	Bodoni Light FORMAL
proton SPORADIC	SYNCHRO SYSTEMATIC
SPATIAL	EMPEROR EIGHT FLAT
PENN STATION STRONG	EPHESVS WEAK
Mrs Eaves D ACTIVE	Mrs Eaves PASSIVE
Moon Regular EXCITING	News Gothic DRY

 Logos showing low (*clean cut*) to high (*BT*) abstraction.

Highway signage must be simple and highly legible from long distances. Type size and spacing have been carefully analyzed and color is used systematically for familiarity and visibility. James Montalbano's *ClearviewHwy* is a type designed for roadside legibility. Tests show it is 25% more legible than Highway Gothic, the face currently used on road signs.

■▶ **Well-built text.** That's right, text is built, one attribute at a time. Weight, size, column width, letter, word, and linespacing, and paragraphing make text either inviting or repelling. Once you've lured and caught me as a reader, don't make me work to read the story. I won't make that much of an effort.

Who's your audience?

Designers stand between the message's sender – the client – and the receiver – the audience. It is our job to interpret content on behalf of the audience so they glean the most meaning and value with the least effort. If you take the designer out of the equation, you have raw messages with a lot of visual static and probably going unreceived because they are sent by people who a) wrongly believe people care about their messages and b) think everyone thinks as they do, so they will respond as they themselves would.

There are many audiences, and each is made of individuals. Individuals are, in turn, members of more than one audience community: a 75-year-old might be a member of a "grandparent" audience, a "frequent traveler" audience, and a "yoga practitioner" audience. How do these audiences differ and what do they have in common? Understanding the individual and the communities to which each individual identifies helps shape a message so it gets through the barriers we all have as readers.

Abstraction and clarity

It has been said that abstraction wins eyeballs while clarity keeps them. Abstraction and clarity are the two ends of a spectrum (*opposite*). Neither is "better" than the other, but each has a time and a place for its use. Attention must be paid to every type's and design's position on the legibility scale.

Display type, including headlines, subheads, captions, and breakouts/pull quotes, are the places where abstraction belongs. Display type that is merely typeset misses the crucial need to lure and reveal content to the reader. Text, on the other hand, is not a place for abstraction. Anything that repels, confuses, or reduces legibility in text hurts the reader.

Identification of the work and artist

General description of the work for the layperson

Additional detail for experts and others. This third level is present, but it's easily skipped by the average guest.

LÍTÁ JAKO
HADR NA HOLI

SCHWARZ
UND WEISS

ARCHITEKTEN
NÁRODNÍ TŘÍDA 25
PRAHA 1
32141

6:60 **IIII Grand jury instructions** The grand jury's legal advisors are the c[...] convened it and the district attorney. [CPL 190.25(6)] It is the pros[...] however, that normally gives instructions to the jury.

6:61 **III Standard: accurate instructions** The grand jury must rece[...] rate legal instructions. For example, there should be an instructi[...] legal presumption is rebuttable. [*People v Williams*, 136 AD2d [...] NYS2d 581 (2d Dept 1988)]

6:62 **II Less precision acceptable** Certain instructions may be [...] however, without endangering the integrity of the proceedings [...] because grand jury instructions need not have the same precisi[...] structions at trial. [*People v Calbud, Inc.*, 49 NY2d 389, 42[...] 232 (1980)]

> **Example** The failure to instruct on the voluntariness of [...] dant's statement is not grounds for dismissal of an indictment[...] *v Davis*, 190 AD2d 987, 593 NYS2d 713 (4th Dept], *leave de[...] NY2d 1071, 601 NYS2d 591 (1993)]

6:63 **III Evidence constituting a defense** For purposes of determini[...] her the grand jury must receive instructions on a defense, case la[...] guishes between defenses that are exculpatory and those that are [...] ing. [*People v Valles*, 62 NY2d 36, 476 NYS2d 50 (1984)]

6:64 **II Exculpatory defense** This type of defense would, if believe[...] in a finding of no criminal liability. The grand jury must be in[...] as to any such defense. Examples include entrapment [*People v[...] 186 AD2d 434, 588 NYS2d 562 (1st Dept 1992)], self-defe[...] agency.

6:65 **I Instructions on alibi evidence** Alibi evidence is in fact [...] tory, but it has sometimes been treated differently from othe[...] patory defenses.
Cases are divided on whether, if this type of evidence co[...] before the grand jury, the prosecutor must give an instructio[...] People's burden of proof on the alibi issue. [*Compare [...] Hughes*, 159 Misc 2d 663, 606 NYS2d 499 (Sup Ct 1992) w[...] *ple v Crump*, 157 Misc 2d 566, 597 NYS2d 1010 (County C[...]

6:66 **II Mitigating defense** This type of defense is offered to re[...] gravity of the offense committed, rather than to avoid liability[...] ample is extreme emotional disturbance. The prosecutor nee[...] struct the grand jury on mitigating defenses. [*People v Valles*, [...] 36, 476 NYS2d 50 (1984)]

6:67 **III Limiting instructions** In some situations the prosecutor shou[...] limiting instruction. Failure to give the instruction may result[...] missal of a subsequent indictment.

❝ Maximum meaning, minimum means." *Abram Games, British designer*

◀ Museum signage (*far left*) typically has three levels so readers can choose how much information they want. A business card from the 1920s uses flush left alignment of the secondary and tertiary type. Aligning the right edge of the primary type establishes unity.

◀ Jan Tschichold illustrates The New Typography with this before and after example of a 1928 small space newspaper ad. The before (*far left*), representing traditional typography, has too many typefaces and seven type sizes, is centered, and is overly ornamented. The after, which Tschichold designed, has improved legibility through disciplined type contrasts. Though tame by today's standards, such clarified thinking was radical in the 1920s.

Hierarchy

Hierarchy means "order, ranking, or sequence." If all the elements in a design were presented as being equally important, it would be the visual equivalent of oatmeal: consistently semi-smooth and gray. That may be tasty for breakfast, but it's not an effective way to lure and keep readers. So we order type and imagery by importance. In general, bigger and darker means more important; smaller and lighter means less important. In practice, though, any element that *agrees with a prevailing visual system* means less important and any element that *breaks the system*, and thus becomes more visible, means more important.

Use type contrasts to show hierarchy. Use type similarities to create unity and make type inviting. Edit copy shorter to make type larger. Make the type's entrances bigger and easiest of all: readers are just browsers at the beginning. Lure readers in and let the content, if it's good, keep them in.

While it is possible to subdivide elements into unlimited strata of importances, readers simply do not need more than *exactly three levels*: most important, least important, and all the rest presented as equivalently middling in importance. There will always be a most and least, so additional subdivisions happen in the middle stuff. These distinctions become meaningless and you're back to semi-lumpy oatmeal, though it is more elaborate.

Design is an "information delivery system." The smoother the transfer of information, the better the design. Multilevel typography organizes thoughts into clear levels of importance and usefulness for readers by using a sequence of indentions (*opposite*), as shown by this page from a legal practice guide. This example shows a sequence from general to specific: general information is level one; an explanation of the general statements is level two; and fine points and reference information is in lesser levels. Multilevel type ensures that some percentage of the message is absorbed by nearly all readers, all of whom will recognize the predigested nature of the text. That goodwill envelops a publication or Web site and make it a valued resource.

Question type	Response	Visual interpretation
Yes/No Be alert to local traditions: Xs in Sweden, for example, mean "yes."	Checking a box	☑ YES ☐ NO
	Writing YES or NO	_YES_ YES or NO
	Circling a choice	(YES) NO
	Deleting a choice	YES ~~NO~~
Multiple choice	Checking a box	☐ Dibble ☐ Edger ☑ Flail ☐ Tongs
	Writing a choice	_C_ A. Dibble C. Flail B. Edger D. Tongs
	Circling a choice	Dibble Edger (Flail) Tongs
	Deleting choices	~~Dibble~~ ~~Edger~~ Flail ~~Tongs~~
Free response Provide enough space for full answers. Character spaces need to be wide enough to accommodate handwriting.	Writing in empty space	CAMSHAFT, CYLINDER & PISTON
	Writing on horizontal lines	FLYWHEEL TO GEARBOX BEARINGS TO CRANKCASE
	Writing in defined character spaces	C Y L I N D E R H E A D │ │ │ │ │ │ │ │ │ │ │ │
Instructions	Instructions at each box	Bistoury Colter Slotter ☒ Single ☐ Single ☐ Double ☐ Double ☒ Twin ☒ Quad
	Instructions grouped near questions	Indicate small or large size for each ☒ Bistoury ☒ Colter ☒ Slotter
Position of answers to questions	Flush right	Air or bar: BAR Fire or loy: FIRE Ditch or drain: DITCH Peat or salt: PEAT
	Following questions	Ball peen, beetle, or claw? BEETLE Drop, end, or Stillson? STILLSON
	Flush left	AUG Auger or bench? GIM Gimlet or keyway? DIS Chamfer or disk? STR Rotary or strap?
	Below questions	Three favorite mills: CIDER, PEPPER & TREAD
	Above questions	CIDER, PEPPER & TREAD Three favorite mills

Information mapping

There are two kinds of printed information: reading matter and reference material. Reading matter is continuous text like an article or other prose. Reference material is documentation, like an owner's manual or a dictionary, and requires the user's ability to find specific information quickly. Readers judge reference material by its utility more than by its aesthetic attributes.

Both reading matter and documentation can be improved by *information mapping*, a technique that uses segmentation and hierarchical styling – using type weight, size, style, indention, and position – to make the material effortless to read.

Reading matter can be mapped by using space, breaker heads, type variations, and ornaments to break text into bite-size pieces. Bulleted lists, for example, are better than grouping short bits in continuous text.

Reference material is information that readers dip into for specific content. It is typically not the kind of reading in which people want to be engrossed: they rarely use it unless a crisis exists, so it's not reading by choice. They just want the facts they're looking for. There are a few design considerations that make documentation more user friendly:

▣ Display type must be as effective as highway signage.

▣ Nothing may be done that hurts clarity and usefulness.

▣ Documentation is often judged on the quality and clarity of its display type.

▣ Hierarchy of decreasingly useful information is critical. Show the category, the most useful text, and the lesser text.

Forms are specialized documents because they require the reader's completion. Forms, whether on paper or on line, represent the asker: it is often the most intimate interaction a respondent has with the asker, so they should be considerate and particularly well thought out. Forms require a variety of responses and the trick to good forms is to make such variety look systematized. A good form makes it easy for the form filler so he or she will be inclined to fill it out willingly and fully.

Dieses neue Zeichen
von Johannes Tzschichhold in
Leipzig entworfen und von uns
handelsgerichtlich eingetragen,
wollen wir in Zukunft an die
Stelle unseres früheren Verlags-
signets treten lassen. Wir bitten
unseren verehrten Kundenkreis,
hiervon Kenntnis zu nehmen.

Leipzig-Reudnitz, am 1. Januar 1923

Fischer & Wittig
Kunstverlag und
Buchdruckerei

*

philobiblon   ei

ner verlag, wien VI (vienna), strohmay

Type and identity

What typefaces represent *101* · **Matching type to job and meaning** *105* · **A type treatment you can own** *107*

> " *Set a page in Fournier against another in Caslon and another in Plantin and it is as if you heard three different people delivering the same discourse – each with impeccable pronunciation and clarity, yet each with through the medium of a different personality."*
> BEATRICE WARDE, 1933

WITH REPETITION, TYPE CAN COME TO REPRESENT its source. An extreme example is provided by the Nazis. Blackletter is a writing style developed in northern Europe beginning about 1200AD. In 1450, when Gutenberg invented movable type in Mainz, he modeled his letters on the prevailing lettering style in the area. Because other parts of Europe adopted types based on the much lighter Italian script writing, blackletter was recognized as Germanic, not least by Germans themselves. Indeed, German typefounders released 218 versions of blackletter typefaces between 1900 and 1940, indicating keen continuing interest in their use. Though difficult to read by those not born to their use, blackletter is a highly legible style that creates more unique word-shapes than roman types.

The Nazi's official adoption of Fraktur, one of five variations of blackletter, in the 1930s was a way to state unequivocally that their political party "stood for Germany." As Germany attacked its neighbors and expanded beyond its own borders, the Nazis recognized that Fraktur's Germanness would not help as much and they stopped using it in 1941. The reason the Nazis gave, however, was that it was a "Jewish invention." This was a total fabrication. Blackletter types have not yet recovered from the Nazi's terrible manipulation of national identity and type style.

◁ Blackletter was widely used in Germany through the first half of the 20th century. Jan Tschichold, the author of *Die neue Typographie*, used it in a student lettering exercise in 1920 (*far left*), a corporate announcement in 1923 (*middle*), and on a Viennese magazine's letterhead in 1940.

◁ A variety of styles were used to illustrate type in a 1928 German type catalog. Each type was given a treatment thought to show off its inherent quality to best effect.

" For me, the alphabet epitomizes culture." *Fritz Gottschalk (1937–)*

Bodoni
Caslon
Clarendon
Fette Fraktur
Franklin Gothic
Frutiger
FUTURA
𝕿𝖎𝖒𝖊𝖘 𝕽𝖔𝖒𝖆𝖓
Trajan

⬚ Type has its own identity. These nine typefaces have been "mis-set" in one of the other types listed.

Jncipit epiſtola ſancti ih
paulinum preſbitecum d
diuine hiſtorie libris·cap

1450
Gutenberg's 34-line Bible and Prague Castle

Quem ad finem sese effr
Nihilne te *nocturnum prae.*
is vigiliae, nihil *timor pop*
um omnium, nihil hic *mun*

1724
Caslon and the Spanish Steps, Rome

'Monotype' TIMES
New Roman Series
327, available from Four and a quarter pt. to

1931
Times New Roman and the Empire State Building

Perched atop stair t
fan rooms accent d
of energy-conservii

1959
Optima and the Sydney Opera House

1998
Tear Drop and the Guggenheim Museum in Bilbao

Caslon Antique and *Italic* are in themselves expressive of

DIGNITY
HONESTY
CHARACTER
Antiquity
Simplicity
Quality
RELIABILITY
Sincerity

In the use of these types
bear in mind
the subject or properties of the message
so that the result may be fitting
and convey
to the customer and his clients
evidence of the printer's
intelligent service

A detail from a 1925 showings book lists nine adjectives for Caslon Antique, all of which culminate in making the printer – in those days the buyer of typefaces and therefore the target of this message – look intelligent.

Sans serif types were avant garde as Tschichold wrote *Die neue Typographie*. This contemporary postcard is by Joost Schmidt.

❝ I have always railed against ideological purity. I've found corruption is more interesting than purity." *Milton Glaser*

What typefaces represent

Do typefaces represent anything beyond their own aesthetic quality? Some designers feel all types have a soul and discuss them as an œnophile describes wines: can a typeface really be *pious*, or *materialistic*, or *gluttonous*? On the other hand, is a typeface merely a tool? The answer, naturally, lies somewhere in the middle. Some types have a soul because one has been bestowed on it. It takes inside knowledge to perceive a type's soul: it isn't built in. Some types are just shapes – and there is certainly nothing wrong with that. It is a question of perception.

Sans serifs represented modern typography in the early 20th century, particularly after Jan Tschichold's 1928 *Die neue Typographie* defined the movement. Tschichold wrote, "The so-called Grotesque (sans serif) is the only one in spiritual accordance with our time. To proclaim sans serif as the typeface of our time is not a question of being fashionable. It expresses the same tendencies to be seen in our architecture… I believe that no single designer can produce the (sans serif) typeface we need, which must be free from all personal characteristics. It will be the work of a group, among whom I think there must be an engineer."

Helvetica represented current sensibility for hundreds of European companies in the latter 20th century. Its appeal comes from two sources: the shapes are highly legible, based as they are on earlier sans serif designs (to some extent, it fulfills Tschichold's call for a type without a personality), but another factor in Helvetica's adoption may be political: the famed neutrality of Switzerland, for which the type was named. This may have played a part during Helvetica's rise to ubiquity during the Cold War decades. It is easy to imagine the same types would have been far less well received if they had been named *Soviet State* or *Stalinist*. In fact, *Helvetica*, a revival of *Akzidenz Grotesk*, was originally called *New Haas Grotesque*, a notably bland name. Antonio Boggeri has called the neutrality of Swiss graphic design "…as perfect as any spider's web, but often of a useless perfection (because it isn't) broken by an entangled fly."

Typeface samples		Symbolism
Caslon Canon	Frutiger Bold	**Power**
Charter	Linoletter	Seriousness
CONDENSED SANS	Miller Display Roman	Sophistication
		Industry
BODONI	Joanna Regular	**Purity**
Electra Cursive	Lucida Handwriti	Truth
Futura No.2 Bold	Post Antiqua	Cleanliness
		Spirituality
Bell Regular	Garamond	**Neutrality**
BOVINE	Officina Serif Book	Tranquility
Eureka Roman	Poppl-Pontifex	Indifference
		Normalcy
ALPFAKLUI	Forte	**Energy**
champollion	Guilty	Excitement
Déformé	Korakuen	Danger
		Vigor
Anatole France	MAQMA	**Creativity**
Armada	Rusch's R-Type	Passion
ARTS & CRAFTS	SCHWITTERS ARCHITYPE	Dignity
		Intelligence
Bureau Grotesque	COPPERPLATE	**Conservatism**
CASLON	FLORIDE	Security
Charpentier Classicistique	Meta Plus Medium	Caution
		Reliability
Asphalt	ECKMANN	**Optimism**
BERNHARD GOTHIC	KLEX	Kindness
CORVINUS BOLD	MOTOR	Vitality
		Enlightenment

Typefaces, like color, can represent more than one idea at a time. These adjective groups are adapted from Jill Morton's very useful *Color Voodoo*. Many of the types are selections from *Indie Fonts 1* and *2*. Please note that subjective associations are to be viewed with skepticism. We perceive through the filters of our own experiences. Using subjective feelings is a risky way to explain or defend design decisions: you will lose as many contests as you win. So I don't expect to convince you on more than about half of my selections on the opposite page.

❝ There are many artists who…see their value and justification in novelty; but they are wrong. Novelty is hardly ever important. What matters is always this one thing: to penetrate to the very heart of a thing, and create it better." *Henri de Toulouse-Lautrec (1864–1901)*

The chart opposite shows seven categories of symbolism, each represented by six typefaces. You may wonder at or disagree with many of my type designations. That is expected: it is the nature of subjective design. It is this subjectivity, this "because *I* like it" – whether the "*I*" is the designer or the client, the author or the reader – that causes discord. After all, *everyone* has an opinion. Some opinions are more fully informed and can be explained. If a type choice is refused by a client or colleague after explaining its symbolism, the designer must make another selection, and another, and frequently, another, until all parties are *reasonably* happy. If, by chance, the designer is not at all happy, symbolism must be applied to the chosen type. For example, if you can't communicate "energy" by using *Déformé* (which is an adaptation of *Clarendon*), you may have to communicate energy by applying some attributes that drew you to *Déformé*. Some types are very hard to read, so concentrate on symbolism but keep some attention on the type's legibility.

There are five considerations when choosing a typeface:

▶ **Readers' needs** What are they used to seeing? Should you consciously stretch their comfort zone? Unless your message *needs* to say "cutting edge," use a time-tested typeface. It may lack novelty, but it will be familiar to your readers and therefore trusted and readable. A type's ability to attract is important in display faces; its ability to be read is essential in text faces.

▶ **Symbolism** Many types represent the time of their design, or have other meanings (*opposite*).

▶ **Knowing your client** If your client needs to project "reliability" with "trustworthiness," select a face that conveys those qualities. Also important is design continuity with the client's previous pieces so the client projects a consistent image.

▶ **Passing fashion** The more popular the type you are considering, the faster and further out of fashion it will soon be. The opposite of fashion is choosing a typeface because of convenience: the font happens to be on your computer.

▶ **Reproduction variables** Fine serifs and extreme stroke contrasts don't hold up on screen or with poor printing.

M⊗THER
(CHILD)

ske?tic

THE FORUM FOR ? CONTEMPORARY HISTORY

Neutral face	Convenient face	Historical face
TITIAN CELEBRATES FIRST BIRTHDAE	TITIAN CELEBRATES FIRST BIRTHDAE	TITIAN CELEBRATES FIRST BIRTHDAE
Times Roman	Centaur	Alvise Brothers, 1478
NATIONAL GALLERY Opens in London	NATIONAL GALLERY Opens in London	NATIONAL GALLERY Opens in London
Impact	Bodoni	Roman X Condensed, 1838
PICASSO PAINTS "THE TWO SISTERS"	PICASSO PAINTS "THE TWO SISTERS"	PICASSO PAINTS ϟTHE TWO SISTERS ϟ
Courier	Cheltenham	Koloman Moser, 1904

That's not a paper cut. It's a finger cut. I'm going to dream about you my whole life. Or maybe
Frutiger 75 w/Californian Roman

That's not a paper cut. It's a finger cut. I'm going to dream about you my whole life. Or maybe
Champion Midweight w/Journal Text

That's not a paper cut. It's a finger cut. I'm going to dream about you my whole life. Or may-
Ignatius w/Linotype Didot

That's not a paper cut. It's a finger cut. I'm going to dream about you my whole life. Or may-
Meta Plus Black w/ITC Baskerville

That's not a paper cut. It's a finger cut. I'm going to dream about you my whole life. Or may-
Colossalis w/Comenius Antiqua

That's not a paper cut. It's a finger cut. I'm going to dream about you my whole life. Or maybe I'll
Griffith Gothic w/Concorde Nova

That's not a paper cut. It's a finger cut. I'm going to dream about you my whole life. Or maybe I'll
Geometric 706 Black w/Eureka Roman

That's not a paper cut. It's a finger cut. I'm going to dream about you my whole life. Or maybe I'll help
Flare Gothic w/Gill Sans Light

THAT'S NOT A PAPER CUT. IT'S A FINGER CUT. I'm going to dream about you my whole life. Or maybe I'll help you wash your car sometime.
Posada w/Oz Handicraft

Matching type to job and meaning

Type selection is usually the second step in a designer's process:

1 Develop the strategy or concept.

2 Choose typefaces that suit the concept: first one family (often for the text because that is where the reader will spend the most time) and then a display face to complement it. Enormous breadth is achieved if one family is serif and the other is sans serif. This gives *inter-family contrasts* of style, weight, posture, in addition to *intra-font contrasts* of size, color, and position.

The content itself often leads to distinctive and appropriate type choices. Two magazine logos by Herb Lubalin (*opposite, top*) use specific typefaces: *Mother & Child* uses *Goudy Oldstyle*, which has organic strokes and an ampersand borrowed from the italic font; *Skeptic* uses *Clearface*, which has ball terminals that relate to the dot under the question mark. Both examples were extensively reworked so the results look inevitable.

Designs describing places or historical periods are relatively easy to evoke. Using actual period samples, generally available as art rather than fonts, will give a degree of authenticity that a design otherwise wouldn't have (*opposite, middle*).

Another way to optimize job and meaning is to produce one design using several different type combinations, then decide which solution is most satisfactory (*opposite, bottom*). In the early years of typesetting, it was impossible to do this: the only fonts available were the ones cut by the printer for his own use. As centuries passed, it became possible but time consuming and expensive to use this technique. Today, the computer makes this a quick and easy process.

Mortimer Leach, author, educator, and designer, said in 1963, "Alphabets can portray a variety of feelings or moods, such as stability, strength, an avant-garde quality or that of a past era… At all times, the designer should seriously consider the use of type styles other than those which are currently in vogue. This is not a project for a lazy mind. There are hundreds of alphabets available and waiting to be gainfully re-employed."

ARCHI **AKERS** TECTS
20 Prospect Street
Summit NJ
908 **555 1956**

Akers
Architects
20 Prospect Street
Summit NJ
908 **555 1956**

AKERS ARCHITECTS
20 Prospect Street
Summit NJ
908 **555 1956**

Akers
Architects
20 Prospect Street
Summit NJ
908 555 1956

AKERS ARCHITECTS

AKERS ARCHI TECTS

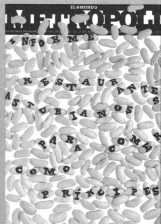

A type treatment you can own

By *own*, I mean developing a type treatment you are recognized for having and is sufficiently recognizeable that others can't copy it. For example, swirly letters are recognized as Coca-Cola's. Swirly letters inside an oval are recognized as Ford's. These are typographic "ownings" on a global level that have taken years and billions of dollars to construct. Fortunately, typographic ownership can be developed at a more local level.

Every client deserves a design treatment for which they can be recognized. Few will admit it, but they want to be clapped on the back by their colleagues and congratulated for their company's well-made materials. So a magazine should have a look that is theirs alone. An ad campaign should sell product while reinforcing the sponsor as a unique entity.

Part of owning a typographic treatment is knowing what the direct competition is doing. The other part is knowing what the broader marketplace is doing. The redesign of a magazine must be noticeable against its *direct* magazine competitors as well as among other magazines with which its readers may come be familiar and the visual noise we get from all other sources.

Develop a type treatment that is recognizable, whose characteristics are yours alone. Repeat them so to buttress your ownership of them.

A few case studies:
▶ **Tiffany & Co.** (*left*) This full-page-wide newspaper ad is a photograph of an iconographic Tiffany light blue box. The ribbon obscures about 90 percent of the logo which suggests the concept of a surprise, and thus, a gift.
▶ **Xerox** (*left*) Their ad campaign runs the Xerox logo across the page or spread. The logo's size is great enough that the O can be replaced by an image which is then discussed in the text.
▶ **Metropoli magazine** (*opposite*) This Madrid newspaper's weekly supplement has created a recognizable design system in which each cover, including the logo, is given a unique treatment. The covers' *alterability* is its distinctive attribute.

Fresh vs familiar

Case studies *113*

> " *The world is full of inadequate design solutions, which merely build on conventional wisdom. If you don't constantly turn over rocks, you'll never notice if something has changed.*" RICHARD SEYMOUR

◀□ An ordinary map is planned for locating streets and buildings. Robert Venturi's map of the Las Vegas strip shows every significant word visible from the road, C1972.

THE ESSENCE OF DESIGN FRESHNESS is recognizing when your work is too comfortable or too familiar.

The definition of *familiar* is safe, automatic, and likely to be accepted. While a familiar presentation may adequately display its message, it does not add value to the message. Some designers are willing to, or are perhaps unaware of, settling for ordinary, familiar design solutions. Often, design looks familiar simply because the designer accepted standard treatments without thinking about them (*see next spread*).

The definition of *fresh* is thoughtful, solves the problem in a unique way, and is risky. A fresh presentation adds value to the message. There is, in fact, a correlation between value added and freshness: the more value added to the message through its design, the fresher the solution. It takes informed and interested minds – both the client's and the designer's – to look for fresh solutions. Freshness springs directly from a full diagnosis of the problem. One needs to get inside the problem and turn it over, looking for the unique aspect that will show off its essence. If your design solutions are not unique, if your solutions are applicable to other problems, you haven't dissected the problem fully.

François Colos, a collagist who did a great number of conceptual op-ed illustrations for the *New York Times*, said his biggest problem was coming up with something fresh every year for recurring subjects. "You have for example now the 98th Congress

Sidebar quotes:

" In my opinion there are three essential things in design: passion, challenge and discovery. Without them, design gets boring. With them, the more excited I become. And work which in enjoyable results in success." *Takenobu Igarashi*

◀□ Problem: a story about Ellis Island, the site of entry for hundeds of thousands of immigrants in the early 20th century. Solution: a typographic cluster that illustrates "islandness" positioned in a vast area of empty image.

" The designer is not an artist, yet he can be one." *Walter Gropius*

◀□ These two poster diagrams by Yukichi Takada use relative type size to indicate quantity and location of energy use (*far left*) and forest area (*left*). What makes these works fresh is the way familiar shapes of landmasses have been abstracted in service to the messages.

Mr. Bedrich Smetana
258 Fulton St.
New York, N.Y. 10038
(212) 555-1645

1 Examine typographic
standards: Ordinary
typesetting following styling inherited from mono-
spaced typewriters.

Mr. Bedrich Smetana
258 Fulton Street
New York, N.Y. 10038
212-555-1645

2 Set in a higher-quality
font; spell out abbrevia-
tion; replace parentheses
with hyphen.

Mr Bedřich Smetana
258 Fulton Street
New York, NY 10038
212/555 1645

3 Remove periods and
hyphen; replace hyphen
with slash; add háček.

The unusual dates on Bedřich Smetana's gravestone
in Vyšehrad Cemetery indicate he was born on
March 2, 1824 and died on May 12, 1884.

Mr Bedřich Smetana
258 Fulton Street
New York, NY 10038
212 555 1645

4 Add 3' (*58 Fulton* and *212 555*) optical linespacing; remove slash.

Mr Bedřich Smetana
258 Fulton Street
New York N Y 10038
212 555 1645

5 Replace lining figures with old style figures; remove comma.

Mr Bedřich Smetana
258 Fulton Street
New York N Y 10038
212 555 1645

6 Add 3' (*New York*) and remove 3' (*212 555*) optical linespacing; italicize telephone for differentiation; reverse zip code in box.

First draft	Second draft	Final design

Freshness is tied to timeliness. What was once fresh becomes trite and what is fresh today will probably show its age in the future. Neon lights were new when this travel poster was designed in 1938, so this was quite an edgy treatment at the time.

of the United States. It comes every year. What are you going to do for the 98th which is a new statement? And a hundred, a thousand on the economy: it's always the same story. Unemployment, inflation: you made one inflation, two inflation, a hundred inflation drawings, what are you doing for the hundred and *first*? That's the big problem."

As Walter Gropius said, design *may* be art. To which I would add, but only if a design is fresh. Design is never art if it is merely familiar. After all, art is defined as making the familiar appear new.

Case studies

Designers usually have to get the familiar out of their systems before the fresh ideas begin to flow. The four designs shown on the opposite page all began with perfectly acceptable studies (*far left column*), each selected from a dozen or more first draft sketches. Second passes (*center column*) show increased individuality and abstraction. Final sketches (*right column*) push abstraction further and add illustrative elements.

Identity sketches for *Lyrica*, a pharmaceutical for neuropathic pain, developed from the client requirement of a triad. The literal quality of the mark was gradually replaced by a simplified, abstract interpretation.

Identity sketches for *Prescott Funding* started with a clean, "trustworthy" typeface in two weights and sizes, an unexpected word break, and visual alignment. The client asked for an eagle to represent "honor and integrity," so it was made slightly transparent. The use of the organic image contrasts with the exosketetal type.

Cia Delas, meaning *"Their Company,"* is a Brazilian theater troupe. They wanted a mark that would define their group as modern and daring, yet serious and respectful of drama's history.

Subtle type changes adjust the importance of secondary type on the GE Halogen Floodlight Bulbs package studies. The GE logo is integrated with the illustration and *HALOGEN* is given a custom letterform treatment.

◁ (*Top*) Robert Massin's 1954 interpretation of Eugene Ionesco's *The Bald Soprano* is an unusual visualization of a play. Each character's dialogue is set in a different font, with typographic size and position used to indicate its delivery. (*Bottom*) Handlettering, or in this case *handcrafting* letters, is Stefan Sagmeister's solution for an Austrian magazine sequence. Though abstract (they read: *Everything I do always comes back to me*), these six designs are astonishingly original.

▷ (*Top*) Value creates order in this near-lifesize design. The logo for *City Ball*, a party in São Paulo, uses contrast of rigid letterform repetition and alignment with looser spiral forms. (*Middle*) Hand lettering and positive/negative contrast of value and baselines reveals editorial meaning on this book jacket. (*Bottom*) Handlettering contrasts with typesetting in this spread from a British design association's annual report.

❝ There should be a kind of impersonal ease about type – type is after all only a medium between writing and reading." *Rudolph Ruzicka*

Section 3

Creativity

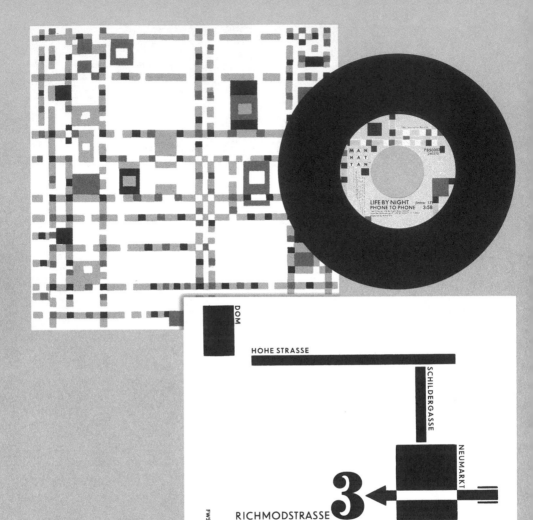

MAN
HAT
TAN

FBS0003
240370

LIFE BY NIGHT (Intro: 17)
PHONE TO PHONE 3:58

DOM

HOHE STRASSE

SCHILDERGASSE

NEUMARKT

3 ←

FWS

RICHMODSTRASSE

weniger Lärm

SÄCHSISCHE
SCHULZEITUNG

POSTKARTE

IM AUFTRAGE: ALWIN OTTO

DRESDEN-LEUBEN

KÖNIGSALLEE 40
RUF: NIEDERSEDLITZ 411

Deutsches Reich 5

Evolving a treatment from existing characteristics

> ❝ *Design requires esthetics, inspiration, and guts. To me nothing is more vibrant than having the power to do something but not having the experience of knowing what's right and what's wrong.*❞ TIBOR KALMAN

EVERY DESIGN EVOLVES from an existing model. The model may be a current or previous incarnation of the object. For a new business or product, the model may be the competitors' design materials. A design is compared to a client's previous design, the client's competitors' designs, and the broader prevailing design sensibilities of the time.

The design industry is great at making the best work viewable. Annuals of the year's best advertising and editorial design and typography flow with regularity. But what doesn't get communicated is the process that produces such great results. Few designers actually get jealousy-inducing results on the first pass. It takes time and editing to make a design look, as composer Aaron Copland said referring to music, *inevitable*.

Most clients want a design to be reminiscent of their existing materials. In a way, they aren't really looking for a design, but an *extension* or a *redesign*.

The development of five projects are shown on the following pages as case studies. They show, among other things, that design is a process in which the final result evolves. Typically, the process proceeds from complex to simple. The results appear obvious and effortless. But having a peek at the process reveals the truth: design is work. Really fun work.

Mondrian's *Broadway Boogie-Woogie* (1942–43) served as inspiration for Paula Scher's identity for Manhattan Records. In response to what Scher thought was a depressing sameness of corporate logos "shoved in the upper right corner," she adapted Mondrian's abstract street map of New York City, which was itself inspired by music.

◀ ❑ Hot metal type had severe limitations which provided creative opportunity for designers in the 1920s. These examples, a diagrammatic map by Franz W. Seiwert, a postcard by Joost Schmidt, and an ad by Walter Dexel (*above*), all use type and printing bars – plus a dynamic use of space – in a revolutionary way to design.

◀ ❑ By using inherent axes in the image, Josef Muller-Brockmann (1914–1996) creates an "x" by crossing the figure's arms and the type in this 1960 poster for the Swiss Committee to Combat Noise. Black and white image with red type.

❝ The secret to creativity is knowing how to hide your sources." *Albert Einstein*

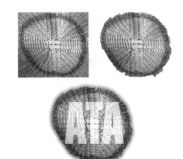

Aid to Artisans

⊡ Logo development, here for a nonprofit arts organization, begins with reinterpreting the existing mark. Clarifying the T/K letterform, "weaving," and roundness are chosen as starting points. ⊡ A basket from the Amazon is scanned and silhouetted in a round shape. Edges are softened and rigid transparent letters are added. ⊡ Final art is a dithered line conversion and the name is set in Trade Gothic Extended beneath the mark.

AID TO
ARTISANS

⊡ A sketch of weaving leads to actual weaving in clay. A crafted symbol like this forces abstraction on the mark. ⊡ The clay model leads to studies of digitally-perfect weaving. ⊡ Final art is a high contrast evolution of the clay model with all-caps TG Expanded, set in clean alignment to contrast the organic mark.

⊡ The letterforms are worked into a relationship that uses negative space. It is put in a circle, maintaining that one similarity to the original mark. ⊡ News Gothic Bold Condensed Italic is given three alternative notches (*top*). The T is extended through the bottom of the circle and the entirety is textured in Photoshop. ⊡ All-caps NG Bold Condensed Italic is angle-aligned beneath the T.

Aid to Artisans

⊡ Weaving and dimensionality leads to another abstraction of the *ATA* letters. Shown here is the first letter *A*.

⊡ An isometric grid is set up and the shapes are prepared. Studies explore value, complexity, and legibility.

⊡ Asymmetrically-set NG Expanded complements the rigidity of the mark with organic shape.

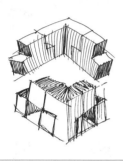

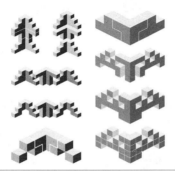

Aid to Artisans

⊡ The dimensionality of the previous studies evolves into greater simplicity and abstraction. ⊡ Using the same isometric grid, the essence of the two letters, *A* and *T*, are explored. Every idea can be expressed as advancing or receding studies. ⊡ The final contrasts the abstract letterforms with a curvilinear shape and an extremely simple setting and exact sizing of the name.

Aid to Artisans

⊡ Weaving and roundness are characteristics that need enhancement, so several previous studies are revisited. ⊡ A new woven pattern is applied in new studies (*top*). The isometric grid is converted to a beehive-like pattern that fits beneath previous marks and suggests a circle. ⊡ Note the typeset capitals are stacked beneath the midpoint of the circle, asymmetrically relating to the symmetrical circle.

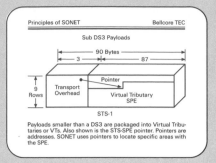

Principles of SONET — Bellcore TEC

Sub DS3 Payloads

90 Bytes
3 — 87

9 Rows

Transport Overhead — Pointer — Virtual Tributary SPE

STS-1

Payloads smaller than a DS3 are packaged into Virtual Tributaries or VTs. Also shown is the STS-SPE pointer. Pointers are addresses. SONET uses pointers to locate specific areas with the SPE.

▪ This is a typical presentation frame prepared by the Bell Telephone training center near Chicago. They provide all coursework for all the Bell companies in the U.S. The question they asked was, "Can our visuals be designed and formatted to communicate better and be easier to produce?" Of course. Here's a step by step how-to. The artwork style and use of Helvetica could not be changed.

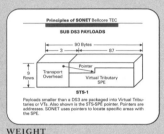

WEIGHT

SIZE

POSITION

▪ Design is a process, so we will consider one type contrast at a time. This is type weight. The size remains unchanged and position is adjusted only to strengthen the title. ▪ This is type size contrast. The weight remains unchanged and position is adjusted only to make room for the headline. ▪ This is type position. The size and weight remain unchanged. This is the best single contrast manipulation.

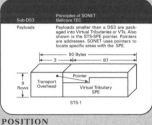

WEIGHT

SIZE

WEIGHT+SIZE

▪▪ This design process next combines individual contrast studies. While it is optimal to try to have, in this case, weight and contrasts each contribute 50% of the design characteristics, it is not necessarily achievable. One contrast may contribute more than the other in order to create a more successful design. ▪ Combining weight plus size yields a better design than either contrast alone.

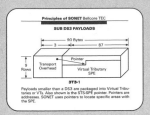

WEIGHT

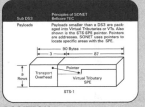

POSITION

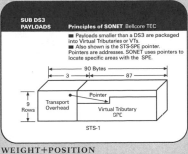

WEIGHT+POSITION

⊡ ⊡ Merging weight again relegates it to lesser status than its partner, in this case position. This is because weight, in my opinion, is a less successful design on its own. The result is that the combined design is heavily skewed to position.

⊡ This is a combination of weight plus position. Note that bullets in the text are invented as an expression of weight.

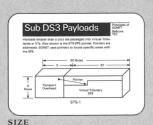

SIZE

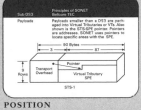

POSITION

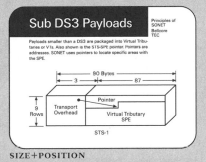

SIZE+POSITION

⊡ ⊡ This process is almost mechanical in nature. It leads to a successful redesign that is based on logical decision making. This combination is closer to a 50-50 split than the other two. The resulting design, though, should be better than either of its constituent designs. ⊡ This is a combination of size plus position. Compare it to the other two combination studies.

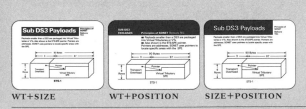

WT+SIZE   **WT+POSITION**   **SIZE+POSITION**

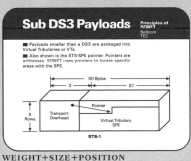

WEIGHT+SIZE+POSITION

⊡ ⊡ This last step combines the best parts of the three combination studies. Note that the illustration has remained unchanged throughout, but its context and the type relationships have changed. ⊡ This is the combination of the three paired contrasts. This final study is considerably more distinctive than the original slide

RISK CAPITAL MANAGEMENT PARTNERS
1750 Broadway, Suite 1900
New York, NY 10019

David C. Shimko

Voice: (212) 988-1817
Cell: (917) 988-1818
Fax: (212) 988-1819
shimko@rcm-rcm.com

◢RCM◢

David C. Shimko
Hang RISK CAPITAL *Skip one line*
Risk Capital Management Partners
1750 Broadway
Suite 1900
NYC NY 10019
212 988 1817
Skip one line
917 988 1818 cell
212 988 1819 fx
shimko@rcm-rcm.com
Equalize optical space on top, bottom, and right

⊡ Typical of many startups, this business got cards from a nearby print shop. The result is unexceptional design, including logo.

⊡ Once the business got on its feet, it needed to be presented more appropriately. This preliminary type study is one of about two dozen. AG OLD FACE

⊡ The original logo (*top*), designed by the founder, needed reinterpretation. The RCM/triangles relationship was an obvious start.

⊡ Cropping in on the edges of RCM makes a neat alignment. Six examples from a series of about twenty variations explored stacking, repetition, and order. ⊡ The final logo. It retains all the elements of the original with the addition of a quirky point of view.

David C. Shimko

Risk Capital Management Partners
1750 Broadway
Suite 1900
NYC NY 10019
212 988 1817

917 988 1818 cell
212 988 1819 fx
shimko@rcm-rcm.com

RCM

David C. Shimko

RCM   **Risk Capital Management Partners**
1750 Broadway
Suite 1900
NYC NY 10019
212 918 1817

917 918 1818 cell
212 988 1819 fx
shimko@rcm-rcm.com

⊡ Corporate design is comparable to a business suit: simplicity and dignity is imperative. Using order and alignments defines success. AG OLD FACE

⊡ Once the direction is determined, a variety of executions are run to compare subtle differences. GRIFFITH GOTHIC

Card 1 (top left)

RCM

David C. Shimko
9179881818 cell

Risk Capital Management Partners
1750 Broadway   2129881817
Suite 1900   2129881819 fx
NYC NY 10019   shimko@rcm-rcm.com

Card 2 (top right)

RCM

**Risk
Capital
Management
Partners**

David C. Shimko

1750 Broadway
Suite 1900
NYC NY 10019

212 988 1817 office
917 988 1818 cell
212 988 1819 fax
shimko@rcm-rcm.com

⊡ The purpose is to identify types that create a unified design and project timeliness, but not faddishness.   *TRADE GOTHIC*

⊡ Information groupings are manipulated, not individual lines. Space is carefully attended to, as in the two examples above.   *URW GROTESK*

Card 3 (middle left)

David C. Shimko

**Risk Capital
Management** Partners

RCM

1750 Broadway
Suite 1900
NYC NY 10019

212 988 1817
917 988 1818 cell
212 988 1819 fax
shimko@rcm-rcm.com

Card 4 (middle right)

David C. Shimko
917 988 1818 cel

1750 Broadway
Suite 1900
NYC NY 10019

212 988 1817
212 988 1819 fax
shimko@rcm-rcm.com

RCM   Risk Capital
Management Partners

⊡ It is decided that the company name will be larger and darker. The alignment of *PARTNERS* unifies the design.   *BARMENO*

⊡ Putting the company name at the bottom of the card is counterintuitive, but suggests the company thinks in fresh, dynamic ways.   *ELLINGTON*

Card 5 (bottom left)

RCM

David C. Shimko

1750 Broadway
Suite 1900
NYC NY 10019

**Risk Capital
Management** Partners

212 988 1817
917 988 1818 cel
212 988 1819 fax
shimko@rcm-rcm.com

Card 6 (bottom right)

RCM

David C. Shimko

1750 Broadway
Suite 1900
NYC NY 10019

**Risk Capital
Management** Partners

212 988 1817
917 988 1818 cel
212 988 1819 fax
shimko@rcm-rcm.com

⊡ Approaching completion, compare this design to the original card. Notice how differently the same company presents itself.   *ROTIS SEMI SANS*

⊡ The mark is centered over the left edge of *RISK* on the final card. This format is adapted to letterhead, envelope, and forms.   *ROTIS SEMI SANS*

⊡ Logo development for a reformulated pharmaceutical product that is long acting (*LA*). The first step is trying varied typographic directions to get familiar with the problem. ⊡ The second pass tries simpler faces which can be used in a supporting role with imagery.

⊡ The third pass adds illustrative ideas to type treatments. Some studies include the drug's generic name, an eventual requirement.

⊡ A highly abstracted L and A that suggest building blocks, strength, and dynamism. Multiple color and ground studies.

⊡ Federal requirements require the drug's generic name at half the logo's point size. Note the alignment of elements and consistency

of sizes. ⊡ Horizontality is chosen over the square format. Branding colors are dark blue and gold. The type is *Interstate*.

⊡ The idea, "What if the *i*'s talk to each other?," came up in an agency meeting. Increased interaction is a benefit of this drug.

⊡ Bending the *i*'s makes them look more human with the dots becoming heads. The cost is a slight decrease in legibility.

⊡ The final mark uses the *NEW ONCE DAILY* "eyebrow" as a conversation between the two *i*'s. The type is *News Gothic*.

⊡ This started as a simple typeset example using a font called *Plastic Man*, which evokes the plastic pieces in a modelmaking kit. Stud-ies were made using alternate types. Modelmaking is age-specific and suggests playfulness and pa-tience. ⊡ The two ancillary "bugs" are incorporated into the primary type. ⊡ *NEW ONCE DAILY* is reduced to the width of *RITALIN*. The type is *News Gothic Rounded*.

⊡ The mark suggests cooperation, playfuless, and process. You may see an abstract face, though this was not promoted as an attribute. ⊡ The cyclic motion of the mark is reiterated in the horizontal bars. These studies tended toward busy-ness more than the others. ⊡ The final logo centers the mark over *RITALIN* and sizes *NEW LONG ACTING* with *RITA*. The type is *Trade Gothic*.

⊡ One of the basic typeset studies evolved to highlight the long-acting properties of the drug. These ear-ly studies were too abstract. ⊡ These are six of the dozens of studies produced in FreeHand. They are better at suggesting day-time and improvement. ⊡ *NEW ONCE DAILY* has been de-emphasized and the dots over the *i*'s imitate the sun's shape. The type is URW Grotesk.

⊡ A magazine redesign is a complex challenge. There are hundreds of little pieces, each of which must be made to agree or, with great care, disagree with the overall format. *Vistazo* is the newsmagazine of Ecuador. Shown are three covers in its evolution over eight years.

⊡ *Vistazo* began as a project to keep the presses busy at a leading printery in Ecuador. The logo at top is from the mid-'90s. The 3D version was to be the last iteration before a redesign. The logo was set in Futura Extra Bold (*bottom left*) and ⊡ various experiments were performed. Colors are red, black, and white. ⊡ The dot over the *I* was getting too much attention, so it was absorbed into the background.

⊡⊡ The logo is the most important typographic element for a magazine. It is most recognizeable (or should be) and it sets the tone for all other display type. Department headings are the second most important type because they connect the cover to the inside pages. These four variations were among several sets prepared. ⊡ The folio/footline is another recurring element that unifies a magazine.

Berling Roman
Last night I took a stroll through the center of Guayaquil. The clouds were dark in the east and I expected rain, but it never came. As six turned into seven, more people crowded the sidewalks. Verandas cover virtually all the sidewalks. They must be there because it rains

Giovanni Book
Last night I took a stroll through the center of Guayaquil. The clouds were dark in the east and I expected rain, but it never came. As six turned into seven, more people crowded the sidewalks. Verandas cover virtually all the sidewalks. They must be there because it rains frequently.

Adobe Caslon Pro
Last night I took a stroll through the center of Guayaquil. The clouds were dark in the east and I expected rain, but it never came. As six turned into seven, more people crowded the sidewalks. Verandas cover virtually all the sidewalks. They must be there because it rains frequently.

Charter Roman
Last night I took a stroll through the center of Guayaquil. The clouds were dark in the east and I expected rain, but it never came. As six turned into seven, more people crowded the sidewalks. Verandas cover virtually all the sidewalks. They must be there because it rains

El éxito genera más éxito

Este Gobierno ha sido el más represivo de todos

ANTONIO VARGAS

Last night I took a stroll through the center of Guayaquil. The clouds were dark in the east and I expected rain, but it never came. As six turned into seven, more people crowded the sidewalks. Verandas cover virtually all the sidewalks. They must be there because it rains frequently.

I visited the cathedral, which abuts the back of the *Grand Hotel*

El éxito genera más éxito

Este Gobierno ha sido el más represivo de todos ANTONIO VARGAS

Last night I took a stroll through the center of Guayaquil. The clouds were dark in the east and I expected rain, but it never came. As six turned into seven, more people crowded the sidewalks. Verandas cover virtually all the sidewalks. They must be there because it rains frequently.

I visited the cathedral, which abuts the back of the *Grand Hotel Guayaquil. Patricia tells me the*

⊡ Text studies at reproduction size must be carefully evaluated: this is where readers spend the most time. Legibility matters the most in these studies. ⊡ *Charter* was chosen for text and many studies have to be done to develop the secondary type characteristics. Shown here are two from opposite ends of the design spectrum. Though workaday, the simplest is preferable to the most complex.

⊡⊡ The cover format encourages imagery to run up into the logo, though it doesn't have to, and cover lines to align in one of three columns at the page's head. Cover composition is relatively easy: select a great photo, write a catchy headline, and use any version of Futura, including the "crazy ones," to make a special piece of typographic art. ⊡ The finished cover is immediate and attention-getting.

⊡⊡ The makeup of the magazine includes departments, which are recurring topics of interest in every issue, and feature stories, which are, by definition, special to that one issue. Departments use a three-column grid to accommodate partial-page ads. Features use any grid, so long as they don't look like departments. ⊡ This feature story looks different from the rest of the editorial matter as it should.

Readability	Legibility
Unconventional	Functional
Unpredictable	Legible
Disorderly	Orderly
Complex	Simple
Original	Banal
Dynamic	Static

jahre nach seinem unfall nahm er wieder eine ahle in die h

f einem würfel angeordnet ● ● ● in einen festen karton.

sechs punkte, so hoffte er, sollten ausreichen,

benötigten kombinationen für alle buchstaben

habets herzustellen. nachdem louis die einzel

nkt-kombinationen für die buchstaben des

ets festgelegt hatte, stach er einen ganzen satz

er blindenschrift. dieses einfache und ebenso

system funktionierte perfekt! mit dieser schrift

n blinde nicht nur schnell lesen,

n und das ist genauso wichtig **auch selbst schreiben!**

J | DAGEN

TORSDAG | 22.08.2002 | No.005 | PRIS 15,- KR.

| A10 | KLOGE KÆRTEGN DAGEN DROPPER LÆSERBREVENE | B14 | LARS KOLIND GÅR TIL HUMOR BEDRE HVIS DER ER MERE TEKST | B12 | BECKUAM OG ZIDANE DAGEN FAVORITERER DE STØRSTE STJERNER FØRST |

STORSEJR TIL ISLAMISTER

Den islamistiske højrefløj vandt fredagens jordskredsvalg i Marokko

A12

Kloge kærtegn dagen dropper laserbreve
A10

Ronaldo forgyldes
B14

Mdiernes saturcensur
A10

Ronaldo forgyldes
B14

Readability, then legibility

Readability *133* · Legibility *137*

> **“** *Readability is likely to be a result of good design, not of type but of text. Not “Times New Roman is readable or unreadable,” but “a newspaper or a book is readable or unreadable.”*
> GERRIT NOORDZIJ

TYPOGRAPHY IS AN INFORMATION-DELIVERY SYSTEM like a cigarette is a tar and nicotine delivery system and a mint is a fresh breath delivery system. Some typography – like some cigarettes and some mints – work better at delivering their content.

Legibility and readability are among the most misunderstood areas of type. Indeed, many use the terms interchangeably, which reduces their usefulness and perpetuates confusion. Let's define terms:

Readability Type's capacity to attract and hold a reader's interest. Readability is *macro-typography*: it applies to the overall reading experience.

Legibility Type's capacity to be read under normal reading conditions; the ease with which it can be read. Legibility is *micro-typography*: it applies to component parts like letters, words, and lines of type. Further, legibility is the condition in which the eyes discern more than the mind can absorb. Conversely, illegibility is the condition in which the mind can absorb faster than the eyes can discern.

First, you have to get browsers to be interested in the type enough to want to read it. You have to make it subconsciously appealing so they become readers. Then you have to make it legible. Readable/illegible type is bad design: you've earned the browsers' attention and desire to read, yet the type can't be deciphered. Legible/unreadable type will simply be ignored.

Cheddar Cheese

THE main characteristics of Cheddar cheese are its clean, mellow flavour and good keeping qualities. The body is firm and smooth, free from gas holes, and the texture close. The colour is uniform and the rind clean and unbroken.

Cheddar cheese is made from evening's and morning's mixed milk ripened with starter. No cream should be removed from the evening's milk, since this results in a lower yield and the production of a "chalky" cheese.

Treatment of Evening's Milk

The milk is strained into the cheese vat or tub, and in warm weather is at once cooled (preferably by running over a cooler) to a temperature of 65–70° F. The use of a cooler ensures that the milk is evenly cooled and aerated, and the action of the acid-forming organisms is not unduly checked. When cooled in a jacketed vat or tub, the milk must be constantly stirred whilst a steady stream of cold water is circulated through the jacket.

During the evening the milk is stirred occasionally. This prevents a too rapid rising of the cream and results in a thinner layer on the milk the following morning. In cold weather it is not necessary to cool the milk, the vat being covered to maintain the temperature, so that by the following morning it will be about 60–62° F.

After the evening's milk has been treated as outlined above, the acidity is tested. At this stage it is generally 0·17–0·19 per cent and determines the subsequent details of manufacture.

Ripening with Starter

Next morning, the evening's milk is carefully skimmed; the cream is raised to a temperature of 90° F., and then strained back into the milk, the temperature of which has been raised to 70° F.* Starter is now added, the amount required varying from 1–2 pints per 25 gal. of milk, according to the acidity of the milk and the time of year. Sufficient should be used, however, to give a correct degree of acidity for renneting in from 1½ to 2 hours after adding.

When the starter has been well mixed in, the morning's milk is added, either in bulk or as it is brought into the dairy.

Acidity Test. The whole is then heated to renneting temperature, i.e., 84–86° F., and the acidity tested. The acidity at this stage (usually 0·19–0·23 per cent) controls the texture, flavour and keeping quality of the cheese and also determines the time taken to complete the making process, which should be 5½–6 hours after renneting. The acidity at renneting should be at least 0·02 per cent above that taken about 30 min. after the evening's milk was received in the dairy. Generally, the acidity of the evening's milk next morning will be from 0·18–0·22 per cent.

BAD Low readability
High legibility

WORSE High readability
Low legibility

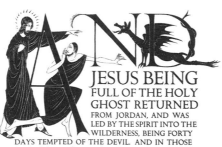

IDEAL High readability
High legibility

Readability

"Readability connotes an aethestic pleasantness that makes the type inviting to read. Legibility, on the other hand, does not mean letter-to-letter identification, but instead the degree of word recognition. Words are, in effect, type-shape associations." *Lester Beall, 1962*

High readability, making something noticeable and interesting, often produces low legibility, that is, the piece becomes hard to read. Pick your moments to develop readability. Catching readers is the job of display type, not text. Display type is primary and secondary type elements, those that are intended to be read first, describe the story contained in the text, and lure the reader into the text. Display type typically includes headlines, subheads, decks, captions, breakouts, and pull quotes. Holding readers is the job of text. It is the destination to which readers have been lured, so once they are there, don't let anything interfere with their reading experience. Increase *readability* in display type; increase *legibility* in text.

How to make display type inviting to read:

▶ Understand the reader's self-interest. Edit the primary and secondary type so value of the content to the reader is obvious.

▶ Make the design look purposeful. Give display type a distinct treatment that adds to or reveals its meaning.

▶ Readability of small point size display type, for example as captions, is a function of brevity. The human mind perceives groups of two or three as "few." More than three is perceived as "many," so keep small display type short or risk having it skipped.

How to make text type inviting to read:

▶ Make it legible: choose a medium weight of a quality face.

▶ Make it legible: give it a comfortable size and column width.

▶ Make it legible: give it invisible, that is to say unselfconscious, spacing attributes.

The following, discussed at length on pages 31–39 and 59–71, are considerations that affect both type's readability and legibility. An accumulation of carelessness in handling these attributes

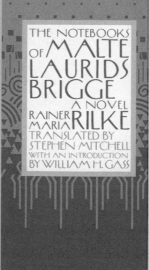

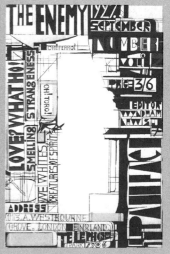

Type size (points)	Min. length (words)	Optimum length (words)	Max. length (words)
6	8	10	12
7	8	11	14
8	9	13	16
9	10	14	18
10	13	16	20
11	13	18	22
12	14	21	24
14	18	24	28

🗋 A rough guide for optimum words per line. In this system, a "word" is considered to be about four characters, including its following word space. Technical terms, for example, are longer and will require fewer words per line.

◁ Combining readability attributes can decrease legibility. *LEFT TO RIGHT:*
3+4+9 = *a decoding game*
1+4+7+8 = *asymmetrical hierarchy*
1+2+4+5+7+8+10 = *an artistic riff on the numeral 1 to announce the first copy of a magazine*

🗋 Max Ernst's 1927 cover for *The Little Review* contrasts type treatments with Massimo Vignelli's 1964 cut paper poster for the 32nd Venice Art Biennale.

creates a sense of unreadability. Overlooking just one of these will not necessarily deter a browser, but neglecting as few as two or three may deter even a committed reader.

▶ **1] Type size** Optimal type size is 10 to 11 point for text. Type that is too *small* repels readers who can't be bothered. Type that is too *big* makes skimming difficult and looks inept.

▶ **2] Type weight** Medium weight produces maximum legibility: the relationship of letterform and counter spaces is balanced.

▶ **3] Type posture** Paragraphs of italic text are harder to read than roman. Use italics only in short sections for emphasis.

▶ **4] Line length** Optimal line length is two alphabets (±52 characters). Fewer than 30 characters interrupts reading and causes too many hyphens and, in a justified column, uneven word spacing. More than 65 characters becomes tedious after three lines.

▶ **5] Letterspacing** Optimal letterspacing is invisible. Experiment with tracking and spacing attributes to eliminate anomalies.

▶ **6] Wordspacing** Wordspacing should be sufficient to separate words but not so much that it weakens lines of type.

▶ **7] Linespacing** Linespacing should increase with line length to maintain reading neutrality.

▶ **8] Justified vs flush left** Consistent word spacing makes flush left easier to read than justified type. A soft right rag is best: set the hyphenation zone to 0p3. Justified type can make rivers of white when large word spaces stack. Have at least six words per line in justified type to absorb uneven wordspaces.

▶ **9] All caps vs lower case** All caps are harder to read because word shapes are more similarly shaped. All caps also takes up about a third more space. Use all caps for brief display type.

▶ **10] Type and background** Black on white is about twice as fast to read as white on black. Reducing contrast between type and background causes loss in legibility and readership.

▶ **11] Serif vs sans serif** Readers prefer serif faces for text reading, so it makes sense to give it to them.

▶ **12] Paper finish** High-gloss paper makes images look great but makes type hard to read. Print on uncoated stock and use spot UV coating on images.

National

Rolan Hoskin was crushed in an accident at Tyler Pipe in Tyler, Tex., in 2000. Ira Cofer, left, lost an arm in 1997.

Agony and Loss at a Texas Foundry

By DAVID BARSTOW and LOWELL BERGMAN

TYLER, Tex. — It is said that only the desperate seek work at Tyler Pipe, a sprawling, rusting pipe foundry out on Route 69, just past the flea market. Behind a high metal fence lies a workplace that is part Dickens and part Darwin, a dim, dirty, hellishly hot place where men are regularly disfigured by amputations and burns, where turnover is so high that convicts are recruited from local prisons, where some workers urinate in their pants because their bosses refuse to let them step away from the manufacturing line for even a few moments.

Rolan Hoskin was from the ranks of the desperate. His life was a tailspin of unemployment, debt and divorce. A master electrician, 48 years old, he had retreated to a low-rent apartment on the outskirts of town and taken an entry-level maintenance job on the graveyard shift at Tyler Pipe.

He would come home covered in fine black soot, utterly drained and dreading the next shift. "I don't know if I'm going to last another week," his twin brother recalls him saying. But the pay was decent, just under $10 an hour, and his electricity was close to being cut off. "He was just trying to make it," his daughter said.

On June 29, 2000, in his second month on the job, Mr. Hoskin descended into a deep pit under a huge molding machine and set to work on an aging, balky conveyor belt that carried sand. Federal regulations require safety guards on conveyor belts to prevent workers from getting caught and crushed. They also require that belts be shut down when maintenance is done on them.

But this belt was not shut down, federal records show. Nor was it protected by metal safety guards. That very night, Mr. Hoskin had been trained to adjust the belt while it was still running. Less downtime that way, the men said. Now it was about 4 a.m., and Mr. Hoskin was alone in the cramped, dark pit. The din was deafening, the footing treacherous. He was found on his knees. His left arm had been crushed. His head had been pulled between belt and rollers.

Mr. Hoskin fell victim to a way of doing business that has produced vast profits and, as the plant's owners have admitted in federal court, deliberate indifference to the safety of workers at Tyler Pipe.

Mr. Hoskin worked for McWane Inc., a privately held company based in Birmingham, Ala., that owns Tyler Pipe and is one of the world's largest manufacturers of cast-iron sewer and water pipe. It is also one of the most dangerous employers in America, according to a nine-month examination by The New York Times, the PBS television program "Frontline" and the Canadian Broadcasting Corporation.

Since 1995, at least 4,600 injuries have been recorded in McWane foundries, many hundreds of them serious ones, company documents show. Nine workers, including Mr. Hoskin, have been killed. McWane plants, which employ about 5,000 workers, have been cited for more than 400 federal health and safety vio lations, far more than their six major compet itors combined.

On Jan. 22, 1997, another maintenance w er, Ira Cofer, descended alone into a mar pit. "Downsizing had ended the earlier prac of entering the pits with a buddy," OSHA in tigators later wrote.

When Mr. Cofer's sleeve snagged in an guarded conveyor belt, he struggled des ately to free himself. It was nearly three he before his screams were heard.

Mr. Cofer's arm had to be amputated.

In their accident report, plant managers the blame squarely on Mr. Cofer: "Keep h away from belt and do not work alone," wrote.

McWane declined repeated requests for terviews. But in a series of written respo the company's president, G. Ruffner Page,

A pipe maker exhibits an indifference to life.

knowledged "serious mistakes" and expres deep regret for Mr. Hoskin's death. "Our in sified focus on safety speaks to less learned," he wrote.

In the last decade, many American corpe tions have cut costs, laid off workers pressed those who remain to labor har longer and more efficiently. But top federal state regulators say McWane has taken idea to the extreme. Describing the compa business, they use the words "lawless" "rogue."

Even now the toughest of Tyler Pipe erans remember the day in 1995 when McW came to town as the day they were, as one them put it, "kicked into hell."

Baskerville	Rockwell	Times	Univers
along	along	along	along
along	**along**	**along**	**along**
along	along	along	along
	2964	2964	2964
2964	**2964**	**2964**	**2964**
2964	2964	2964	2964

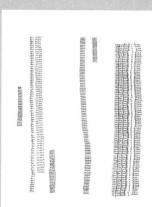

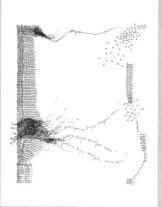

Legibility

Type is used in the furtherance of communication. Type's legibility, therefore, largely determines the success or failure of communication. If type is more legible, the communication succeeds. If type is less legible, it is a barrier to communication.

How to make type legible:

▶ Text type has a greater need for legibility than does display type because text type is smaller, so character and word recognition is made more difficult. Anything that gives hard-won readers the slightest awareness of reading text type is bad design.

▶ Type size is the most abused legibility attribute. Make type too small and you instantly lose all readers for whom small type is hard to see, let alone read. The New York Times, among a few other newspapers, has a large print edition that comes out weekly. Stories are edited about in half to make room for the 18-point text, which gives the paper a digest feel. (Their famous "All the News That's Fit to Print" is notably missing from the cover.) Similarly, popular books are available in large print editions. They, too, look a bit like books for kids, in which text is set large so individual letters and word shapes can be easily discerned.

▶ Type's legibility is determined in part by the spaces within and immediately surrounding each character. As type's size gets smaller, the spaces must be increased.

▶ It is thought that serif is easier to read than sans serif in part because it has a built-in horizontal emphasis. Compensate for this by opening the letter and wordspacing just a bit to make sans serif equally legible.

▶ The alphabet has four letter shapes: vertical, round, vertical/round combination, and angular. Letters in each group can be mistaken for each another: choose a typeface where distinctions are clear.

▶ As Adrian Frutiger said, "Smooth roads, soft beds, large windows, and sound-proof walls spell comfort to the average human being. The same feelings may be applied to optimum reading comfort of the printed word: suitable paper, sharp printing, well-justfied composition, and clean, open, universally recognized letterforms guarantee optimum legibility."

Typographic creativity grows from taking the rules in this chapter and turning them on their heads. Informed rule-breaking makes a design visible. Remember, a designer can do anything *so long as it looks like it was done on purpose*.

Egyptian hieroglyphics c2500BC

German woodblock page 1470

Pains of love
be sweeter far
Than all other
pleasures are.
JOHN DRYDEN

Saint-Gaudens sculpture c1895
John Dryden quote 1675

Ballets
de Paris
Roland
Petit
Théâtre de l'Empire

WILLY. Wonderful coffee. Meal in itself.
LINDA. Let me fix you some eggs?
WILLY. No. Take a breath.
LINDA. You look so rested, dear.
WILLY. I slept like a dead one. First
sleeping till ten on a Tuesday mornin
nice and early, heh?

Anton Clave poster 1953
Arthur Miller excerpt 1948

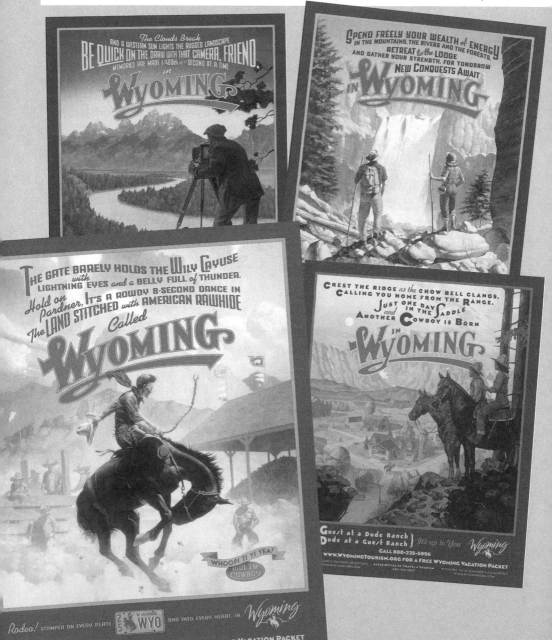

Type and imagery

Relating type to image *141* · **Type as image** *143* · **Texture and dimensionality** *145* · **Preparing display type** *147*

○ Design is interesting when developed in the areas between the three elements designers use: type, image, and space.

◁□ Each type treatment was developed from the words and the meaning of its illustration in this poster series by Michael Doret and Monte Mead. The photography poster headline suggests light through a lens, the hikers emphasizes panoramic breadth, the bronc rider has a few unexpected kicks in the curves, and the cowboys combines types like an Old West "wanted" poster.

❝❝ Design should be used to communicate ideas with wit, simplicity, and intelligence." *Marcello Minale*

○ A detail of a page from Francesco Petrarch's (1304–1374) sonnets, written in north Italy about 1370, uses an elaborately-drawn intial as a focal point.

❝❝ *In special cases the particular way type is used makes the difference in the communication. But unless typography is being used as central to the communication – as the pivotal illustration – what makes the communication work is always the content."* SAUL BASS

TYPE AND IMAGE. IMAGE AND TYPE. These are the two *visible* elements of design. Though inherently different, they are almost always seen together. They come with plenty of contrast. What takes thought, though, is how to make them harmonize by sharing attributes.

Scott McCloud, author of *Understanding Comics, The Invisible Art*, offers the following evolution of type and imagery. Egyptians placed their hieroglyphics near images, like extensive captions, so the words and pictures would work together for clear communication (*opposite, top*). Early European woodblock printing matched pictures with textual captions. As images increased in representational quality, type increased its power to express abstract thoughts using its abstract characters. Finally, with both representational and abstract issues achieved, there was nowhere left but for words and images to begin their inevitable journey back to a central, shared language. Imagery would become more abstract as type became more representational. This happened in the early 20th century, first by the Expressionists, then by the other avant garde movements. Art became abstract and expressed ideas. Writing became specific and vernacular.

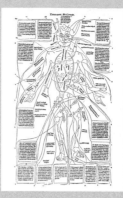
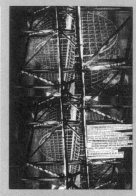

O Livro dos Espíritos
allan kardec

Cardinal Health

Der Vor Leser
Bernhard Schlink

de fraîcheur
les vallées

Dans toutes

GRAFIK
Ausstellung des Verbandes Schweizerischer Grafiker
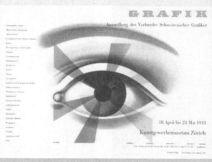
18. April bis 23. Mai 1943
Kunstgewerbemuseum Zürich

GIANT
GIANT

SIGHT UNSEEN
SIGHT UNSEEN by DONALD MARGULIES with BYRON JENNINGS LAURA LINNEY
ANA REEDER BEN SHENKMAN
PREVIEWS BEGIN MAY 6, 2004

A cheese lover is called a
TUROPHILE.
OENOPHILE
is what a wine lover is called. Usually they're both the same.

sirenella

cycle
Brillan

◁ **Position** The caption surrounds the image in a 1519 book; captions are directly linked to parts of a 1491 "exploded view" diagram; and individual lines of type in a caption are cut apart and positioned on top of the image.

◁ **Layering** Image dominates over type in crafting an American flag; odor wafting in the foreground on a book cover; and a logo's symbol. Type dominates over image on a re-purposed map and a book cover (with a backward title adding depth).

◁ **Space/alignment** An experimental study using a 5x5 unit grid imposes space on both the image and the type; and strict order using flush left and flush right alignment at the perimeter of the page contrasts with a slightly off-center radial image.

◁ **Shared characteristic** Type and image are both cut and refit in an ad for a Broadway show; O's are replaced by round objects; type encircles a cactus on a calendar; secondary type explodes from a drummer; and type matches a leaning bicycle's angle.

Relating type to image

The first step in developing a type and image relationship is recognizing that type and image are different and our job is to develop similarities to achieve design unity.

The second step is deciding whether the type or the image will be dominant. The image, as a default "non-decision," is usually dominant. Dominance ordinarily refers to quantity: an image is said to dominate when it is the largest element on a page. But dominance can also be applied when one element imposes itself on another element, which is to say, it *gives* the pain. A subordinate element is one that is imposed on by another: it *takes* the pain.

The third step is to recognize that the subordinate element must be made to agree with the dominant element. There are four basic relationships, with an infinite number of ways to execute them:

▶ **Relate by position** TYPE NEAR IMAGE Captions, whether as little clots of type beneath pictures or as headlines splashed across the page, are read before the text. They are therefore display type: that which is meant to entice and lure. Captions satisfy readers' curiosity and help them understand what they are seeing and how they are to interpret the picture. As tools for enticement, captions should be carefully worded and not very long.

▶ **Relate by layering** The ultimate *nearness* position is *on top of*, so this might be considered a subset of the preceding relationship. IMAGE OVER TYPE makes image look more real by making it look dimensional. If too much type is covered, it makes type hard to read. TYPE OVER IMAGE is much less persuasive. It negates the reality of the image and invariably makes the type hard – or impossible – to read.

▶ **Relate by space and alignment** POSITION, SIZE When type and image are both affected by space, they are unified. When the height or width of an image is equal to type, they are unified.

▶ **Relate by shared characteristic** TREATMENT, SHAPE, DIRECTION, ANGLE, COLOR, AND TEXTURE This is a huge category. One example may suffice: if the headline that goes with a picture of, say, a beach scene is given a sand treatment, the two elements will be unified.

ABC
ABC
ABC

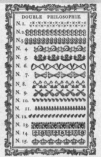

GUGGENHEIM

MUSEUM
OPEN FREE TUESDAY
EVENINGS

89th St & 5th Ave
5 to 8 pm
Made possible
by a grant from Mobil

Virclude®

DOUBLE PHILOSOPHIE

BROOM
BROOM

PAULA
SCHER

Wolfgang Amadeus
MDZ
Symphony
ART
NO.

BROOM
5 3

BROOM
5 3

wordplay

America's answer!

PRODUCTION

BIANO

MARRIAGE

QUINTET

MADISON
SQUARE

Experiment

1 2 3 4 5 6 7 8 9 10 11 12 13 14

Type as image

Sometimes the best way to tell a story is with type alone. The meaning and power of language is most persuasive. In these circumstances, simple letters simply arranged are enough.

Sometimes type is enhanced by *developing* it into the focal point. There are eight ways to do this and each one of them takes a toll on legibility. Consequently, practice these ideas on display type only. Text is too fine, and readers too harried, to tolerate much fooling around at small sizes.

▶ **Image in the shape of type** Non-letterforms are arranged into readable letters and words. The emphasis is on imagery. If letterforms are too subordinate, legibility suffers. Be sure that the illustrative subject is appropriate to your message.

▶ **Letterforms and images joined into characters** These are augmented letterforms. Type forms and images are about equal in emphasis.

▶ **Type overwhelmed by image so it nearly disappears** By definition, type plays a very subordinate role in this category.

▶ **Type chopped and arranged as image** The image is entirely made of parts of letterforms.

▶ **Picture fonts** These are collections of keystroke-accessible images. They can be used as bullets for emphasis or, when repeated, as borders and separators. The first picture font was a set of movable type *fleurons* ("flowers"), made by Giovanni and Alberto Alvise in 1478. Picture fonts are also called *symbol fonts, ornament fonts,* or *dingbats.*

▶ **Type so interestingly treated, it becomes an image** The ultimate expression of *readability*. As in all these categories, matching treatment with meaning is essential.

▶ **Type as part of the image** Type inserted into or substituted for a part of an image. This is particularly effective when meaning and execution are unified.

▶ **Type arranged to illustrate its meaning** Keen observation, free imagination, plus strong intention can turn many words insideout so they show what they mean. This is harder than it looks.

◁ Image in the shape of type; letterforms and images joined into characters; type overwhelmed by image.

❝ An idea makes the strange familiar or the familiar strange." *David Bernstein*

◁ Type chopped and arranged as image: the LWA of Leading Web Advertisers becomes a digital man; a *v* becomes activated as a virus; a building's form is shown; a face is "drawn"; early picture fonts.

◁ Type that becomes image through abstraction: five examples that trade readability for legibility.

❝ Unless typography is being used as the pivotal illustration, the content makes the communication work." *Saul Bass*

◁ Type as part of the image: letterforms permuted into illustrative elements.

❝ Typography of swirling patterns, shapes trapped in texture are sophisticated examples of expressionism." *Tom Carnase*

◁ Type arranged to illustrate its meaning: purposeful illustrations using only letterforms to both state and show their meaning.

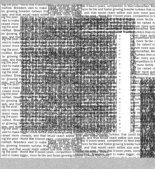

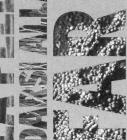

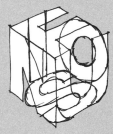

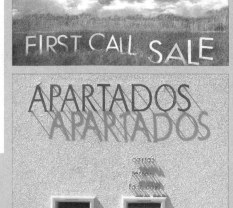

Texture and dimensionality

Text type is said to have "color" and texture,* which are closely related. These days, we speak more often of a type's "color" than its texture, perhaps because more realistic texture – the flat rendering of a dimensional surface – is easily achieved.

Texture can differentiate areas of text type, as shown by the student studies on the opposite page. Texture can also be used as a fill on display letterforms.

In this age of increased visual competition, display type must be provocative. One technique that makes type stand out (literally) is dimensionality. With the proliferation of three-dimensional (height+width+depth) rendering software, dimensional display type has become almost ordinary. As with all type treatments, the purposefulness of a particular technique defines its success or failure as mere noisiness. In other words, does the dimensionality express appropriate meaning, or is it only a trick?

Three-dimensional type can be digitally made, or it can be crafted and photographed.

When applied to type, texture and dimensionality are illustrative approaches, subsets of the previous spread's categories of *type overwhelmed by image until it nearly disappears* and *letterform and image joined into single entity*. These treatment can be used as bridges to connect headlines to images and thereby achieve design unity, the Holy Grail of visual communicators.

* About 800 years ago in what is now Germany, handwriting evolved from Carolingian – an open and light style – into a very dark and condensed style. This was in part to make most efficient use of precious vellum. It became known as *textura* because, writing being fairly uncommon, and with little with which to compare it, Europeans thought it looked something like the texture of rough fabric. This bit of history illustrates that type has inherent texture. We are so familiar with type today that its textural quality has become all but invisible. But it is still there for useful exploitation.

Textile
Rental

Large point size typesetting

Textile
Rental

Value-added display type crafting

Developing perfect display type (in this case a magazine flag) begins with a sketch. After setting the type in Illustrator or FreeHand (*opposite top*), convert to paths and finesse the *shapes* (*opposite bottom*). This type is ITC Berkeley Oldstyle, a digital interpretation of Frederic W. Goudy's 1938 face for the University of California Press. Note the spacing improvements made between every character pair, the joining of the *XT* and the *EN* into ligatures, and the shortening of ascenders to get tighter line spacing.

Preparing display type

Display is usually the big stuff, so every mistake or oversight that you might get away with in text is magnified. The most significant thing to do to finesse display type is not just typeset it as if it were merely big text. It isn't big text. Instead of typing in the copy, designating its point size, and allowing the defaults to make all the other decisions, prepare the type as an outline file in either Illustrator or FreeHand. An outline file can be scaled without losing resolution. A file made in Photoshop, by comparison, is a bitmap file that will degrade if enlarged.

An outline file will force you to attend to every letter-to-letter, word-to-word, and line-to-line relationship, ensuring that nothing is overlooked. Adjust letter shapes for the best optical alignment, kerning, minus linespacing, hung punctuation, and to avoid accidental alignments. Taking the extra time on display type preparation reveals design quality and care.

To achieve the next level of typographic excellence, the letterforms themselves should be changed at display sizes. From 1450 through the 1950s, metal type had to be cut in specific sizes. (This is, by the way, the source of the sizes listed on a computer's pull-down font menu.) The typefounder made subtle differences to type proportions and spacing for each size as he cut the fonts. Larger type sizes allowed greater detail while smaller sizes required larger counters and weightier thin strokes. Beginning in the 1950s, the phototype process set type of any size using a single negative, usually optimized for an average setting of 12 points. This forced a significant compromise at the largest and smallest sizes.

For the first 15 years of its existence, digital type has continued that palliative model. More types are now being made that have two or three family "lines" to be used at small, text, and display sizes. *ITC Bodoni*, for example, comes in three lines, each based on Bodoni's original types at these sizes and having optimized spacing attributes: *ITC Bodoni Six* for small settings, *ITC Bodoni Twelve* for text, and *ITC Bodoni Seventy-two* for display settings.

Section 4

The evolution of typography

> " *Type evolved as a way of putting the word into non-face to face communication. Electronic media have (made) the relation of type to sound more meaningful. There's a kinship between expressiveness in typography and sound through control of such elements as rhythm, volume, montage, pauses, pace, style, accent, clarity, and tone.*" TONY SCHWARTZ

A 22,000-year-old cave painting of a bison. Highly detailed images were representational. Some simple line drawings, more stylized than representational, date from this time and might be considered "pre-writing." Cave paintings were messages made for the community to see. Such works are today called *murals* or *graffiti*.

STYLIZED DRAWINGS OF THINGS BECAME SYMBOLS, or *pictographs* (*picto*=image, *graph*=drawing) around 3,000BC. Pictographs show things, so a pictograph of a cow, for example, could

A variety of proto-writing styles: African rock paintings, Northern European cave painting, and more symbolic renderings on stone and bone. All show drawing preceded writing. The oldest known proto-writing dates from C3000 BC, though notched baboon bones found in South Africa have been dated to 37,000BC.

C1800BC Mesopotamia (present-day Iraq) is home to Akkadians, Sumerians, and Assyrians in such legendary settlements as Babylon, Ur, and Nineveh. By inventing notations for his own use, a livestock trader records his inventory on this small clay pad.

C1200BC Sumerian cuneiform (from the Latin *cuneus*, meaning "a wedge," after the tool used to make the marks) used stylized pictograms, top. A wedge-cut reed in use, here indicating "tens." *Photo by Marvin A. Powell*

c3,000BC Egyptian hieroglyphics

c3,000BC Hittite hieroglyphics

c2,000BC Babylonian cuneiform

c1,600BC Linear script from Crete

c1,100BC Phoenician "soundscript"

c1,000BC Cuneiform script

c1,000BC Egyptian hieratic script

c1,000BC Late Phoenician script

Egyptian hieratic script (*left*) and hieroglyphics (*right*) on a papyrus scroll. Hieroglyphics were almost always placed near images as lengthy captions.

The edged pen, made from hollow cane, reed, or quill, was the primary writing instrument for centuries.

mean either an animal used for food or a unit of wealth, since cows were used for trading. Pictographs couldn't represent ideas very well, so ideographs, which show ideas and actions, evolved. Ideographs had to be learned because the marks were symbolic. Society grew into two distinct groups: those who could understand ideographs, and those who couldn't. Eventually, ideographs could no longer describe the increasingly complex societies in which they were used. There was a huge difference between spoken and written languages. Around 1800BC, the Phoenicians, a successful trading society on the eastern shores of the Mediterranean Sea, reasoned that if symbols represented specific sounds, they could be joined as sounds were. Their revolutionary system directly connected spoken sounds to writing. Instead of two distinct languages, only one needed to be learned. They spread their system as they traded with others. The Greeks adopted their system around 800BC and added vowels and named the letters. The Romans adopted the Greek system within two hundred years and added the *G* and *Z*.

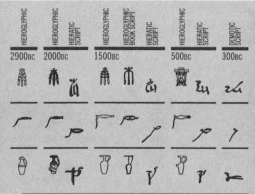

The development of Egyptian hieroglyphics ("*sacred writing*") begin as a symbol system that is unrelated to spoken language.

Hieroglyphic	Meaning	Linearized	Written	Modern
	Camel			גמל
	Righteous			צדיק
	King			מלך
	Not			לא
	Hear			שמע

Hieroglyphics and a quicker writing style, hieratic script, develop in parallel, culminating in a cursive abstract system.

The development of Hebrew hieroglyphics shows a transition from representational to abstract. *Chart by linguist Zev Bar-Lev*

YEAR		CHARACTERS IN ALPHABET
1600BC	Phoenicians (Syria and Lebanon) develop alphabet that represents specific sounds.	22
800BC	Greeks adopt Phoenician alphabet, taking 15 characters and adding 9 of their own. Greeks also add word spaces and punctuation.	24
700BC	Etruscans, then Romans, adopt Greek alphabet, taking 18 characters and adding 7 of their own.	25
400BC	Anglo-Saxons (northern Europeans) adopt Roman alphabet, adding two characters and later dropping one.	26

c2000BC Sheets of papyrus, a giant swamp grass, begin to be used as writing material. Layers of the inner fiber are cut into strips, dried, then interwoven and soaked and dried again. Papyrus can't be folded without cracking, so it has to be rolled. Papyrus rolls are called *volumes* (Latin *volvere, to roll*). Papyrus strips can be glued into wide sheets as in this detail of a Greek example that measures over 12 feet long. Because of grain, only one side can be written on.

c1600BC First alphabet developed in the Middle East. Though it contains no vowels, its characters represent spoken sounds relating written and spoken language. **c1500BC** Chinese develop ideographs. **c1400BC** Ten Commandments incised on stone tablets. **c950BC** The Phoenicians, building on alphabets by the Egyptians and Chaldeans, take a very significant step further, directly linking specific sounds to nonrepresentational symbols. Phoenician traders bring their alphabet to the Greeks, who then carry it to the Etruscans and Romans. **c850BC** Semites use first punctuation | vertical strokes separating phrases. **c600BC** Earliest dictionary written in central Mesopotamia, indicating need for various peoples to understand growing lexicon. ▷ Torah, first five books of the Bible, written by exiles in Babylon. ▷ As societies develop, the only writing is either God's or the King's words, giving *all* writing great significance.

IN THE 6TH CENTURY BC, THE GREEKS, WHO AT THE TIME HAD ONLY CAPITAL LETTERS, USED A METHOD OF WRITING IN WHICH ONE LINE LED IMMEDIATELY TO THE NEXT, WHICH THEN BECAME BACK-
-DAƎᴙ THƎИ TO THE NEXT, WHICH BECAME ИOIЗ, ᗡᴙAWᴙAᗡ-

474BC Etruscan inscription from Syracuse shows earliest roman interpretation of Greek letters.

MOFVISE·VIRO
LJOS BARBATI
IDILIS·HIC FVE
ALERIAQVE·VR

Remnants of Greek letters can be seen in this c200BC Roman tomb. These letters are incised in the stone grave marker of L. Cornelius Scipio.

Scrolls were first written across the width of the roll, which was held vertically. Later, the characters were written parallel to the roll, which was held horizontally, in groups that could be thought of as "pages."

9AD Tomb inscription of a Centurion shows developing roman monumental capital. A skilled craftsman could carve three characters per hour.

C50AD Roman Cursive from Pompeii shows flamboyant ascenders and descenders.

130AD Roman Monumental Capitals are inscribed on a gateway honoring Emperor Hadrian in Shropshire, England.

Early Christian capitals use ligatures and abbreviations to make the lettering hard to read on purpose: outsiders would be unable to decipher the message.

The evolution of Greek to Latin (Roman) letters.

ING, THEN FOREWARDS AND BACKWARDS ON DOWN THE COL-UMN. THIS WAS KNOWN AS BOUSTROPHEDON, OR, "AS THE OX PLOWS." IT HAS BEEN SUGGESTED THAT SUCH WRITING WOULD TODAY BE MORE EFFICIENT WITH THE ADDITION OF BRACKETS AS GUIDES. SHORTLY AFTER THE ADVENT OF BOUSTROPHEDON, *STOICHEDON*, A TERM THAT MEANS '*BY ORDERLY RANKS*,' BEGAN TO BE USED IN SOME PARTS OF GREECE. LETTERS WERE WRITTEN IN ONE DIRECTION AND THEY WERE EVENLY SPACED. SUCH PRECISION WAS SOON PROVED INEFFICIENT AND THE PRACTICE ENDED.

c300BC Alexandria, the world's cultural center, has two libraries with 500,000 scrolls, which are burned to the ground by Roman soldiers in 48AD. ▷ Chinese invent paintbrushes made of hair. **c250BC** An Egyptian papyrus embargo forces the need for an alternative in Greece and Rome. Parchment, made from sheep and goat skins, is invented in Bergama. Parchment can be written on both sides and folded, so *codices* and *books* replace rolls. Requiring the skins of 300 animals for a single Bible, and running out of livestock, scribes use the Chinese technique of breaking down cotton fiber in water and flattening the slurry

c700BC Early Greek looks much like the Phoenician alphabet.

560BC Demotic script.

c400BC Greek Lapidary ("carved") type is the Greek's interpretation of the Phoenician alphabet.

c300BC Formal Roman Lapidary type adapting Etruscan and Greek alphabets, written right to left.

c200BC Early Classical Roman Capitals.

72AD Roman Monumental Capitals from the *Arch of Titus*.

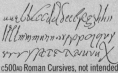

114AD Roman Monumental Capitals from the *Trajan Column*. This is the source of all serif fonts.

c150AD Handwritten *Quadrata*, or "Square Capitals." Vellum's smoother surface was preferred over papyrus at this time.

c300AD Rustic Capitals, a condensed square capital, saved valuable vellum and was quicker to write.

c350AD Uncials ("Inch High"), with curves and rudimentary ascenders and descenders.

c450AD Half Uncials, the precursors of today's lowercase letters, resulted from ever-quicker writing.

c500AD Roman Cursives, not intended for permanence, were a faster, more fluid writing style. This shows variations of each character.

A *codex*, the earliest book-form with folded pages, c250AD. Made from parchment, animal hides glued together into a long strip then folded, they opened to two facing pages. The modern equivalent is called a *French fold* (top left). A *folio* is a single sheet folded once (four faces); a *quarto* is a sheet folded twice (eight faces); an *octavo* is a sheet folded three times (sixteen faces); four quartos stitched together are a 16-page *signature*.

500AD Monks illuminate hand-copied manuscripts as the early Middle Ages begin, developing dozens of character variations to make each line equal in length. This "justification," or evenness of column edges, is thought to please God with its perfection. At about this time, St. Jerome invents a punctuation system, breaking text into logical segments, while he translates the Bible into Latin.

cob. ſeptuaginta quinque
gypto erat Quomodo et
nuſ omniq: cognatio eſua.
. et quaſi germinanteſ multi
proximi miſimpleuerunt terra
et renouuſ super aegyptum
b. et ita ad populum ſuum.

790AD Carolingian Minuscule ("Small Letter") develops at the dictate of King Charlemagne to unify holy texts. He appoints Englishman Alcuin of York to live in Tours, France, while overseeing the rewriting of all available manuscripts. The lettering Alcuin uses, efficient to write and beautiful to read, becomes the source of our minuscule letters.

into sheets. ▷ The surface of valuable parchment can be scraped and the hide used again. Such manuscripts come to be called *palimpsest*, or "scraped." Some famous works have been discovered beneath later writings, including Cicero's long-lost 51BC *On the State* under a 7th century copy of a Saint Augustine work. That a pagan work was erased to make room for a Christian one is typical of a palimpsest book. **59BC** Posted in public spaces, first daily news document founded in Rome. **c400AD** Wood blocks used to print textiles in Egypt. ▷ Black ink invented in China.

500–999AD

c476AD With the fall of the Roman Empire, the skill of writing is practiced almost exclusively in monasteries. With the exception of illuminated manuscripts, not much other writing is produced for nearly 1,000 years, when movable type is invented. ▷ Letters have always been made in the way that is easiest, given the materials in use. Angular letters resulted from chisels on stone. Curved letters developed after papyrus and vellum accommo-

IVLIVS CAESAR
114AD Trajan Column

IULIUS CAESAR
900AD *U* replaces *V* within words

JULIUS CAESAR
1400AD *J* replaces *I* at beginning of words

```
- = ≡ ✱  ౧ ౩  ౪
c250AD India Nana ghat

౭ ౩ ౮ ౪ ౬ ౦ ౦ ౦
814AD Arabs adopt Indian numerals

౧ ౨ ౩ ౪ ౫ ౬ ౧ ౯ ౦
c900AD India Devangari

౧౨౩౪౫౬౭౮౯౦
950AD Eastern Arabic

౧౨౩౪౫౬౧౮౯౦
976AD Spain Ghobar

1 2 3 4 5 6 7 8 9 0
1400 Italy

1 2 3 4 5 6 7 8 9 0
1545 Paris Claude Garamont

1234567890
1908 New York Morris Fuller Benton, News Gothic
```

c100AD Romans write on wax-covered wood with a metal stylus. Wax tablets are still in use in the Middle Ages. Speed causes letters to be joined and to become angled. The pages are tied together into a *codex*. Extremely difficult to read until two Oxford scientists in 2002 use computers and complex lighting to reveal what is hidden. Two samples of this temporary, quick writing are shown. The top example is from a heptaptych, or a codex of seven pages. The illustration beneath shows an octoptych, or an eight-page codex.

c230AD The Gospel According to St. John

Numerals develop quickly after the concept of zero is invented in India. Renamed, "Arabic" numerals are introduced in Spain in about 950AD and brought to France 40 years later.

868AD Wood, clay, and stone are early printing materials using a raised surface for relief rubbings and printing. *The Diamond Sutra*, the earliest dated printed book, is block-printed in China on seven sheets of paper glued into a single strip. It is an exceptional example and indicates years of block printing experience. The technique is brought to Europe by traders around 1420.

date pen and ink. **c500AD** Ornamental initials, from the Latin *initialis* meaning *beginning*, are used by monastic scribes in the 5th and 6th centuries to give their manuscripts an unusual treatment. These enlarged letters evolve into illustrations and, over centuries, become identified with book making of the highest quality. Gutenberg includes such decorative initials in his books, and they have been used by designers ever since. ▷ The dot over the letter 'i' introduced. It is used initially as an accent to indicate a double 'i'. **c700AD** The Chinese develop block printing. **c860AD** Cyrillic alphabet, based on Greek, developed by missionaries to Moravia, now part of the Czech Republic. **c875AD** The Middle Ages bring more rounded letters and a more condensed style, which formalizes in the next 300 years into *Textura*, the northern European lettering that Gutenberg copied for his type. **c950AD** At about the time of the turn of the first millenium, books and reading were held in such high esteem that, typically in monasteries throughout Europe, an annual book exchange took place. The head librarian would

c780AD Merovingian Script, from the Rhone River area of France.

c900AD Roman cursive script.

c700AD The Book of Kells (Latin Gospels), Ireland. It is the most highly regarded book of the Dark Ages (500–1450AD) because of its perfected minuscule letters. According to *Calligraphia Latina*, a 1756 book, "The man who could write, or the *scribe*, was held in high honor." Irish law "metes out the same price for the shed blood of a scribe as for a bishop or a king. It also inflicts the same punishment upon anyone bold enough to steal the property of a king or a bishop or a scribe."

975AD A psalter from southern England shows more rounded letters.

Carolingian Minuscules become more formalized between c750AD (*top*) and c850AD.

931AD Certificate in *Scriptura Longior* minuscules.

c975AD Runic characters are brought from south-east Europe around 250AD. Based on the Latin alphabet, it is simplified from 24 to 16 characters.

T TO TI STI ATI RTI TTR

ma mb mc md me mf mg mh mi mj mm mmo mp mr ms mt mx my mz

Late roman cursive shows many variations of a single letter, here the letter *t* from one manuscript. Given the coarse papyrus paper imported from Egypt, writing requires changes to make the pens work as smoothly as possible. Simply changing the way the pen is held increases writing speed and changes the way letters are shaped.

solemnly read the book title that each monk had borrowed the previous year, collect the book, and assign the next year's book, one per person. It is likely that the monastic residents read more than a single book per year, but this was their minimum, and those who didn't finish their one book "shall confess his fault prostrate and ask for pardon," according to Francis Wormald's *The Year 1200: A Background Survey.*

1000–1399

The letters we use today are derived from two distinct sources: capitals from Roman inscriptions and lowercase letters from Medieval handwriting. ▢ Roman letters are today used by about a third of the world's population. The other two thirds use a variety of languages. ▢ The 1,000 years prior to type's invention, about 500–1450AD, are the Dark Ages, so called because the increase in mankind's knowledge had slowed to nearly nothing. Books, copied one at a time by hand, couldn't keep up with increasing demand. With type's invention, knowledge became immediately accessible to many more people. Movable type is

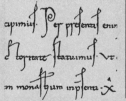

c1100 Late Carolingian Minuscules from northern Italy.

c1100 Typical "civil" minuscule script.

12th C. English pontifical shows condensed characters and heavy strokes, which lead to gothic letters.

c1350 A page from a Mongolian-Chinese dictionary. Mongolians need a new alphabet after converting to Buddhism.

Byzantine letters were considered literary art at the time of their writing. Shown here are samples from four dated c1000, c1325, c1350, and c1425.

Byzantium is the eastern part of the Roman Empire and is governed from Constantinople. It exists between 330AD and 1453AD.

c1300 Every monastery had a scriptorium. It was sometimes the only heated room. *Scriptores* wrote about four large pages per day using goose-quill pens. The monastery at Murano includes the exhortation,

"The pious man should copy books and render them more plentiful: he should improve upon their writing, he should ornament them and annotate them: for the spiritual life is nothing without books."

umæthrmeljorumæ
c350AD Late Roman cursive

atnon fytnoicu
c450AD Semiunical

greca confentiant uen
c900AD Carolingian script

go. Emulare g æ ponitent
c1050 Carolingian script

ad o conuflif. feralif arti aliq
c1200 Carolingian script

cor pcem profecto funtfe
c1250 Early Gothic script

Magnus dominus et
c1400 Angled Gothic script

niete familie me. Quefumus do
c1450 Textura type

quorum maieftate fug
c1480 Humanistic script

Sic splendente domo, claris na-
c1500 Humanistic type

---

c1200 Condensed letters with pronounced vertical strokes become exaggerated into Gothic blackletter in northern Europe.

one of the most important developments in human history. **1000** Beowulf manuscript written on vellum in Anglo-Saxon, a precursor to English language. **1041** Pi Sheng invents movable type made of baked clay and glue in China. The sculpted letters are glued onto a metal sheet, printed, and removed from the sheet for reuse. His characters are words rather than letters. **1200** *Textura*, or *Gothic*, script develops. So named because it looks like woven fabric. Legibility is not the chief concern of this heavy, condensed handwriting style: fitting many characters into a small space is. In fact, it fits about twice as many characters into the same space as its predecessor, *Carolingian*. **1221** Chinese develop movable type from carved wood. ▷ Goose quill first used for writing. **1253** Arabic numerals introduced in England.

1400–1499

Written materials until now are notably scarce. Reading by the ordinary person is limited to inscriptions on buildings. The invention of movable type printing changed everything. With

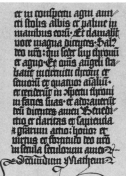

Books become among the most treasured and beautiful of artistic expressions. Illuminated letters are compact visual narratives.

IOANNES WICLEFVS Ang

1300 German manuscript writing with flourishes. This is called *textura* or *blackletter* because of its darkness and density. By the late 1400s, the letters are so condensed and dark they have become hard to read. Textura is the lettering style used in France and Germany when, in 1450, Gutenberg makes his first movable types there.

1328 *The Book of Hours of Jeanne d'Évreux*, a tiny personal prayer book created for the queen of France, is an intricately illuminated work of art.

1380 The first translation of the Bible into English by John Wyclif is not welcomed by clergy: "This Master John Wyclif translated from Latin into English… so the pearl of the Gospel is scattered abroad and trodden underfoot by swine."

c1390 The Incas' "writing" system consists of tying knots in string. *Khipu* are first thought to be only for accounting, but research indicates the possibility of a unique three-dimensional binary code, similar to modern computer language. Incas may have had over 1500 "characters," a few more than Sumerian cuneiform writing and twice as many as Egyptian hieroglyphics.

The initial of every sentence is illuminated in this small, beautifully lettered personal prayerbook from Bourgogne, c1450.

10th C.   15th C.

Playing cards were among the earliest block printing.

printing – primarily in the form of books from its inception in 1450 through the mid-1800s – is the greatest development in history: it makes knowledge available to everyone. It is a revolution that causes regional languages to be standardized, drawing the public away from Latin and the religious structure that has shaped society. By stimulating thinking, it leads directly to the Rennaissance. ▷ The demand for books increases: one Florentine bookseller employes up to 50 scribes at one time. *Writing* books is about to be supplanted by *printing* books. ▷ Block printed, or *xylographic*, books are the world's first mass-produced objects. Each page was carved as a complete entity. ▷ Playing cards were among the earliest instances of block printing in both the east (China) and the west (France, Germany, and Italy). ▷ Wood, widely available and easily worked, begins to be replaced by metal, which can be cast, engraved, and etched – and used for more impressions without degradation. **1440-1450** Gutenberg takes the existing printing press, a repurposed grape press for winemaking (and block printing), oil-based ink, and

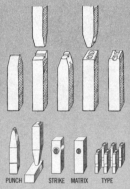

1423 Earliest dated wood block printing in Europe. The type and illustration of St. Christopher are on a single block.

c1440 Gutenberg begins experimenting with movable type in Strassburg, where he lives from 1434 to 1444. He produces the *Sibyllene Legend*, a short booklet, that prophecies a political event. Strassburg has a claim to the earliest movable type printing, but Mainz is where Gutenberg printed the first *book* with movable type.

1452 Gutenberg checks a page proof (*top*). A sample of Gutenberg's type and a spread from the 42-line Bible, the first book printed with movable type.

That Gutenberg is a goldsmith makes his invention of movable type a natural evolution: he is accustomed to working with molds and duplicating metal masters. Type founding is the process of striking a punch, a carved relief letter, into softer metal to make a female (called a *matrix*), into which molten metal is poured to make multiple copies of the original letterform.

PUNCH   STRIKE   MATRIX   TYPE

1452 Johannes Gutenberg (1394-1468) creates movable, reusable type and prints 160 copies of his "42-line Bible," a 1300-page work in two volumes. Marking the birth of typography, such an ambitious and beautiful piece couldn't have been his first attempt at printing. The round gothic above is Gutenberg's second type, cut in 1460 and called *Lettre de Somme*. It has many roman features and looks less like blackletter.

the eastern invention of movable type, and adds the crucial component: a way to manufacture many copies of letters quickly in metal molds. As a jeweler, he was an expert at casting. ▷ Laurens Coster of Holland begins cutting the letters from used blocks for reuse on subsequent pages. While some think he, rather than Gutenberg, may have invented movable type, Coster's own community doesn't seek credit for his work until the mid-1500s. Gutenberg, working at the same time, develops his movable letters from scratch. ▷ The greatest type designers are all masters of both printing technique and letterform artistry, and their letters show their understanding of technology. Punches, the original master letters, continue to be handmade until the 1890s, when an American company introduces a punch cutting machine. **1460** Albrecht Pfister of Bamberg produces the first book including both woodcut illustrations and type. **1464** Earliest printed books are reprints of existing works and are made to look as similar to the manuscript works as possible for market acceptance. Printers soon

1452 Gutenberg's first type is a copy of *Textura*, the heavy black manuscipt writing in Germany at the time. His typeface has over 300 letters, ligatures, and abbreviations, necessary for justification *(top)*. Gutenberg printed only the text. The initials were hand-lettered afterwards.

ACEGMORTY
Spabefgomty w
1234560
Trajanus Semi-Bold

ACEGMORTY
Spabefgomty w
1234560
Goudy Thirty

ACEGMORTY
Spabefgomty wuns
12345670
Poliphilus
(facsimile of Aldus' 1499 type)

1465 Sweynheym and Pannartz cut type in Subiaco, Italy. Their first, Cicero's *De Oratore (top)*, looks like a cross between blackletter and local humanistic lettering. Their second, *Speculum Humanae Vitae* in 1467, shows more Latin characteristics. This trend continues, rapidly diverging from northern European blackletter *(left)* to more readable Italian letterforms.

1470 A page from a blockbook showing the Gospels looks like a modern comic book. Rough paper kept woodcuts relatively rough as well. Block printing is used by many printers on title pages to show their artistry after Peter Schöffer invents the idea in 1463.

Sweynheym and Pannartz — Subiaco Italy 1465	Johann and Wendelin da Spira — Venice 1469	Aldus Roman cut by Griffi — Venice 1495	Aldus Italic cut by Griffi — Venice 1514
A A a	A A a	A A a	a
B B b	B B b	b	b
C C c	C C	C C c	c
D D d	d	D D d	d
E E e	e	E E e	e
f	ff	F F f	f
G G g	g	G G g	g
H H h	h	H H h	h
I I i	I I i	I I i	i
L L l	l	L L l	l
M M m	M M m	M M m	m
N N n	n	N N n	n
O o	o	O O o	o
P P p	P P p	P P p	p
Q Q q	q	q	q
R R r	r	R R r	r
S S fs		S S f s	ſs
T T t	t	T T t	t
V V u	V V u	V V u	u
x	x	x	x
		Y y	y
		z	

begin making changes in letters and style that make printing its own art. ▷ Arnold Pannartz and Conrad Sweynheym become "journeymen" and move to Subiaco, near Rome, with their press and blackletter types from Mainz. But Italians aren't accustomed to such letters and Pannartz and Sweynheym are forced to craft letters designed after the region's manuscript writing. In due course Blackletter is used for religious material while Littera Antiqua is used for secular content. ▷ Movable type printers institute type changes to reduce cost and increase efficiency. Initials become smaller, ornamentation and illustrations are added and printed in a single pressing with the type. **1470** Johannes de Spira (a transplanted German originally named Johann von Speyer) opens the first printery in Venice, one of the most active trading centers in Europe, and produces the first fully roman typeface, basing it on humanistic handwriting of the area. This marks the shift from Gothic to roman typefaces throughout Europe. ▷ Nicolas Jenson, a Frenchman, begins printing and making types based on manuscript writing in Ven-

iſſimi dei ſacerdos iu

rorū appellatus eſt: a

la mentio erat . Quar

ntiles: quoniam non

hræos proprie noiam

inſitiuos ſig

ſcripta ad c

rectam uita

tius generis

ſtitiā quā nc

oſes naſci t

1470 Nicolas Jenson (1420-1480) was a Frenchman who moved to Venice. This was his first type (shown actual size, about 16pt), and was made for his *Eusebius*. It is the first true Roman, rather than blackletter, type. Its proportions and elegance remain a standard by which all text types may be measured.

1476 Erhard Ratdolt's ornamented title page (*top*) is the first time author, title, printer, place, and date are listed. Two years later, Giovanni and Alberto Alvise produce some of the earliest fleurons.

1484 William Caxton (1421-1491), prints Chaucer's *Canterbury Tales* (*above*). The type is actual size from *Prologue to Eneydos*, 1490. England's first printer, Caxton learns the art in Belgium in 1472, where he prints the first book in English. Imports *blackletter* fonts to London, then develops his own faces which become known as *Old English*.

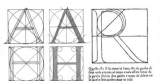

1480 The Renaissance brings about letterform perfection based on geometry and numerical proportion. The earliest studies are by Felice Felicianus, Andrea Mantegna, and Damianus Moyllus (l-r). In his complete alphabecedarium, Moyllus writes: "This R is made like the letter B… The shank below should be distant from the upright shank two and a half thicknesses at top and is seven thicknesses below as thou seest." More famous studies will be completed by Pacioli, Fanti, Vicentino, Dürer, and Tory.

ice. Rather than perfecting the beauty of individual characters, Jenson sets out to create an even typographic color in multiple lines of type. His interest is equally in the spaces within and surrounding letters as in the letter shapes themselves (*below left*). **1476** For the first 20 years of movable type printing (1450-1470), books have no title pages. They don't need them because there are still so few books. After twenty years, there are more than 100 printers in Europe, primarily in northern Italy and southern Germany (*see map, below*). Competition among printers becomes fierce. Partly to stay ahead of the crowd, in 1476 Venetian printer Erhard Ratdolt produces the first ornamented title page for Johannes Montenegro's *Calendarium*, a treatment that is immediately and widely copied. Ornamented title pages evolve into today's book covers. Just two years later, Giovanni and Alberto Alvise design movable type illustrations of flowers and leaves that can be repeated as borders. *Fleurons* or "flowers" are initially rejected by fellow printers, but shortly become popular because they are fun to make and allow

LONDON • ANTWERP
PARIS • FRANKFURT
STRASSBURG • MAINZ
VERONA • VENICE
SUBIACO

1499-1500 Aldus Manutius (1450-1515) is the first to recognize that the printed book's character is different than a manuscript book's. He and his typecutter, Francesco Griffo de Bologna (1450-1518), base their roman type on Jenson's (its modern interpretation is *Bembo*). A shrewd businessman, Manutius creates a graceful, slanted type (*left*) to fit more characters on

a page for his new 3½"x 6" "pocketbook" line, a portable series that emulates handwriting of the region. Their new type has over 60 ligatures because their source, a manuscript by Petrarch, was written that way. Making only lowercase letters, Manutius uses his type with roman capitals. This slanted style became known as *italic*.

ABCDEFGHIJKLMN
OPQRSTUVWXYZ
&abcdefghijklmnopqrs
tuvwxyzæœfffiflffiffl Æ
1234567890.,;!:'"()ŒŁ

Aldus Manutius designs *Bembo*, named for Cardinal Pietro Bembo, the author of *De Aetna*, the first book set in the face.

1493 Anton Koberger's sketch (*left*) and printed page of his *Nuremburg Chronicle*, shows the detail to which printers planned the complex craft of making a page.

Johann Trithemius of Sponheim (1462-1516)

Handsetting type from an early type case. After each page was printed, the letters would be distributed back into the case for reuse. A modern example, fully stocked.

self expression. **1485** As a consequence of William Caxton's efforts in England, Theodore Rood of Oxford writes (in Latin) in the first edition of *Letters of Phalaris*: "The art which the Venetians had to be taught by the Frenchman Jenson, Britain has learned by its native genius. Cease, ye Venetians, sending us any more printed books, for now we sell them to others." **1488** Moritz Brandis of Leipzig invents type families by creating the first semibold version of an existing text face. **1490** Ludolf Borchtorp, a mathematician and engraver, cuts the first Cyrillic types for the printer Szwajpolt Fiol in Kraków. **1500** The first 50 years of movable type printing (1450-1500) are called the *Incunabula* (*swaddling clothes*, or *infancy*). The books printed then were by about 1,000 scholars who became craftsmen so they could print and educate others, spread among 200 cities. On the cusp of the Renaissance, they sensed that their communities were ready for learning. In this 50-year period, 35,000 titles are printed, for a total of 10 to 12 million copies. The average "run" of a book's printing is 250 copies.

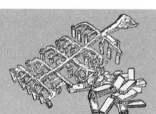

c1500 Typecast matrices from Prague show how letters are made in a mold, then separated and finished.

1526 Giovanni Baptista Verini draws a complex, interwoven composition using seven letters.

1507 Old technology vs new technology: this is the earliest known drawing of a printing press.

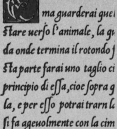

1523 Arrighi's capital alphabet (*top*) and italic lowercase are from *Il modo de temperare le penn*. The capitals are considered perfected Latin letterforms.

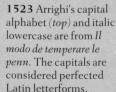

1525 Albrecht Dürer (1471-1528) spends a good deal of his creativity on letterforms and type. These sketches are among his studies of perfected letterforms. His calligraphic handwriting is shown above.

droitte, quõ dit corbee en rond
ngle. Qne ceft que Rond, Qne
, que Triangle. et cõfequamét
:he les figures plus generales
metrie. Car nofdittes lettres At
n font toutes faictes & figurees
ie le mõftreray aidãt noftre fei:
Et afin quon naye caufe digno:
n efcripray cy les diffinitiõs de
:cs laultre, & les figureray felõ

c1520 Geoffroy Tory (1480-1533), a French printer and calligrapher, helps move France from blackletter to Roman type *(top)*. His studies of letterform proportions based on the human body are inspired by da Vinci's sketches. Tory introduces printed decoration and ornament, and teaches Claude Garamont.

1500-1599

1500 Page numbers are used for the first time. ▷ Abbot Johann Trithemius of Sponheim, near Mainz, Germany (1462-1516) writes: "In the city of Mainz, located in Germany on the banks of the Rhine (and thus not in Italy as some have falsely written), was invented and devised by the Mainz citizen Johann Gutenberg that marvelous and previously unheard-of art of printing and the impression of books… O blessed art of printing, long to be remembered as belonging to our age!… Now that this marvelous art has been discovered, it is henceforth permitted to an unlettered person to become as learned as he will." Printed books were nevertheless thought of as second rate well into the 16th century. **1516** As the development of printing types begins to replace monastic scribes, Trithemius builds a library that, at his death, numbered 2,000 volumes, half handcopied and half printed. Trithemius writes that the handcopying of texts is better than printing, but, ironically, he uses a Mainz printer, Peter von Friedberg, to duplicate his *Praise of Scribes*. In it, he writes, "Nobody

iæ, Mediolani principem locu
Galuanius in id tempus quo M
AEnobarbo deletũ eft, vir fu
gloria, & quod in fatis fuit, ir
rabilis. Captus
iam ductus fuif
is catenas fregit

ABCDEFGHIJK
LMNOPQRSTUV
WXYZQUabcdefg
hijklmnopqrstuvw
xyzQu1234567890

1535 Claude Garamont (1500-1567), whose name was changed to *Garamond* on a 1592 Frankfort specimen sheet, opens a foundry and is first to sell his types to other printers, thus creating type founding as a separate activity. Brings Roman types to France, where they replace *Blackletter* in use. Creates first italic capitals. His types have been called "Universal Romans" because of their proportional perfection. Shown are samples of Garamont's printing *(top)* and *Garamond 156*, a 1922 Monotype interpretation under the direction of Stanley Morison.

*du créateur de la tj
Gutenberg (comm.
wriers imprimeurs)
l'Europe, nouveau:
ris notamment, qui
udit, & les preffes*

1540 Robert Estienne uses Claude Garamont's types at the *Imprimerie Nationale*. He refers to printers as "Children of Gutenberg."

Mayan syllabari, 16th century. Phonetic equivalencies of Mayan and Spanish. The sound of a Spanish *a* is translated as the Mayan *ak*, meaning *turtle*, and written as a turtle's head.

sed insbeciles funt et inermes) facil
ramus brevi Sophinn ad fidem pfu
et pro maiori parte chriftianis vtitu
wfumqʒ Senen: Patvie Futurâ ·
obnixe obftcro: ut mc Servitove
Eti dignetue: et opera mea ubi v
lo habbiamo reftituito, percio che
mo pellegrini foreftieri, fi come fon
noftri paffati; la uita noftra in que
uuole ascendere La scala, pima il
La terra: cofi nella diuina scuola n̄
principio al bene, se non col prim

Samples of 16th century italic handwriting *(top to bottom)*: 1516 Cardinal Caravaial to Henry VIII; 1517 Archbishop of Sienna to Henry VIII; 1530 formal italic book hand; 1570 italic chancery.

1611 The First Edition of the King James Bible. The completion of this translation represents the most significant step toward standardizing the English language. Two versions were printed, the "He Bible" and the "She Bible," due to a typographic error in Ruth 3:15.

should say or think: 'What is the sense of bothering with copying by hand when the art of printing has brought to light so many important books; a huge library can be acquired inexpensively.' I tell you, the man who says this only tries to conceal his own laziness." Trithemius offers four reasons that handcopying is better than printing: parchment lasts longer ("Parchment will last a thousand years, the most you can expect a book of paper to survive is two hundred years."); handcopied texts are more aesthetically pleasing; they are beautifully illuminated; and they are more accurate in their spelling and syntax. **1550** It takes about six months to produce a complete font. The punches take three months; striking, justifying (cleaning up) the matrices and making the molds takes about four weeks. **1569** Christophe Plantin of Antwerp begins his *Polyglot Bible*, showing simultaneous translations in Latin, Greek, Hebrew, Aramaic, and Syriac. He publishes it three years later. **1592** The first known typeface "showing," or sampler, is printed in Frankfurt.

de l'Eternel eſt le che
ſent ſapiéce &inſtru
nt graces enſilees ton ch
ol. Mon fils, ſi les pecheu

GARAMOND, JEAN JANNON 1621

)etical writing, P
with much comp
ns, the invention of a
, Plato did not look i

GARAMOND 156, MONOTYPE

1632 Richard Shorleyker, London, title page of printer's showings book.

1640 Shakespeare's poems were first printed 25 years after his death in this pocket-sized edition.

Initial caps in a variety of styles:

K	1464	France	
B	1485	Paris	
L	1499	Venice	
O	1521	Augsberg	
S	1554	Venice	
X	1580	Italy	
N	1611	London	
Q	1640	Paris	
E	1700	Nuremberg	
D	1750	Austria	
Y	1843	Paris	
U	1891	London	

1621 Jean Jannon's (1580-1658) *Antiqua*, after Claude Garamont (*top*). Jannon's types are mistakenly used in an early 1900s revival of *Garamond*.

CLAUDE GARAMOND PARIS 1530		PHILIP GRANDJEAN romain du roi PARIS 1693	
A a	*A a*	A a	*A a*
B b	*B b*	B b	*B b*
C c	*C c*	C c	*C c*
D d	*D d*	D d	*D d*
E e	*E e*	E e	*E e*
F f	*F f*	F f	*F f*
G g	*G g*	G g	*G g*
H h	*H h*	H h	*H h*
I i	*I i*	I i	*I i*
j	*j*	J j	*J j*
K k	*K k*	K k	*K k*
L l	*L l*	L l	*L l*
M m	*M m*	M m	*M m*
N n	*N n*	N n	*N n*
O o	*O o*	O o	*O o*
P p	*P p*	P p	*P p*
Q q	*Q q*	Q q	*Q q*
R r	*R r*	R r	*R r*
S f s	*S s*	S f s	*S s*
T t	*T t*	T t	*T t*
u	*u*	U u	*U u*
V v	*U v*	V v	*V v*
X x	*X x*	X x	*X x*
Y y	*Y y*	Y y	*Y y*
Z z	*Z z*	Z z	*Z z*

King's Roman is the first geometric type.

Russia and some of its neighbors use Cyrillic, an invented alphabet in the 9th century AD. Based on Greek, it has additional letters to accommodate the sounds of Slavic speech. ▷ Since 1450, when Gutenberg invented movable type, improvements in typecasting and type use are stylistic, but don't really make the system more efficient. Paper gets smoother, ink becomes more consistent, and type gets finer and more even in color. But type is still set one letter at a time. **1605** First public library is founded in Rome. ▷ First true newsapaper, *Niewe Tijdinghen*, founded in Holland. Contains political and social news, trials, births and deaths, sports, theater reviews, and international news delivered by Dutch seafarers. **1609** First weekly newspaper appears in Strasbourg, the *Avisa Relation Oder Zeitung*. **1620** Gutenberg's press has been in use for almost 200 years without much alteration. But its impressions are uneven, requiring letters that have little contrast, and they fade in spots. The Blaeu press gives even pressure and permits letterform

1640 First book printed in America by Stephen Day in Cambridge, Massachusetts and his press, the first in America.

1660 Venetian Francesco Cavalli's *Xerxes* is performed at Louis XIV's marriage in France. This is the first page of the opera's synopsis.

1663 The Bible is translated into Algonquin and printed in Boston by Samuel Green and Marmaduke Johnson.

1682 Peter de Walpergen *Fell Roman* and *Italic*, a Dutch Old Face bought for the Oxford University Press.

A labyrinth poem, a new year's gift to the king from J.C. Zetsching in 1666 *(top)*. Portuguese poet J.T.M. de Távora commemorated the 1738 wedding of the King's granddaughter with this labyrinth poem.

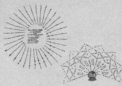

1684 Nicholas Kis (1650–1702), a Hungarian who moves to Holland, produces a Bible in Hungarian. His types are incorrectly attributed to Anton Janson when Kis's matrices are bought by D. Stempel AG in 1919

pend pas quelqu'un qu
de cent mille écus
s passerent dans le ca
tant après , Monsieu
n sortit persuadé qu

ABCDEFGHIJK
LMNOPQRSTU
VWXYZ&123456
7890abcdefghijkl
mnopqrstuvwxyz?

1742 Forbidden by law to copy the Romain du Roi of Grandjean, Pierre Simon Fournier (1712-1768) develops similar, though more condensed, high contrast types, which in turn lead to Bodoni's even crisper types. Fournier's types are used by W. A. Dwiggins to create Electra in 1949.

development. **1621** First English newspaper is a translation of the Dutch *News Currents*, which includes "Newes from Italy, Germany, Hungarie, Spaine and France." Newspapers appeared across Europe in this period: 1620 in Austria, 1634 in Denmark, 1636 in Italy, 1645 in Sweden, and 1661 in Poland. **1663** London has 60 printers. ▷ First true magazine, containing specific information tailored for a particular audience, is published in Germany. **1690** First American papermill founded in Philadelphia. ▷ Printing is firmly positioned as a business rather than as a personal cause. **1695** After three year's work on the order of Louis XIV for the Royal Printing House, the first typeface that transitions from old face to modern is readied. A conscious effort to build letters using geometry rather than humanistic structure and to relate roman and italic versions, Philippe Grandjean (1666-1714) used a 48x48 unit grid on his *Romain du Roi*. This is the first important change in printing types in 250 years and precedes Baskerville in England, Firmin Didot in France, and Giambattista Bodoni in Italy by decades.

ABCDEFGHIKLMNO
PQRSTUWXYZ
ABCDEFGHIKLMNOPQ
RSTUVWXYZ
AaBbCcDd EeFfGgHhIiKkLl
MmNnOoPpQqRrSsfTtVvUu
WwXxYyZz
AaBbCcDdEcFfGgHhIiKkLlMmNnOo
PpQqRrSsfTtVvUuWwXxYyZz

c1700 Anonymous specimen sheet from England shows fairly rough letters. There are four sizes of roman letters and one size of Old English.

SARAH SELLS,
Muffin-Maker, in Broad-Street;
TAKES this Method of informing her Friends, and the Publick in general, that the continues making MUFFINS and CRUMPETS hot twice every Day; humbly thanks her Friends for their former Favours, and intreats the Continuance of them, which she will make it her constant Endeavour to deserve, and which will be ever gratefully acknowledged.

1718 The first color printing in America, by Andrew Bradford, uses red and black inks.

Russian *poluustav* type of the 16th century is an imitation of medieval script (*top*). But it echoes the old ways and Czar Peter I wants a modern alphabet. After three years of development, he still finds characters he "doesn't like" and crosses them out. He approves this final version of *Civil Type* in 1710.

ABCDEFGHIJK
LMNOPQRSTU
VWXYZ12345
abcdefghijklmnop
qrstuvwxyz6789

1724 William Caslon's (1692-1766) *Old Face*, based on Dutch types of the time. Caslon's types advance text setting perfection by producing even type color. This is the first significant type to be made in England and become recognizeable as "English" types. It is still in wide use today, which attests to its beautiful proportions and balance.

PRIVILEGIUM
CÆSAREUM.

NOS FRANCISCUS DIVINA FAVENTE CLEMENTIA ELECTUS ROMANORUM IMPERATOR, SEMPER AUGUSTUS, AC GERMANIÆ, ET HIEROSOLYMARUM REX, DUX LOTHARINGIÆ, ET BARRI, MAGNUS HETRURIÆ DUX, PRINCEPS CAROLOPOLIS, MARCHIO NOMENEI, COMES FALCKENSTEINEI, &c. &c.

Agluglione, & votum facimus tenore præsentium universo : Quod, cum Nobis facтам insignis expositum Oratorir, cui Titulus : CALLIGRAPHIA LATINA, humillime exponendum curavit, illud elaborationis falius Publici onoere liberalior in se felicissife, quandoque jam plenoque artes tabulae unclaeis Sculptoris manu magisti sumptibus & labore aliphitaz prelo propediem commissarum esse : timeri autem, ne alis quaepiam cupiditate illi laboris sui literalatæ alents, id iis quæ suo ingenio ejus dehmentum fere integrum, fire fissifsa per quandam partes electri recudiqe concurar, itaque Nobis præfatæ Auctor demissifsime supplicavit, ut que indemnibati PRIVILEGIO

1756 Johann Georg Schwandner (1716-1791) publishes *Calligraphia Latina*, a lengthy and lavishly illustrated engraved book of calligraphic initials and decorations. The title page warns of copyright infringement at the cost of "six marks of pure gold."

ABCDEFGHIJK
LMNOPQRSTU
VWXYZ&123456
7890abcdefghijklm
nopqrstuvwxyz?!;:

"Having been an early ad-
mirer of the beauty of letters, I became insensibly
desirous of contributing
to the perfection of them."
*John Baskerville (1706–
1775)* Baskerville was a
perfectionist. Fellow printers found his types unat-
tractive, though their
opinions may have been
affected by his disdain for
religion, which was then
central to English life.
Didot and Bodoni found
great inspiration in Baskerville's work, which bridges
Caslon's *Old Style* types
and their own *Moderns*.

1700–1799

1702 The *Daily Courant*, England's first daily newspaper, is founded. **1714** Henry Mill receives an English patent on his typewriter. **1719** Wood first proposed as a paper source by a Frenchman, who recognizes the wasp's ability to chew wood and regurgitate it for their nests. Wood is used as paper in 1801 by Mathias Koops in England. Paper is at the time made of cotton and linen rags, but there isn't enough cloth to keep up with the ever-increasing needs of printers. The linen wraps from Egyptian mummies, each of which provided about 30 pounds of fabric, are used, and *rag pickers* are paid to find remnants in the garbage, sometimes drying them on clotheslines. Wood becomes economical in 1860, after a German invents a wood grinding machine, and a Canadian processes a sheet of paper made from ground wood. **1742** Pierre Simon Fournier produces his first specimen sheet in Paris. His shaded and ornamented letters bring fresh vitality to printing. **1796** Archibald Binney and James Ronaldson start the first permanent type foundry in the

Tandem a
A B C D 1
Tandem
A B C D E

ABCDEFGHIJKL
MNOPQRSTUVW
XYZ&123456789
0abcdefghijklmn
opqrstuvwxyz?!;:

ABCDEF
LMNOPQ
VWXYZ&
7890abcde
mnopqrstu

1757 John Baskerville (1706-1775), a wealthy amateur from Birming-ham, improves the printing press and ink-making and develops smooth paper. It complements his type (straight serifs, extreme contrast and vertical emphasis), which transitions from *Old Style* faces to the *Moderns* of Bodoni and others. Baskerville's types (*above, top*) are used privately until his death, then sold and used only occasionally. Monotype releases a version in 1923 and *Baskerville* is now one of the most used text faces in the world.

1760 Giambattista (*John the Baptist*) Bodoni (1740–1813) becomes head of the royal printing house in Parma. Designs the first of many versions of what became known as *Modern* faces, with hair-line serifs and heavy vertical strokes. Hermann Zapf says "If Bodoni had merely continued to copy Fournier – as he did dur-ing his first years – his books would not be out-standing achievements. It was not until he used printing types in the style of his time that his books became truly represen-tative of his age."

1776 William Caslon's types are adopted by many Colonial printers and are used for the original set-tings of the Declaration of Independence (1776) and the U.S. Constitu-tion (1787). Caslon's type is revived by the Ameri-can Type Founders in 1892 as *Old Style*, then renamed *Caslon 471*.

1783 Firmin Didot (1764–1836), a third-generation printer and type founder, begins cutting types based on his father's (François Ambroise Didot) roman alphabets. In 1812 he be-comes director of the Im-primerie Impériale.

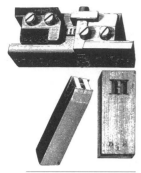

Making metal type: a master letter "punch" (*top left*) is crafted out of metal, then hardened. It is punched into a softer metal "matrix" to make a reverse female mold (*top right*), into which molten metal is poured to make multiple copies to be used as printing characters. The punch is held in a vise.

United States. Ronaldson writes to Thomas Jefferson on July 3, 1822, "...the genius of Arch Binney simplified the [typefounding] process, and by putting it within the reach of a greater range of talent, there are now in the U.S. six letter foundries." Binney invents a way to eject type from its mold, making it possible to produce 6,000 characters per day, up a full 50 percent. ▷ Making metal type: The punch-cutter would reproduce letters by making a master, called the punch, from steel. First, the spaces enclosed within the letter were formed with a "counter punch," then the outer parts of the letter were cut away. The letter was tested with ink on paper as it progressed to ensure an accurate rendition of the original drawn letterform. The finished letter punch was then tempered to harden it. It was then punched into a softer metal, which became the female mold. The mold was worked to accommodate the type's width, then placed in a holder into which molten metal was poured to create multiple male copies that would be used on the printing press. **1798** Aloys Senefelder invents lithographic printing.

1817 Vincent Figgins (1766-1844) develops the first *slab serif* types, calling them "Antiques."

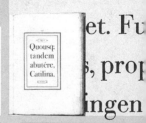

1808 Robert Thorne's *French Canon* (top), and **1822** Thorowgood's *Canon Modern* show the transition from bold face to fat face, introduced in 1810.

1816 Sans serif ("grotesque") letterforms existed for hundreds of years before William Caslon IV's *Egyptian*, which had only capitals. Designs followed by others through the 1830s.

1820 A rebus, the combination of pictures and text, is represented in this German work from 1820.

1818 Bodoni's *Manuale Tipografico* is published posthumously by his widow, Margherita, in an edition of 250 copies. It contains 142 roman alphabets with many more italic and decorative types and ornaments.

nostrà ? quamdiu etiar
furor iste tuus nos elu
det ? quem ad finem ses
effrenata jáctabit aude
cia? nihilne te nocturnui

1818 Giambattista Bodoni
creates succession of high
contrast types. Shown are
hardened punches Bodoni
cut. Bodoni's refinements
culminate in what many
believe are the most elegant
letterforms ever designed.
William Morris, for one,
disagreed: "The sweltering
hideousness of the Bodoni
letter: the most illegible
type that was ever cut."

1800–1899

During the 1800s, readership in the United States explodes from
5.2 million to 75 million. The public school system is introduced,
papermaking begins using wood pulp, and steam and electric-
ity replace foot-powered presses. ▷ Industrial Revolution
brings *hot type*, type made by forcing molten lead into casts of
each character. Mechanical typesetting technologies evolve
throughout the century as competing systems vie for dominance. This speeds the printing process and spurs expanded
typestyle offerings for use in the newly-formed advertising business. ▷ The Arab world uses three writing systems, each of
which can be written very quickly: Naskh, the universal language, and two styles used for headings and inscriptions: Sol-
loss and Kufic, used in many of the greatest mosques. **1816**
William Caslon IV (the great, great grandson of William Caslon)
uses first sans serif *type*, though the Greeks used sans serif *let-*
ters 1,400 years earlier. ▷ Graphic design evolves markedly
during the 19th century, as industrialization sweeps the western

ABCDEFG
HIJKLMN
OPQRSTU
VWXYZ;,.

c1825 *Schreeflooze Kapi-*
talen, Series 510 from Enschedé en Zonen, a Dutch
type house started in 1703.

1834 Johann Heinrig's
title page showing his
sans serif face.

ABCDEFGHIJKL
MNOPQRSTUVW
XYZ&abcdefghij
klmnopqrstuvwx
yz1234567890!?

1845 *Clarendon*, first
slab serif, introduced in
England as a display face.
It is distinguished by
greater stroke contrast
and bracketed serifs.

A B C D E F G
H I J K L M N
O P Q R S T
U V W X Y Z
1 2 3 4 5 6 7 8 9 0

1847 Sans serif from
Vincent Figgins, a style
that was widely copied
by other founders.

ABCDEFGHI
KLMN
STUVWXYZ

1827 Darius Wells in-
vents a way to mass pro-
duce wooden display
letters, making large-
scale printing common.
There are three basic
styles: Roman, Antique
(with heavy serifs), and
Gothic (sans serf).

1840 The "Pianotype"
composing machine,
made by James Hadden
Young and Adrien
Delcambre, had justifi-
cation and matrix distri-
bution capabilities.

Setting type by hand
requires placing indi-
vidual characters into a
composing stick. The
lever on the left is
moved to set the mea-
sure, or line length.

A B C D E F
G H I J K L
M N O P O R S
T U V X Y Z

1850s Machine-carved
wooden display faces
proliferate in quantity
and exuberance through
the second half of the
19th century. Wood
types used extensively in
posters, the "mass mar-
keting" of the time.

1865 The "writing ball" was invented by the director of a school for the deaf in Copenhagen (*top*). Remington begins developing typewriters in 1829, with the first model made of wood. In 1873 Remington begins to sell the first commercially-available typewriter. The Remington *Model 7*, shown above, is from the early 1900s.

world. **1839** Niepce and Daguerre invent photography in France. ▷ Large wooden letters used for printing and for sand casting to make metal copies, which lasted far longer. ▷ Progressively ugly type used because of Industrial Revolution, in which speed and cost were paramount concerns. ▷ The industrial revolution brings major speed improvements in typesetting for the first time since Gutenberg invented movable type. As speed increased, cost decreased and generated even more information to readers worldwide. Knowledge increased at a startling rate. But automated typesetting machines, which still made bits of metal with raised characters on them, could not kern, so what we would consider open letterspacing was normal. **c1860** Printing quality suffered in the throes of the Industrial Revolution. Henry Stevens, a Vermont-born rare-book seller in London and recognized proponent of fine printing, wrote, "The disagreeable fact that our books are deteriorating in quality is assumed for the present and taken for granted. The fault exists and is daily becoming more and more manifest…

1866 *Alden Typesetter and Distributor #2*, a steam-driven machine, uses a rotating wheel (*right rear*) to return characters to storage channels.

1851 This poster shows the cacophony of types that printers use in the mid- to late 1800s.

1867 *Fette Fraktur*, an updated blackletter, is released by Bauer in Frankfurt. Blackletter, which has come to represent Germany, is the typographic equivalent of Gothic architecture.

1885 *Lagerman Composer, Justifier and Distributor*, by Swedish inventor Alexander Lagerman, is a two-man machine: one to load font casettes and one to pull a three-ring letter selector.

Upper- and lowercase are blended together in this type designed by Andrew Tuer in the 1880s. Similar to earlier unicase faces, Tuer was experimenting with maximum x-height to save space for uses like "the crowded columns of a newspaper."

1892 American Type Founders forms when 23 small foundries merge. This brings the American type foundry business into alignment and profitability. In 1893, ATF releases *Jenson Oldstyle*, a revival of the 1460 face, shown here in two spreads from ATF's 1912 catalog. Fonts cost from $9.10 for 72 point to $2.00 for 6 point.

Our printing presses are teeming and steaming with books of all sorts (with some striking exceptions) not up to the mark of the high calling of book-making. It is no excuse to say that the rapidity of production has been largely increased. That amounts merely to confessing that we are now consuming two bad books in the place of one good one... It is not the amiable public that is so hungry for cheap printing and cheap books; but the greedy provider of cheap and cheaper books with which the public is crammed like Strasburg geese, that are in fault. This downward tendency is not so much the fault of the consumers as the manufacturers. The manufacture of a beautiful and durable book costs little if anything more, it is believed, than it does to manufacture a clumsy and unsightly one. Good taste, skill, and severe training are as requisite and necessary in the proper production of books as in any other of the fine arts." **1886** After several attempts, Ottmar Mergenthaler perfects his *Linotype* matrix and type casting machine. As the keyboard operator types, letter molds drop into position and entire lines are cast at once. Because

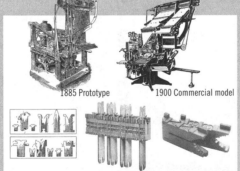

1885 Prototype   1900 Commercial model

1886 The Blower Linotype machine is the first line-casting machine in the world and replaces letter-by-letter typesetting. This prototype evolved into a refined machine within 12 months. By 1960, there are 100,000 Linotype machines around the world.

1886 Ottmar Mergenthaler perfects his *Linotype* matrix and type casting machine. A keyboard operator types, releasing female letter molds from a rack placed at the top of the machine. Gravity drops them into position and, with the push of a button, entire lines are cast at once. Spacing bands, which progressively thicken, adjust word spaces to justify lines (*bottom, left*). Each letter has a key-like matrix on the back (*bottom, center*), making the return of matrices easy, though very noisy.

1894 *La Revue Blanch*, magazine cover by Pierre Bonnard, Paris, uses wonderfully organic type with uneven baselines and extended ascenders.

HATE THE DRE[AD]
HOLLOW BEHI[ND]
LITTLE WOOD,
IN THE FIELD
ARE DABBLED
BLOOD-RED HE[...]
THE RED-RIBB'[...]
ES DRIP WITH A
HORROR OF BL[...]
ECHO THERE,
EVER IS ASK'D H[...]
SWERS DEATH

2.

FOR THERE IN THE G[...]
PIT LONG SINCE A BO[...]
FOUND, HIS WHO HAD
ME LIFE: O FATHER! O GO[...]
IT WELL? MANGLED AN[...]
TEN'D AND CRUSH'D AN[...]
ED INTO THE GROUND:

of the key-like matrix on each letter, returning the characters is now automated, too. Until the Linotype machine, all type has been handset one letter at a time, a method essentially unchanged since Gutenberg's invention in 1450. **1890** In a response to sweeping industrialization and mass market design, William Morris (1834-1896) commits himself to craftsmanship, beauty, and quality. In addition to furniture, fabric, and stained glass design, Morris' Kelmscott Press revives the art of fine printing. Morris designs three typefaces: *Golden Type* in 1890, *Troy Type* in 1892, and *Chaucer Type* in 1893. His politics are as illustrative of the man as his art: Morris declines an Oxford University professorship and naming as poet laureate. **1892** Faced with industry-wide

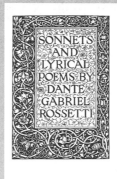

of the Frankeleyns Tale
HISE olde gentil
Britons in hir dayes
Of diverse aventures
maden layes,
Rymeyed in hir firste
Briton tonge;
Whiche layes with hir
instruments they
songe,
Or elles redden hem
[...];
[...]em have I in remembraunce,
[...]seyn with good wyl as I kan.

1890 William Morris (1834-1896) *Golden Type* (*top, actual size*) and *Chaucer* (1893, *above* and *left*): "This type (of Nicolas Jenson) I studied with much care, getting it photographed to a big scale, and drawing it over many times before I began designing my own letter."

1894 William Morris overwhelms type with gorgeous floral patterning (*above left*). Morris spends about 20 years designing jewelry, wallpaper, and stained glass windows before turning to type design in 1890. This helps explain his attraction to decorative design. Erhard Ratdolt

worked similar territory in 1477 (*above right*) with a wood-block-framed page. Ratdolt was a punchcutter who moved from Augsberg (in southern Germany) to Venice. He produced in 1486 the first type specimen "showing," a complete one-sheet sample of the types and sizes he had made.

frustration at the lack of manufacturing standards, American type manufacturers agree to adopt a single point system for type measurement. Then more than half merge into a new entity, The American Type Founders, which dominates the type design and manufacturing field for decades to follow. ATF consolidates its many existing types, discarding near duplicates, and has an intial offering of about 750 faces (*left*). ATF expands many existing typefaces into families and begins designing all its new typefaces in families. By 1923, its catalog displays over 8,000 faces. It isn't difficult to imagine the enormity of the task of composing those pages, one line, or one letter, at a time. ATF begins to decline in importance – succumbing to competition though proving the viability of type founding as a profit-making business – in 1935. **1893** Joseph Phinney of The Dickenson Type Foundry in Boston, one of the brand-new members of ATF, begins development of a type family based on Nicolas Jenson's 15th century types. This revival results in Jenson Oldstyle. ▷ Halftone printing begins to replace line art illustrations.

1890s Unknown artist *Tobaccos of Popov's Tobacco Factory and Trading House, Moscow.*

ABCDEFGHIJKL
MNOPQRSTUV:
WXYZ&123456?
7890abcdefghijk;
lmnopqrstuvwxyz!

1896 German type foundry Berthold releases *Akzidenz Grotesk. Akzidenz* is the source in a revival as *Helvetica* in 1957.

**ENRQ
abegn**

1898 Eleisha Pechey *Grotesque 8* for Stephenson Blake Foundry. "Grot 8" is available in only one weight and has various quirks in its design.

1896 Henri de Toulouse-Lautrec uses unsophisticated letterforms to emphasize the sheer joy of living, as in this cover for *Les Affiches Illustres*, a book about the art of the poster.

ABCDEFGHIJKL
MNOPQRSTUV
WXYZ&abcdefg
hijklmnopqrstuvw
xyz1234567890!?

1896 Bertram G. Goodhue *Cheltenham* for the Cheltenham Press in New York City. The face, redrawn by Matthew Carter in 2003, is adopted by the *New York Times* as their display face.

1897 *The Inland Printer* magazine cover, by Joseph Christian Leyendecker, USA. IP is the first magazine to use a changing cover design. It responds to its critics by stating, "That covers of periodicals should be of permanent design is the opinion of the many… (But) this is certainly not true of a magazine designed to exploit the inventions and arts of printing."

1900-1913

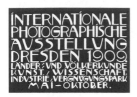

Letterforms went through dynamic reinvention in the early 20th century. These are samples from posters made in Europe between 1902 and 1926.

Type, design, and society had stagnated at the end of the 19th century, with relatively few typefaces available. Bookmakers and artists who care have to make their own types for their private presses. They use 15th century types and contemporary calligraphy as models. The Germans and French lead the way with the most idiosyncratic type designs, often as direct statements against the machine age that is quickly forming around them. ▷ Type is still in the domain of the printer. Indeed, the typesetter and the typographer are the same craftsman. Designing as a separate practice has not yet broken away from the printery. **1902** There are about 6,000 Linotype machines in use since their introduction in 1886. ▷ Otto Eckmann and Peter Behrens design faces for the Klingspor foundry in Germany. Behrens is an early practitioner of what comes to be known as corporate identity, developing a logo and its application for AllgemeineElektrizitäts Gesellschaft, or AEG. ▷ In anticipation of the First World War – and in response to it – some artists in

ABCDEFGHIJK
LMNOPQRSTUV
WXYZ&12345678
90abcdefghijklmn
opqrstuvwxyz?!;:

1900 Morris Fuller Benton *Century Expanded*, based on Linn Boyd Benton's and Theodore Lowe DeVinne's *Century* for *Century Magazine* in 1894.

ABCDEFGHIJK
LMNOPQRSTU
VWXYZ&abcd
efghijklmnopqr
stuvwxyz1234
567890$.,-';:!?

1903 Morris Fuller Benton *Franklin Gothic*, initially offered in a single weight. Named for Benjamin Franklin, this is America's first sans serif.

The **INTERNATIONAL STVDIO** An Illustrated Monthly Magazine of FINE & APPLIED ART *Edited by* CHARLES HOLME *Published by* JOHN LANE The Bodley Head at 140 Fifth Ave New York Price 35 cents Yearly Subscription $3.50 post paid

ABCDEFGHIJKL
MNOPQRSTUVW
XYZ&12345678
90abcdefghijklm
nopqrstuvwxyz?!;:

1907 Morris Fuller Benton *Clearface*, here shown in ITC's revival version of 1979. Benton headed the ATF type development team for 35 years and oversaw the design of dozens of typefaces, many of which have become standards. Under his guidance, ATF developed the largest type catalogue in the world.

ABCDEFGHI
JKLMNOPQR
STUVWXYZ&
1234567890?

1902 Frederic Goudy (1865-1947) *Copperplate*. Goudy began designing types only after he turned 30, and produced about a dozen American classics including *Californian* and *Deepdene*.

1907 George C. Blickensdorfer's American-made *Model 8* typewriter.

1905 Will Bradley (1868-1962), having sold his printing set in Chicago to Frederic W. Goudy, moves near Boston and opens Wayside Press. His posters change America's design sensibility and he is hailed as "one of those who have helped develop culture in this country."

1902 Felix Vallotton's periodical covers relate image and type and help define the Viennese Art Nouveau movement.

Europe conclude that the times need a new way of communicating. Eleven movements overlap and succeed each other in the first half of the 20th century. Steven Heller writes, "There is *always* an artistic avant garde. Once accepted, that avant garde becomes fashionable and, after its turn on the fashion wheel, becomes mainstream." ▷ The early 20th century is a time of a succession of avant garde art movements, almost entirely in Europe. Artists and designers intently follow each others' work and either add to it or refute it in their own works. Each movement is a response to what has come before, and each is intent on overthrowing the prevailing attitudes and values of the Victorian and Arts & Crafts movements that survived until the turn of the century. Between 1905 and 1935, Expressionism is followed by Cubism, Futurism, Dadism, de Stijl, Constructivism, the Bauhaus — which introduces the clean, uncluttered typography that is still a standard — Art Deco, Surrealism, and Modernism.

ABCDEFGHIJKLM
NOPQRSTUVWXY
Z&abcdefghijklmn
opqrstuvwxyz1234
567890$.,"-;,!?""

1908 Morris Fuller Benton *News Gothic*, the first type designed as a family and redrawn for optical equivalency at each size.

ABCDEFGHIJ
KLMNOPQR
STUVWXYZ
abcdefghijklmn

1911 Frederic Goudy *Kennerly*. Commissioned and first used in a book published by Mitchell Kennerly, a British publisher.

1913 Alphonse Mucha's lettering is indicative of the Art Nouveau movement. This poster is for a daughter of the family with whom he stayed in Chicago in 1906.

ABCDEFGHIJKLM
NOPQRSTUVWXY
Zabcdefghijklmnopqr
stuvwxyzæœffffifflffifffl&
1234567890.,;:!?ÆŒ£

1913 Monotype's *Plantin*, a revival of a 1500s Dutch type.

ABCDEFGHIJKL
MNOPQRRSTT
UVWXYZabcdef
ghijklmnopqrstuvw
xyz&Qu&abcdefghij

1913 Morris Fuller Benton *Cloister Old Style*. An early interpretation of Nicolas Jenson's 1469 roman. Comparable to *Centaur*, Adobe *Jenson*, *Legacy*, and *Venezia*.

1913 Ludwig Hohlwein's *Das Plakat* magazine cover, Germany, shows a new spatial structure and type and image contrast.

❝ *In the sense in which architecture is an art, typography is an art… Every work of architecture, every work of typography, depends for its success on the clear conveyance of intentions from one human mind to others.*❞

BEATRICE WARDE

THE CONSTRUCTIVISTS HAD THE MOST INTEREST in typography of the avant garde artists in the early twentieth century. This may be a reflection of their belief that their works are art objects. ▷ Bruce Rogers (1870–1957), one of the most influential typographers in American history, is an artist who designs types for new manufacturing techniques without compromising the highest standards of form and color. Rogers designs *Centaur* and *Metropolitan*, among several others. Raised in

c1915 The Merganthaler Linotype machine (*top*) is adopted across the Unites States and the world, replacing handset type (*above*).

ABCDEFGHI
JKLMNOPQ
RSTUVWXY
Zabcdefghijklm
nopqrstuvwxyz

1914 Bruce Rogers *Centaur*, for a book called *The Centaur*.

ABCDEFGHIJKLM
NOPQRSTUVWXYZ
&abcdefghijklmnopq
rstuvwxyzfifflffifflffifl123
4567890$.,"-:;!?"'"

1915 Morris Fuller Benton *Century Schoolbook*, based on 1890s *Century* by Linn Boyd Benton. This design is the result of early legibility studies.

erano gente ff ffl
.Tuctiquefti fl ffi
lalunga moffeno efi
giote sforzo italman
hati &fossi inpiu l
ssi ne uscire ne etrare

Nicolas Jenson's 1470 *Eusebius* (*top*) inspired Bruce Rogers *Centaur* in 1915 (*center*) and Emery Walker's *Doves* (for his Doves Press) in 1900.

ABCDEFGHIJKLMN
OPQRSTUVWXYZ
abcdefghijklmnopqrst
uvwxyzæœfifflffffifflffl&
1234567890.,:;!?'ÆŒ£

1916 Frederic Goudy *Goudy Old Style*. Drawn after the Venetian Old Style model, *G.O.S.* has a slightly enlarged x-height.

Handlettered effects are seldom attempted in type but the designer of this face was very successful
Colwell Handletter Italie

1916 ATF releases the first type designed by an American woman, Elizabeth Colwell.

Il Pleut (It's Raining), Guillaume Apollinaire's 1918 visual poem, translated from the French, shows type and meaning joined by form. Concrete poetry can be "understood" merely by looking at the image it creates. *Link*, an English arts magazine, said in 1964: "Do not try to read (concrete poetry) at all, just look at it …as an image."

Wood types were used by artists in several movements: Cubism, Dadaism, Futurism, and Constructivism. Victorian letters, which took great advantage of the figure/ground relationship, were especially valued. Shown here are two works by Filippo Tommaso Marinetti from 1915 and 1919. (This is a love poem: *chair* means *flesh* in French.)

Indiana, he moves to Indianapolis, then Boston for his primary client, a quarterly arts magazine. He becomes a trade book designer, then the director of fine editions at Houghton Mifflin. He designs his own versions of *Jenson* and *Caslon* for use in specific books. A few years later he reworks Jenson's *Eusebius* and creates *Centaur* for the Metropolitan Museum Press (although its first use is on Guérin's *The Centaur*) followed by the *Oxford Lectern Bible*, *Fra Luca de Pacioli*, and a new translation of *The Odyssey*. Rogers has been called a master at achieving Beatrice Warde's acclaimed typographic crystal goblet: "the vessel which contains without distortion the thought of the author." In fact, Rogers is a refined reader and thinker and comes to advise – and even edit – his authors, among them Winston Churchill, Ezra Pound, and Willa Cather. ▷ Walter Gropius, German architect and teacher, helps found the Bauhaus in Weimar after the First World War. Gropius sees a more integrated relationship between the artist and industry. He seeks to reduce the compromises that machines imposed while bringing

ABCDEFGH
IJKLMNOPQ
RSTUVWXY
Zabcdefghijklm
nopqrstuvwxyz
1234567890ß&æ

1919 Anton Janson (1620-1687) *Janson Antiqua*, made from the original matrices by D. Stempel AG in Frankfurt.

1920 Lazar M. Lisitskii (1890–1941) *Red's Wedge is the White's Death*. This is a powerful revolutionary statement in a constructivist poster.

c1920 Dadaism born in Switzerland. *"Dada,"* a term which has no meaning, identifies an anti-art avant garde movement, identifiable by its anarchic type. This example, *The Bearded Heart*, is a 1922 composition by Francis Picabia and emphasizes absurdity by using the printer's on-hand stock art.

1921 Ladislaw Medges' *Broom* magazine cover, USA *(also see page 142)*. *Broom* is a poetry and literary magazine that offers opportunities to many artists who will later become famous.

ABCDEFGHIJ
MNOPQRSTUV
XYZ&1234567
90abcdefghijk
nopqrstuvwx

1921 Oswald B. Cooper *Cooper Black*. Designing types was a sideline for Cooper, who thought of himself as a lettering artist. His lettering jobs were typically expanded into complete typefaces. "No one has done more than Cooper to combat ugliness in American advertising... He understands the anatomy of letters, their 'bones' as he calls them. He has an unerring sense of the fitness of things." *Thomas J. Erwin, Art Director, J. Walter Thompson Co.,* c1923

Dutch Moderne logos
from the 1920s and 1930s.

the artist into the business mode and to "humanize the rigid, almost exclusively material mind of the businessman." This is a conscious effort to attack the artistically vapid terrain of the industrial revolution, in which speed and cost are the primary concerns. The Bauhaus strives to invent new standards for an age that is examining time and space by reexamining the purpose of design in society. ▷ Stanley Morison and Eric Gill are central to the development of typography between the two World Wars, 1917–1940. Morison oversees typeface design for the Monotype Corporation. Gill designs a sans serif that remains one of the most popular faces in use today: *Gill Sans*. ▷ Linotype and Monotype machines compete for business by offering differing technologies. Both machines have limitations: maximum type size is 48 and 60 points respectively; the maximum line length is 36 and 60 picas respectively, and the Linotype requires that bold and italic characters be the same width as roman, forcing some undesirable compromises in counterform shapes and spacing attributes.

c1921 Dadaism spreads to Germany then Holland, where Theo van Doesburg evolves it into de Stijl (*The Style*).

1925 Eric Gill's carved alphabets, an unequaled modern standard.

1925 Jan Tschichold's *Typographischen Mitteilungen*, in black and red, shows the new dynamic, asymmetrical typography.

1925 Alexander M. Rodchenko (1891–1956) *Lengiz Publisher: Books on All Sorts of Knowledge*.

1925 Herbert Bayer (1900–1985) *Bayer*, a unicameral type (only one case).

c1926 Kurt Schwitters' Pelikan symbol and Piet Zwart's (meaning "Black") personal mark use combinations of letters and metal printing shapes.

1925 Paul Renner (1878–1956) *Futura* with a page from the original 1928 Bauer Type Foundry catalog and a showing of Renner's original letters with the replacements suggested and adopted by the foundry. Futura popularizes sans serif types. It's geometric simplicity and lack of obvious weight change makes it an especially clean-looking type.

1928 Fantastic letterforms are the style in Europe.

1920-1929

The early 1900s are a time of freeing typography from the strictures of the previous century. The Arts and Crafts movement of the late 1800s is an example of the classic refinement that has been achieved. ▷ The world is now changing rapidly at the close of WWI. Cubism, de Stijl, Suprematicism, and Dadism are flourishing. The Russian Revolution in 1917 propels Russian artists to new ways of seeing. The revolution ruins nearly every physical tool they have to work with, so imaginative use of what is left lying around is essential. Printing sizes, for example, depended entirely on what paper is already at a print shop. ▷ Lazar (El) Lissitzky meets and becomes enormously impressed with Malevich, who is pressing Cubism and Futurism to their ultimate ends: abstract art. Lissitzky emphasizes space, simplicity, the tension between objects and typography, and photomontage. He develops a list of requirements of good typography: 1) Printed words are seen and not heard; 2) Concepts are communicated through words and letters; 3) Concepts should be

ABCDEFGHIJKLM
NOPQRSTUVWXY
Z&abcdefghijklmn
opqrstuvwxyzfiffffl
1234567890$.,'-:;!?"'

1926 Heinrich Jost (1889-1948) *Bauer Bodoni*. This may be the best of many Bodoni interpretations.

1926 The Bauhaus ethic is shown in this magazine cover by Herbert Bayer.

ABCDEFGHIJK!?
I.MNOPQRSTU
VWXYZ&abcde;¡
fghijklmnopqrstuv
wxyzff1234567890

1926 Emil Rudolph Weiss (1875-1942) *Weiss*. Notable for its top heavy vertical strokes and the quirky cap *B*, *M*, *S*, and *U*.

1927 Moholy-Nagy develops "typophoto," combining type and image into "the new visual literature," as in his 1929 collaged cover for a brochure for *14 Bauhaus Books*. Moholy-Nagy helps found the Bauhaus school in 1923, eventually leaving for the United States, where he founds the New Bauhaus in Chicago (now named the *Institute of Design*).

1926 Rudolph Koch *Wilhelm Klingspor*, named after the German Klingspor type foundry. Koch also designed *Kabel* and *Neuland*, among other faces.

1926 A chart shows the relationship of metal type to printed letter and the names of common type sizes.

c1927 Several initials show great fluidity and imagination when compared to earlier examples (*see pages 164 and 169*).

1928 Stenbergs' *Berlin, Symphony of a Great City*, a photomontage that depicts man and machine working as one (*top*) compares with one of Piet Zwart's *de Stijl* experiments from the same year.

expressed with the greatest optical (not phonetic) economy; 4) The layout must reflect the content's rhythm; 5) Sequence of pages are like a cinematographical book; 6) The page and the endless number of books must be overcome. **1923** The Bauhaus School, led by transplanted Hungarian László Moholy-Nagy (pronounced *Mahóy-Náj*), Theo van Doesberg, Walter Gropius, and Herbert Bayer, expand on Lissitzky's ideas and address the problem of mechanization head on. From 1919 to 1933, when it is closed by the Nazis, the Bauhaus makes an indispensable contribution to the arts. The Bauhaus marks the birth of graphic design as a separate academic discipline and profession. At its closing, most of its artists move to the United States and, in 1937, Moholy-Nagy establishes the new Bauhaus in Chicago. Other U.S. schools begin offering graphic design in the late 1940s. The American Bauhaus evolves into the International Style, which has prevailed since 1950. ▷ Magazine design is a significant part of the design revolution, particularly the covers, where it is believed readers are most pliable. Art

1928 Eric Gill (1882–1940) *Gill Sans*, loosely based on his teacher Edward Johnston's London Underground signage (*rear*). Gill, a prolific sculptor, painter, calligrapher, and stone-cutter, was commissioned by the Monotype Corporation to create a sans serif to compete with Futura. He made a humanistic sans that remains one of the most legible sans serif faces, as shown by the preliminary sketch of *R* and *S*, to ensure proportional consistency. Gill's theories about letterform shapes and design grew directly from his experience as a stone-carver: extreme limitations must be accepted when chiseling from inflexible stone. There are 36 members of the Gill Sans family.

1929 Stanley Morison *Bembo*, a revival of the 1495 original by Griffo. It is named after the author of the manuscript Griffo used, Pietro Bembo.

1929 Jan Tschichold *Tschichold*, a unicameral type. This is an exceptionally geometric sans serif. Note the alternate *ε* characters.

1930 Eric Gill *Perpetua*. Sketches for Perpetua are begun before Gill Sans, but the sans serif face progresses more quickly and is finished first. Beatrice Warde wrote in 1930, "*Perpetua* is a letter designed by a stone-carver... (It) results not from a designer's whim of the moment, but from the experience gained in a hundred arguments with stubborn stone and metal."

Calligraphic experience, shared by all type designers in the early 20th century, is shown in sketches by Rudolph Koch.

66 There is no essential difference between the artist and the craftsman. Proficiency in craft is essential to every artist." *Bauhaus statement*

Nouveau with its organic curves evolves into a more geometric style which becomes known as Art Deco, named after the International Exhibition of Decorative Arts in 1925. ▷ The poster is a commonplace event in Russia. Posters are used to make political, social, and marketing announcements and color every town, factory, and school. They promote Russia's achievements, wealth, amd dreams until the late 1980s, when posters are replaced by television as the primary means of mass communicating in Russian society. **1929** Herbert Matter works with A.M. Cassandre and Le Corbousier in Paris. He moves to Zurich to work with Anton Stankowski and Walter Herdeg before moving to the United States and reinventing *Vogue* and *Harper's Bazaar* magazines. ▷ Perhaps as a result of the Industrial Revolution, Eric Gill is a critic of commerce and of machines and, most interestingly, of typography. He is quite a curmudgeon: "The only way to reform modern lettering is to abolish it." "There are as many different varieties of letters as there are fools." Master printers are "a bunch of morons."

ABCDEFGHI JKLMNOPQR STUVWXYZ& abcdefghijklm nopqrstyuvwx zæ1234567890

ABCDEFGI
Memphis Medium (Linotype)

ABCDEFGI
Cairo (Intertype)

ABCDEFGI
Karnak (Ludlow)

ABCDEFGH
Beton Light (Bauer)

ABCDEFGI
Rockwell Medium (Monotype)

ADBCEFGF
Scarab (Stephenson Blake)

1930 Rudolf Wolf (1895-1942) *Memphis* (top), essentially a slab serifed Futura, inspires many similar interpretations of sans serif types in the 1930s.

ABCDEFGHIJKLM NOPQRSTUVWX YZ&abcdefghijklm nopqrstuvwxyz12 34567890$.,!?()[]%

1930 R. Hunter Middleton (1898-1985) *Tempo*. Middleton is the Type Director of the Ludlow foundry for 50 years.

Metro
Electra
Caledonia

1930 William Addison Dwiggins (1880-1956) *Metro*. Dwiggins designs Metro, his first typeface, on a dare by Merganthaler Linotype. He designs 300 book covers and coins the term "graphic design."

1930 Wladyslaw Strzeminski *From Beyond* book cover reduces letters to their stylized shapes. Original in red, yellow, two blues, and black.

a b c d e f g h i
j k l m n o p q r
s t u v w x y z

1931 Herbert Bayer *Bayer-type*, a serifed "universal" experiment.

BERNHARD GOTHIC MEDIUM CONDENSED
ABCDEFGHIJKLMNOPQRSTUVWXYZ&
abcdefghijklmnopqrstuvwxyz ...'"::!? $1234567890¢
$1234567890 ÆEFKMNW

HE WHO FIRS
he who first short
HE WHO FIRST

1931 Lucian Bernhard *Bernhard Gothic*. This is a detail from the original 4-page booklet announcing the release.

ABCDEFGHIJKLM
NOPQRSTUVWX
YZabcdefghijklmn
opqrstuvwxyzfiflff
1234567890&ÆŒ

1931 Eric Gill *Joanna*. Named for his daughter, Joan, this face is designed for use at his private press. *Joanna* has consistent weight, though it is very legible. Its italic, really an obliqued roman, is notably condensed.

Italian logos from the 1930s and 1940s.

In December 1936 *Time* magazine reports: "In Budapest, surgeons operated on Printer's Apprentice Gyoergyi Szabo, 17, who, brooding over the loss of a sweetheart, had set her name in type and swallowed it." ▷ In the same year, the most popular types in the *British Fifty* books competition are: *Baskerville* (8 winners); *Bembo* (6); *Fournier* (5); *Perpetua, Poliphilus, Walbaum* (4 each); *Centaur, Caslon* (3 each); and *Times New Roman, Lutetia, Imprint, Bell* (2 each). ▷ Tony Stan, a type designer in the 1970s and 1980s, primarily for the International Typeface Corporation, says of his typographic education, "In the late 1930s, three typefaces were used the most: Bodoni, Caslon, and Futura. I soon discovered the balance of each letter and how one form reacted next to another. It became apparent that balance was synonymous with legibility, readability, and beauty." Similarly, Imre Reiner (1900-1987), designer of fifteen faces, says, "A typographer should never limit himself to being modern in the sense of current fashion. He should strive to produce work

VÖLKER AM 2.Ji
M OPERNhAUS
ER dJRJGeNT V

ABCDEFGHIJ
KLMNOPQRS
TUVWXYZ&ab
cdefghijklmnopq
rstuvwxyzfiffflffi
ffl1234567890$.,!?

c1932 Kurt Schwitters, a leading Dadaist, makes the *Systematic Letter*. Consonants are narrow and square and the vowels are fatter and round.

ABCDEFGHIJKLMN
OPQRSTUVWXYZ&
abcdefghijklmnopqrst
uvwxyzfiffflffiffl12345

1932 Berthold Wolpe *Albertus*. This glyphic face, based on stone inscriptions rather than handwriting, becomes popular for use as in all-capitals settings.

1932 Stanley Morison (1889-1968) *Times New Roman*. Morison serves as the typographic advisor to Monotype Corporation for 25 years and oversees the development of dozens of great faces. Times Roman, commissioned by the *Times* of London. Morison writes the new typeface will be "worthy of the *Times*: masculine, English, direct, simple, not more novel than it behoveth to be novel, and absolutely free from faddishness and frivolity." The set of new fonts weighs 35 tons.

1934 Xanti Schawinsky (1904-1979), a leading design educator and avant gardist, works in Milan and emigrates to the United States in 1936. This poster celebrates the 12th year of fascist rule in Italy, a sentiment at odds with Schawinsky's personal politics, which suggests any assignment is a job as long as it pays.

c1930s Czech typographer Vojtech Preissig produces types and designs book-plates, here for himself and a friend.

ABCDEFGHIJKL
MNOPQRSTUVW
XYZ&123456789
0abcdefghijklmn
opqrstuvwxyz?!;:

1934 Stanley Morison *Rockwell*.

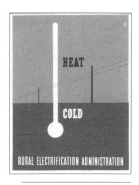

1937 Lester Beall (1903–1969) designs a series of posters for the Rural Electrification Administration. Others in the series are on Running Water, Radio, and Wash Day. Beall is inspired by the Bauhaus and designs this poster the same year he has a one-man show at the Museum of Modern Art, the first American designer to be so honored.

which will stay unaffected in its artistic value by the tastes of future generations." **1942** Isidore Isou develops his ideas for Letterist poetry in Romania. "Letterism" is an avant garde movement and its core idea is that language requires the deconstruction of words into letters. Isou moves to Paris in 1945 and affects a wider audience. One Letterist insight is that, given an abstract work, a representational element will become the focal point; given a realistic work of, say, a landscape, a human being will become the focal point; and given a portrait, letters will become the focal point. Letters, they conclude, are therefore the most potent symbols in any art. **c1945** Photographic advances make phototypesetting practical. A film negative of each character is exposed through a lens onto light-sensitive paper. The same negative can make any size letter, ending the need for optical adjustments in letterform design as the size changes, and leading to a slight diminution of type standards. *Phototype*, also called *cold type*, sparks a flood of new typefaces, most for display use.

1934 *Nationalist poster*, Ladislav Sutnar, Prague.

1936 Heinrich Jost *Beton*. This announcement poster is designed by Alexey Brodovitch. 'Beton' means *concrete*.

1938 Lucian Bernhard (born Emil Kahn, 1883–1972) *Bernhard Modern*. Self-taught type designer and artist. Moving to New York in 1922 to work for the ATF, he jokes, "A city that leads the world in the number of beautiful women per block can't be all bad."

1941 Alexey Brodovitch art directs *Harper's Bazaar*, expanding the possibilities of all magazines.

1941 Bert van der Leck's De Stijl-inspired type used in *Flax* magazine. Though fairly ordinary by today's standards, this was a progressive effort in the mid-20th century.

ABCDEFGH
IJKLMNOP
QRSTUVWX
YZ&123456
7890$.,-';:!?

1938 R. Hunter Middleton *Stencil*.

A B C D E F G H I
J K L M N O P Q
R S T U V W X Y Z
a b c d e f g h i j k l m n
o p q r s t u v w x y z

1939 W.A. Dwiggins *Caledonia*.

1942 "Letterism" develops in Romania and Paris. This 1966 example is by Maurice Lamaitre.

> " *Typography, a perfect fusion of form and meaning in which beauty is born, is raised from mere craft and can claim the title of a philosophy; for it also includes ethics, that enobling factor of man's destiny. Thus the printed word is in touch with the spirit.*" RAUL MARIO ROSA-RIVO, 1951

AT THE END OF THE SECOND WORLD WAR, the economies of the western world began to grow and people had more money, more time, and a higher quality of life than ever before in history. Books, advertising, and magazines all become far more plentiful, in part aided by the development of better quality printing and color reproduction. Television is introduced in the 1950s, bringing an entirely new medium that requires lots of

Handset type requires sure fingers, patience, and eye-to-hand coordination (*top*). Setting lines and locking them in a chase has remained essentially unchanged since Gutenberg's invention in 1450.

1946 Czech designer Oldrich Menhart's *Manuscript Antikva* and *Kursiva*, two of his many calligraphic typefaces (*top*). Menhart also drafted several sets of initials.

Three Dutch stamps from the middle of the 20th century: 1945, Otto Treumann; 1947, Eva Besnyö; 1962, Car van Weele.

1947 Viktor B. Koretskii (1909–1998) *Let's Reconstruct!* The headline is drawn to look like wood shavings.

ABCDEFGHIJKL
MNOPQRSTUVW
XYZ&12345678
90abcdefghijklm
nopqrstuvwxyz?!;

1948 Jackson Burke *Trade Gothic*, released by Mergenthaler Linotype. Because of its elegant simplicity and mildly condensed form, *Trade Gothic* becomes one of the most versatile types ever drawn.

1948 Lester Beall *(1903–1969)* designs *Scope* magazine for Upjohn. He uses collages of old steel engravings and flat areas of transparent color. Beall lays a foundation for Will Burtin, who replaces him later this year. Beall is the first American designer to have his work published in Germany's *Gebrauchsgraphik*.

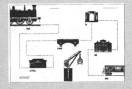

⌂ Italian logos from the 1940s and 1950s.

visual presentation. Graphic design becomes an increasingly important aspect of differentiating competing goods and services. **1946** Photosetter introduced by Intertype. **1947** "Formerly, pictures were used to supplement or amplify words. Now words supplement and amplify pictures." Clayton Whitehill, *The Moods of Type.* **1950** The first phototype face is developed as a cost-saving prototype. Ed Rondthaler, President of Photo-Lettering Inc., says, "Cutting a new typeface has always been the typefounder's most hazardous gamble. To convert a new alphabet from drawing to metal type is an expensive undertaking, and no foundry dares embark on such a project until it is absolutely sure that the style will more than pay for itself. Photo typesetting removes the gamble: a test run of the proposed type will determine its popularity and disclose any design flaws. This approach was first used in 1950, with a commercial testing of Dom Casual by Photo-Lettering for a full year before metal casting was undertaken." ▷ Regarding type, design, and communication, Walter Zerbe writes in *Typographische Monatsblatter,* "In

1949 Handlettered poster for the International Mediterranean Games in Palermo.

1950 Bradbury Thompson (1911–1995) proposes this experimental "alphabet 26" as a solution to different upper and lowercase character shapes. The black letters use uppercase design; light gray use lowercase design; dark gray letters have only one design.

"In publications of the 1940s, everything had to be fitted to two or three columns. But I was privileged to produce designs where images and words were synonymous." *Bradbury Thompson* on his *Westvaco Inspirations* series.

1950 Hermann Zapf (1918–) *Palatino* (named for a 16th century scribe). This is Zapf's first typeface design.

1950 *Dom Casual* is the first phototype face. Its use is as a prototype to reduce the risk of introducing a new metal face.

1954 Georg Trump (1896–1985) *Trump Mediæval.* Also called *Imperial* when released by C.E. Weber in Stuttgart.

1954 Viktor B. Koretskii (1909–1998) *Careless Talk – Enemies Help!* uses calligraphic lettering to imply looseness and typeset words to imply organization and government.

13 **185**

The best typography never gets noticed.

When a good ad is set right, no one notices the letters—they're too busy reading the words.

let type talk

Some ads must whisper, some must shout. But whatever the tone of voice, creative typography speaks with a distinction that sets your advertising above the clamor of competing messages. Type is just one of the creative tools used with skill and imagination at Sadler & Hennessy. Some of the results may be seen in the Type Directors Club awards section in this issue. Call us and let's...

let's talk type

❝ The realization came to many of us in the early '50s that type was not just a mechanical means of setting words on a page. It was, rather, a creative and expressive instrument."
Herb Lubalin (1918–1981)

typographical design the artist's whole personality is revealed… carefulness or superficiality, expert knowledge or ignorance, whether he acts subjectively or objectively. With the objective outlook, he will make typography subordinate to the content: the content decides the form… But with the subjective approach, the content is always subordinated to the form." **1954** First phototypesetting machine sold for commercial use. This begins a revolution in letterspacing and typographic flexibility impossible with metal type. Compugraphic broadens the market by selling a lower-cost machine beginning in 1968. ▷ Perhaps the most significant change in the post-war period is the introduction of television. Herb Lubalin, one of America's most notable designers, says "Television has had its effect on the reading habits of the American people. We are becoming more accustomed to looking at pictures and less interested in reading lengthy copy. These influences have created a need for experimentation with new graphic forms. One important result is what I refer to as the 'typographic image.' The use of typog-

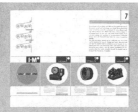

1954 Ladislav Sutnar designs brochures for Marquardt Paper. This spread is from an issue on "Controlled Visual Flow."

1955 Saul Bass's poster and titles from *The Man with the Golden Arm* has become iconic of the mid-1950s. Bass alternated between movie titles and trademark design throughout his career.

1956 Sutnar's poster for Addo-X, a Swedish adding machine manufacturer. Part of a corporate identity plan, the original is in lime, red, blue, and black on white.

1956 Emil J. Klumpp (1912–1997) *Murray Hill Bold*. Named for an area of NYC where advertising agencies are located.

ABCDEFGHIJKL MNOPQRSTUV& WXYZabcdefghi jklmnopqrstuvwx yz1234567890?

1957 Adrian Frutiger *Univers*. This is the first type family completely planned before fonts are drawn. Phototype reduces the cost of development so all 21 weights can be introduced at once. "Frutiger has designed a sans serif in 21 weights and widths, each cut in sizes up to 48 point. Univers (is) the most versatile gothic to be found in metal. It is a costly and heroic achievement." Ed Rondthaler, quoted in 1962.

ABCDEFGHIJK LMNOPQRRST UVWXYZ&abcd efghimnopqrstu vwxyz123456789

1957 Konrad Bauer & Walter Baum *Folio*. Note the alternate cap R.

1957 Charles Loupot (1892–1962) produces a series of restaurant posters for St. Raphael that become increasingly abstract. Original in red and black on yellow.

ABCDE FGHIJKL
NOPQRSTUV
WXYZabcdefghi
klmnopqrstuvw
yz1234567890

1957 Max Miedinger (1900-1980) & Edouard Hoffmann *New Haas Grotesque,* a revival of *Akzidenz Grotesk* (1898). It is rereleased in 1960 by D. Stempel AG as *Helvetica.* Twenty years later, Herb Lubalin says, "Helvetica is for designers, design students, and design instructors, and a few intellectuals and clients, and for the population of Switzerland." Helvetica becomes ubiquitous—and invisible—when it is adopted as the native sans serif on personal computers in the 1980s.

raphy as a word-picture gives designers greater creative scope. In composing a typographic picture, a tight-knit unity of elements is necessary. We have therefore had to take liberties with many traditional rules which have come to be accepted as criteria for good typography. Sometimes, this 'playing' with type has resulted in the loss of a certain amount of legibility. Some consider this a deplorable state of affairs, but the excitement created by an image sometimes more than compensates for the slight difficulty in readability… Typography is not an end product. But, for the first time, we have emerged with typography that is distinctly American and which is contributing its influence to the rest of the world." **1958** The first international seminar on typography, *The Art and Science of Typography,* is hosted by Aaron Burns (future co-founder of the International Typeface Corporation) and Will Burtin in Connecticut. **1959** Photo-Lettering Inc., in New York publishes *Alphabet Thesaurus No. 1,* containing 3,000 faces. It is a revelation and an immediate hit with designers.

ABCDEFGHIJKLM
NOPQRSTUVWX
YZ&abcdefghijklm
nopqrstuvwxyz123
4567890$!?¢ß£;:,.

1958 Hermann Zapf *Optima,* a semi-sans, wanted to name his "serifless roman" *New Antiqua,* but the marketing director at his typefounder wanted a catchier name. The forms, nearly none of which have straight lines, are based on inscribed letterforms dating from 1530 in the Florentine church of Santa Croce. Optima becomes one of the most popular and copied faces in the world.

A B C D E F
G H I L M Æ
N O P Q R
S T V X Y

1958 Zapf's *Optima* looks a lot like Lucca della Robbia's sans serif script from 1438.

1958 Slug casting operators type in characters so their matrixes fall into place and the line of type is then cast from molten metal into a "slug."

Craw Clarendon Book

Craw Clarendon

Craw Clarendon Condensed

Craw Modern

Craw Modern Italic

Craw Modern Bold

Ad Lib

CBS SANS

CBS-DIDOT

Craw Canterbury

1960 Freeman "Jerry" Craw (1917-) *Craw Clarendon.* Of his motivation to design types, Craw says, "If I need it to achieve a certain style or mood, somebody else needs it (too)." Craw begins his career as a designer at a printery, then opens his own design firm.

1960 Gene Federico designs an elegant 16-page booklet in a series on *Experimental Typography by American Designers.*

ABCDEFGHIJ
KLMNOPQRS
TUVWXYZ&
abcdefghijklmn
opqrstuvwxyz
1234567890

1962 Aldo Novarese *Eurostile,* which starts as an all-caps face called *Microgramma.* "The chief problem in creating typefaces is to conciliate the creator's taste with that of the user," says Novarese.

1960–1969

1961 Ladislav Sutnar publishes *Visual Design in Action*, an expansion of an exhibit he co-planned. Sutnar describes three attributes of design: 1) **Visual interest** A force of inventive design which will excite and hold attention. 2) **Visual simplicity** A simple design through precision and ordering has the power to communicate directly. 3) **Visual continuity** A smooth flow with rhythm, direction, and unity for increased comprehension. **1962** Newly-emerging phototype, first tried about 1910, can be leaded in as little as half-point increments, giving designers new-found flexibility. Phototype provides the technology to minus letter and line space, previously impossible because of the physical limitations of working with blocks of metal. As Ed Rondthaler, President of Photo-Lettering, says, "The irregular shapes of many letters do not easily conform to the rectangular blocks of metal type. The letter *H* forms a perfect rectangle and fits naturally on a rectangle, a *V* does not. It should be placed on a triangle, and *O* on an oval. Forcing every letter onto a metal

❝ Design is a problem-solving business. It provides a means of clarifying, synthesizing, and dramatizing a word, a picture, a product, or an event." *Paul Rand*. Shown is a selection of his work from 1961–1968.

1962 Formatt type sheets introduced. The letters are printed on adhesive-backed clear plastic sheets. Individual letters are cut out and composed on a board, then photographed. The flexibility to determine display type spacing is put directly into the designer's hands, resulting in the novelty of very tightly spaced words (and a decrease in legibility).

1963 Letraset dry transfer type sheets introduced. The letters are printed on the back of a clear plastic sheet and coated with low-tack adhesive. Letters are rubbed down as a headline is composed. This leads to type treatments of cracked and torn letters, which happens when the carrier sheet is moved. Letraset's first typeface is *Compacta*.

1964 Corporate identity grows in importance as industry begins to globalize. F.H.K. Henrion's *Royal Dutch Airlines*, Tom Geismar's *Mobil*, and Raymond Loewy's *Exxon* logos set the tone for a new, more generic, less specific corporate look.

1964 Jan Tschichold *Sabon*, based on Rennaisance types, with preliminary sketches. The design of the roman is based on *Garamond* and the italic is based on a Granjon type. Tschichold designed three other types decades earlier, in the early 1930s, but they were unsuccessful.

Would you believe Avis is No.1½?

Well, in a manner of speaking, we're still No.2. But technically, we're No.1½%. After four years of trying harder, we've cut No.1's lead almost in half. (Based on the latest figures from 26 major airports.) And do you know what happens when you get that close to the top? Your people try even harder. Take Ernie Foote, for example. A customer showed up with an expired out-of-state driver's license. So Ernie took him to the highway patrol for a driver's test. He passed. Got a Mississippi license. And was off in a shiny, new Plymouth. Obviously, our people are keeping score. And they can smell the pennant.

An example of "all-display type advertising."

A phototypesetting negative contains one type size.

rectangle cramps the type designer's style, and virtually guarantees poor spacing." ▷ The 20th century sees the split between type as a structural material and type's visual appearance. Until the development of phototype, setting type is an exercise in manipulating bits of metal, whether as the letters or as the spacing between them. This imposes very limiting constraints on what is possible. But as a consequence of the freeing theories of Constructivism and Dadaism in the 1920s and the Bauhaus in the 1930s, type becomes more plastic – formable – resulting in typographic playfulness and experimentation with the artist's, rather than the reader's, needs chiefly in mind. As early as 1962, critics complain that typographers are showing contempt for readers by developing visual riddles, a compulsion to appear original, and a disconnection between the message and the type that expresses it. **c1964** The mid-1960s sees typography evolve from "the old one-two ad presentation" (getting attention then presenting the sales pitch) into what came to be known as "all-display type advertising (*above left*)," in

---

ABCDEFGHIJK
LMNÓPǪŘSTU
VWXYZÄÖŒ
ábcdĕfghijklm
nopqrstuvwx
yzäöü œßî Œ«&

1967 Adrian Frutiger *Serifa*, a slab serif version of his *Univers*. Three weights (45, 55, and 65) are shown here.

ABCDEFG HIJKLMN	ABCDEFG HIJKLMN
ABCDEFG HIJKLMN	ABCDEFG HIJKLMN

1967 CBS News develops two typefaces that won't degrade on screen. One has light traps at all inside corners to counteract the tendency of screens to fill in. The other is a heavier weight to counteract reversed type's weight gain.

Near illegibility is used as an identifying style in the "Art Eureka" poster movement in the mid- to late 1960s. The intense concert experience, generally enhanced by recreational drugs, was implied by the psychedelic type and imagery.

1968 Figured text, a technique that is thousands of years old, is used in Claus Bremer's *Taube* ("Dove"). The form contrasts with the text, which rants various war phrases.

a a a a a ꟸ ꟸ
High   Printer Resolution   Low

1969 The first digital typesetting machine is installed in the U.S. Government Printing Office. Developed by

ABCDEFGH abcdefgh
IJKLMNOP ijklmnop
QRSTUVWX qrstuvwx
YZ*+0123456789 £$
[@!#&,]:;<%>?↑≤≥

ABCDEFGHIJKLMNOPQRST
UVWXYZ%?&$1234567890

1968 Adrian Frutiger *OCR-B* (Optical Character Recognition, *top*), a computer-legible font, replaces *OCR-A*, a less human-legible all-caps face.

Linotype and CBS, the Linotron 1010 can set the Old and New Testaments in 18 minutes, slow by today's standards.

which the entire message was immediately presented. All-display typography was defined as dramatic headlines and text exceeding 18 points. Critics asserted that "excessively large" type was now shouting at readers and that such treatment was a passing fad. **1965** Dr Rudolf Hell introduces *Digiset* and merges with Linotype Corporation, making Linotype/Hell. The *Digiset* can process 6,000 characters per second through a cathode ray tube (CRT) onto photo paper. ▷ Herb Lubalin is a source of amusing and insightful quotes: "Unfortunately, too much is said about good typography and not enough set;" "If what we do with type is effective, we don't care if it is called pretty, ugly, or pretty ugly;" "When a good ad is set right, no one notices the letters – they're too busy reading the words." **1969** International Typeface Corporation is founded. Because ITC types are licensed only to select typesetting manufacturers, they become known and valued for the ability to be set consistently anywhere, a boon to national and international corporations. ITC nurtures revivals and original types from designers worldwide.

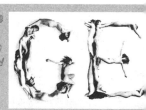

1970 International Typeface Corporation (ITC) founded by Aaron Burns, Ed Gotschall, and Herb Lubalin. They publish compelling promotional materials for each new typeface they release as well as *U&lc*, an outstanding typographic quarterly. Many of ITC's types have an enlarged x-height for increased legibility.

1970 Herb Lubalin & Tom Carnase *Avant Garde*, which grew out of the 1962 logo and a series of headline applications for *Avant Garde* magazine. Lubalin created over 100 types and oversaw the development of dozens more.

1971 Vidifont 28-line, an interpretation of the 1967 CBS News 36 alphabet, is the first cathode ray tube font developed for immediate on-screen needs. Satisfying television's need for a proportional-width and spaced font, Vidifont made a step forward in solving the problems of curved and angled letterforms. The 28-line designation refers to the number of scanning lines used to render the characters.

Belles-Lettres, a complete photo-alphabet of twelve nude models, was a 1971 "typeface" by a group of five Dutch artists.

c1971 Tom Carnase *New York* magazine logo. Carnase is an expert at hand lettering as well as type design, having created 17 faces.

ABCDEFGHIJKL
MNOPQRSTUV
WXYZ&abcdefg
hijklmnopqrstu
vwxyz1234567

1981 Bitstream's *Charter*, designed for low-resolution legibility.

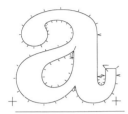

1974 Ikarus, the first program to outline characters for making digital fonts, begins its 12-year run as the industry standard. Ikarus interpolates characteristics to quickly form type families.

1970-1982

Phototype dispenses with the practice of altering versions of a typeface as its size increases in order to maintain optical consistency. Generally, a face would get lighter as it got larger. Instead, phototype uses a single master font, usually 12 point, and uses a lens to enlarge or reduce the type size. **1972** A group at MIT develops a way to render type in grayscale on screen, reducing pixelation and increasing legibility. **1974** Digital type gets a boost with the invention of *Ikarus*, a program that uses vectored outlines to create type. **1975** Steve Jobs' and Steve Wozniak's Apple I developed. **1976** Monotype Lasercomp introduced, the first laser phototypesetter. **1977** Xerox 9700 printer uses digital fonts at 300dpi. **1980** New Wave and Deconstruction grow in popularity. **1981** Matthew Carter and Mike Parker found Bitstream, the first all-digital independent type foundry, in Cambridge MA. **1982** Adobe founded. Their first offering is *PostScript*, a language that allows type and images to be combined in a single document, making *desktop publishing* possible.

ABCDEFGHIJKL
MNOPQRSTUV
WXYZ&abcdefgh
ijklmnopqrstuvwx
yz1234567890;!?¢

1971 International Typeface Corporation releases new version of Morris Fuller Benton's 1914 *Souvenir*. A version is prepared for exclusive use by a Photo-Lettering client in 1967. Eastern Airlines commissions another version in 1969. The ITC version released two years later, drawn by Ed Benguiat, becomes so popular that it is symbolic of 1970s graphic design.

ABCDEFGGHI
JKLMNOPQRS
TUVWXYZÆŒ
1234567890&V
AACAEFAGHT
KALAMMNTR
RASSTHUVVN

1974 Herb Lubalin *Lubalin Graph*, *Avant Garde* with serifs, shown with alternate characters and ligatures.

ABCDEFGHIJKL
MNOPQRSTUVW
XYZ&12345678;:
90abcdefghijklm
nopqrstuvwxyz?!

1974 Adrian Frutiger *Frutiger*. Designed as *Roissy* for signage at de Gaulle Airport in Paris and converted to five weights plus italics.

WHICHEVER
IS IN THE
HAS FOUND
ABCDEFG
ABCDEFG

1974 Dot matrix printers have pins that push inked ribbon against the paper (*top*). They can print 165 characters per second and 60 lines per minute of wall-to-wall text. The trade off is the obvious lack of resolution. Nonimpact printers (*above*), the forebears of today's ink jet printers, have higher character resolution, but need special paper to catch electrostatically charged ink droplets.

ABCDEFGHIJK
LMNOPQRSTU
VWXYZ&12345
67890abcdefghij
klmnopqrstuvwx

1978 Matthew Carter *Galliard*, an interpretation of a 16th century type by Robert Granjon. It is identifiable for its extraordinarily long serifs.

ABCDEFGHIJKLM
NOPQRSTUVWXY
Z&1234567890
abcdefghijklmnop

1979 Erik Spiekermann *Berliner Grotesk*. Founds MetaDesign studio with two partners in Berlin at the same time.

14

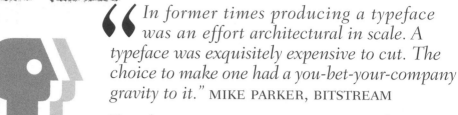

PBS

1984 Tom Geismar *Public Broadcasting System* logo. By flopping the *P* and adding two profiles, "What had been the initial *P* became an image of 'everyman' to represent the idea of public television."

" *In former times producing a typeface was an effort architectural in scale. A typeface was exquisitely expensive to cut. The choice to make one had a you-bet-your-company gravity to it."* MIKE PARKER, BITSTREAM

TODAY'S USE OF TYPE IS BASED ON CENTURIES of typographic evolution, on thousands of improvements based on our need to record ideas and share knowledge. Each major step forward – from the development of the characters themselves to the technology of presses, paper, and inks – is driven by the opportunity to increase efficiency and lower the cost of production. The digital revolution that begins in the 1980s is the most significant change in written communication since Gutenberg's invention of movable type in 1450.

ABCDEFGHIJKLMN
VWXYZ&abcdefgh
stuvwxyz$12345
ABCDEFGHIJKLMN
WXYZ&abcdefghij
tuvwxyz$123456

1985 Charles Bigelow and Kris Holmes *Lucida* and *Lucida Sans*, the first types designed for then-common 72 and 300dpi low-resolution printers. Bigelow and Holmes reduce contrast and remove details – like swelling stems, brackets, and serifs – that can't be rendered well by early laser printers. *Lucida* grows to include over 80 family members, including some designed for *Scientific American* magazine.

ABCDEFGHIJKL
MNOPQRSTUVW
XYZ&12345678;:
90abcdefghijklm
nopqrstuvwxyz?!

1986 Adrian Frutiger *Linotype Centennial*, commissioned to celebrate the 100th anniversary of Linotype, is an update of the Century family. Linotype had a total of 150 hot metal faces, and now adds about 100 new digital faces *per year*. Industry-wide, the need for digitized versions of existing typefaces exceeds the ability of specialized designers and their firms to provide them.

… und ich will bei euch wohnen

1987 Blackletter is used for both its religious and German nationalistic meanings by Manfred Butzmann in his poster. The headline reads "*…and I will live among thee.*" The image is a detail of the handle on a railroad boxcar.

A B C D E F G H
J K L M N O P
R S T U V W X Y
abcdefghijklm
opqrstuvwxy

1987 Sumner Stone *Stone Sans*, part of a family that includes sans, serif, and semi-serif versions in a full range of weights, and, like the *Lucida* family, all designed for low-resolution printers. At 300 dpi, printers render curves with jaggies, step-like angles. These could be minimized by avoiding certain angles and curve diameters.

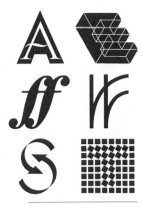

1985–89 Six logos using letterforms in unusual ways by Pentagram Design. *A* for an organization bringing together artists and architects; *E* for Ealing Electro-Optics; *F* for Faber and Faber music publishers; *R* for a fictitious railroad company; *S* for the Scottish Trade Centre; and *T* for Tactics, a line of men's toiletries.

1983–1989

Adobe introduces Type 1 PostScript for Apple computers. ▷ Apple develops the Lisa, the first computer to have windows, pulldown menus, and a mouse. **1984** Apple introduces the Macintosh computer. **1985** Aldus introduces PageMaker 1.0, a program that combines text and graphics, for the Macintosh. With it, the "desktop publishing" revolution begins. ▷ The Apple LaserWriter is the first printer to use the PostScript language. **1986** Altsys introduces Fontographer, a program that allows typefaces to be made entirely on the computer. Now anyone with a Mac can make typefaces – and they do. Over the next decade, so-called *grunge fonts*, type designs of roughly-drawn and butchered characters, become wildly popular. **1987** Postmodernism reacts against the cleanliness and precision of the International Style. ▷ Adobe introduces Illustrator, an outline-based drawing program. ▷ QuarkXPress begins competing with PageMaker. **1989** Canon introduces the first color laser printer. Apple begins making color computers and monitors.

ABCDEFGHI
JKLMNOPQ
RSTUVWXY
Z&12345678
90abcdefghij

1988 Adrian Frutiger *Avenir.* Two-story lowercase *a* and other features makes this a more legible geometric sans serif face than *Futura* or *Avant Garde,* two popular faces at the time. Frutiger receives the Gutenberg Prize from the city of Mainz as he develops his sketches for *Avenir.* Linotype releases a completely redrawn and expanded version of *Avenir* in 2004.

ABCDEFGH;
IJKLMNOP?!
QRSTUVWX
YZ&1234567

1989 Carol Twombly *Trajan,* an accurate reproduction of the 114AD capitals on the Trajan Column in Rome.

ABCDEFGHIJKLM
NOPQRSTUVWX
YZ&tabcdefghijkl
mnopqrstuvwxy

1988 Otl Aicher (1922–1991) *Rotis,* an extensive family similar to *Lucida* and *Stone. Rotis* is named for the German town in which Aicher lives.

1989 Newspapers worldwide (here from Detroit, Washington, and Norway) use shorter stories, more graphics, photos, and adopt magazine-like typography to lure readers.

ABCDEFGabcdefghijl
ABCDEFGabcdefghijklmnop
ABCDEFGabcdefghi

1989 Arthur Baker *Amigo, Marigold,* and *Visigoth,* three of several calligraphic faces he designs.

1990–1996 Rudy Vanderlans tests legibility and typographic standards in *Emigré*, his avant garde magazine. The types he commissions for the magazine become iconic of the period.

1990–1999

Adobe introduces Photoshop for Macintosh, the image manipulation program that becomes the industry standard with the addition of a PC version. **1992** Adobe introduces Multiple Master font technology. The user selects variations between one, two, or three pairs of design characteristics, spectrums whose breadth are created by the type designer. Choices may include weight, width, posture, and serif. **1993** According to the Type Directors Club Call for Entries to their worldwide typography competition, the goal of typographic invisibility is changing. "Typographic standards that have been around for 500 years are now coming under fresh scrutiny from creative, resourceful designers." ▷ TrueType GX font encoding introduced by Apple. Automatically replacing ligatures and alternate characters, TrueType GX provides optical character alignment. Apple licenses TrueType to Microsoft. TrueType GX becomes AAT, or *Apple Advanced Typography*, a few years later. **1994** Luc(as) de Groot completes *FF Thesis*, a type family with 144 fonts, the most com-

Architype Albers
ARCHITYPE AUBETTE
architype ballmer
architype bayer-type
Architype Renner
Architype Renner Bold
ARCHITYPE SCHWITTERS
ARCHJTYPE SCHWJTTERS
ARCHITYPE VAN DER LECK

1990 Freda Sack and David Quay form The Foundry in London, where they research and develop the *Architype* revival series of 20th century types. Type applications antithetical to the original artists' intentions quickly follow.

EEEEE
EEEEE
EEEEE
EEEEE

1990 Erik von Blokland & Just van Rossum *Beowolf*, in which each character iteration is changed as it is placed.

ABCDEFGHIJKLM
NOPQRSTUVWXY
Z&1234567890abcde
fghijklmnopqrstuv
wxyz*ABC*ABCDEFG

1990 Robert Slimbach *Minion*. First released as a Type 1 font, then reissued in 1992 as a Multiple Master font.

ABCDEFGHIJKLM
NOPQRSTUVWX
YZ&abcdefghijkl
mnopqrstuvwxy
z?!1234567890

1991 Erik Spiekermann *Meta*. A popular example of a humanist sans.

ABCDEFGHIJK
LMNOPQRSTUV
WXYZ&abcdefghi
jklmnopqrstuvwx
yz;?!1234567890

1991 Brian Willson *Attic Antique*. Willson says, "It resembles the broken serif type you might find in a hundred-year-old textbook. Like the Century faces, Attic is legible even at tiny sizes."

1992 Nancy Skolos and Tom Wedell craft actual dimensional typography, photograph it, and add secondary type. Initially mistaken for work that has been manipulated in Photoshop, it is hailed as examples of fine craft in a digital world in which all designers seem to use the same materials.

Basketcase

DEVOTION

erasure

Garish Monde

OSKAR

Thickhead

violation

Where'sMarty

Wooly Bully

Fontographer allows any-
one with a Mac to make
typefaces. The random
and scratchy results be-
come known as *grunge
fonts*, above. These came
with Robin Williams' *A
Blip in the Continuum*.

prehensive family ever produced at one time. It contains three
groups: sans serif, semi-serif, and serif. Each of these is available in eight weights, from Extra Light to Black, and each weight
is available in six variants: Plain, Italic, Small Caps, Small Caps
Italic, Expert, and Expert Italic. De Groot includes five styles
of numerals: old style figures in the plain font, lining figures in
the small caps font, and tabular figures (mono-width lining
figures to help set columns) in the expert font, plus superior and
inferior numerals for setting fractions. ▷ Rudy Vanderlans says,
"There is a new generation of graphic designers who, before ever
considering what their favorite typeface is, will design a new
one. I rank myself among them." **1997** Adobe and Microsoft
merge Type 1 and TrueType font formats. **1998** Adobe introduces
InDesign, its page makeup program that offers superior type
controls over either QuarkXPress or PageMaker. ▷ The quickly
expanding universe of digital resources provides limitless choices.
Handcrafting is on the decline as designers sit habitually in front
of blank screens waiting for creative inspiration.

BCDEFGHIJK
OPQRSTUVW;
OMEHIJQLMNTU
ŒÆHLATYŒTI
Y&OI234567

1994 Matthew Carter
Mantinius, featuring an
extensive set of ligatures
and enlarged capitals.

AaBbCcDdEeFfGg
HhIiJjKkLlMmNn
OoPpQqRrSsTtUu
VvWwXxYyZz1234
567890;:!#$%&?*

1995 Bob Aufuldish
Whiplash. Aufuldish says
of this face, "Baroque
modernism for the new
millenium."

[decorative ornament glyphs]

1994 Nancy Mazzei and
Brian Kelly *Backspacer*.
Mazzei and Kelly have
said, "Backspacer is an
homage to the 1930s
typewriter… the late day
shadows symbolize the
passing of time for these
extinct beauties."

ABCDEFGHIJKLM
NOPQRSTUVWX
YZabcdefghijklm
nopqrstuvwxyz1
234567890&ABCD

1995 Peter Matthias
Noordzij *PMN Caecilia*.
It has many weights, all
with small caps and old
style figures.

ABCDEFGHIJKL
MNOPQRSTUV?
WXYZ&abcdefgh
ijklmnopqrstuvwxyz
1 2 3 4 5 6 7 8 9 0

1996 Jean Lochu *Loire*,
an updated Didone, or
Modern, face. Its small
x-height makes this a
somewhat inefficient
face, but it is handsome,
distinctive, and quite
readable as text.

1997 A spread from the
Font Bureau's catalog is
reminiscent of type
showings at the turn of
the 20th century. Found-
ed by David Berlow and
Roger Black, FB is staffed
by some of the most re-
spected names in type
design.

OpenType font format develops. Adobe and Microsoft join to extend Apple's TrueType encoding to accommodate larger character sets (from 256 glyphs to 65,000) and increase their fonts' functionality. It is no longer necessary, for example, to change fonts for foreign languages, to access expert sets for special characters or to replace ligatures. They can be substituted automatically and be "read" during spell checks and searches. OpenType is built on Unicode, which allows for cross-platform use. **2001** Adobe discontinues Multiple Master fonts. ▷ The New Testament of the Bible – all 180,568 words – is engraved on the face of a 5mm (³⁄₁₆" or ▮) square silicon chip by a team from MIT and a private archiving software firm. **2002** The *New York Times* reports that humans stored five exabytes (5 billion gigabytes) of new information this year. This one year activity is equivalent to *every word ever spoken in the history of mankind.* Telephone use in this one year adds another 17 exabytes. This is proof that we are in information overload and that typo-

2001 The OpenType format allows far more glyphs per font, and thus is more useful. This update of 1992's *Myriad Pro* by Robert Slimbach, Carol Twombly, and Fred Brady includes oldstyle figures and additional diacritical marks for worldwide Latin-based alphabets, as well as Greek and Cyrillic glyphs.

ABCDEFGHIJK
LMNOPQRSTU;
VWXYZÆŒ&¶
abcdefghijklmno
pqrstuvwxyzﬁﬂ?!
1234567890æœ

2000 *ITC Bodoni Seventy-two*, a revival from the 1818 *Manuale Tipografico*. Three versions, *Six*, *Twelve*, and *Seventy-two*, accurately represent Bodoni's original size-sensitive types.

§,>) (.-(¶:-, ‡:-(
¶;-/I (;-) ‼-• ß:-I

2000 *Emoticons*, faces made with key-stroke characters, evolve to add humanity to e-mail, used by early adopters since 1983, but more generally since 1994.

2001 *Sumeria*, a digital font for a presumably limited readership, becomes available.

Hail Mary full of grace, walking up the stairs, *I can't go* through with it. I've got to get out of it.

2001 Frank Heine's *Dalliance* is released by Emigré Fonts. It is based on writing on a 1799 map.

The New York Times

2002 By contrasting handlettering with the typical newspaper typography, Brad Holland gives his ad for the Newspaper Association of America humanity, personality, and, perhaps most important of all, readability. This "type" receives recognition by the Type Directors Club competition.

OHAÄME
HOOFTN
ESAUHRS

2002 Linotype releases *Optima nova*, a completely redrawn version of Hermann Zapf's 1958 hot metal type. The original italic was merely an obliqued roman and the spacing, inconsistent and having few kerning pairs, was determined by the requirements of metal type. The new version has 40 fonts in eight weights, a true italic, a titling font (*above*), and improved, digitally perfected spacing attributes.

ЛАБВГДДЕЖЗ
ЗИКЛМНОНО
ПРГТУФХЦЧ
ЧЪШЩЬІЇЪЬ
ЭЮЯЇІЇІЁНѲЙ
1234567890

2002 Innokenty Keleini-kov *Letopis* ("*Chronicle*"), a revised 16th century *poluustav*-style cyrillic alphabet.

❝ I found it unnecessary to adapt an earlier decade's styles. If I did do this, then I used these styles only as a quotation." *Olaf Leu*

graphic messages *must* be compelling and clear. **2003** *Unicode Standard 4.0* released. Begun in 1990, Unicode is *a single font* containing every alphabet of every language in the world. A transparent program, it allows people to use computers to communicate worldwide in any language without actively participating in its translation. Called the most far-reaching and ambitious multilingual project in history, Unicode 4.0 contains 96,000 characters. It encodes characters for 55 languages, including the Mediterranean Linear B, Cherokee, Cypriot, Limbu, ogham, Osmania, Sinhala, Tai Le, Tagalog, Tibetan, and Ugaritic. The project will be complete when all 148 languages now in use worldwide are included so that anyone, anywhere, can use a computer in their own language. ▷ All of Adobe's fonts are released only in OpenType format. **2004** Macs and PCs use the exact same font files, a remarkable achievement in coding that cements OpenType's role in the future. ▷ Saad D. Abulhab develops a simplified Arabic alphabet that is bidirectional, making it easier to read for Westerners – and computers.

ABCDEFGHIJKLMNOPQRST
ABCDEFGHIJKLMNOPQRST
2003 DIGITAL MONTICELLO, 12 PT.

ABCDEFGHIJKLMNOPQRST
ABCDEFGHIJKLMNOPQRST
1892 OXFORD, 12 PT.

ABCDEFGHIJKLMNOPQRST
ABCDEFGHIJKLMNOPQRST
1949 LINOTYPE MONTICELLO, 12 PT.

2003 Binney & Ronaldson's 1796 "Pica Roman No.1" revived as Linotype's *Digital Monticello* on commission for Thomas Jefferson's papers (*top*). Previous versions include ATF's *Oxford* as hand-set type in 1892 and Linotype's *Monticello* as machine-set type in 1949. Though the differences are subtle, this newest version is true to the original 200-year-old type.

2003 Display typefaces from a variety of designers, through veer.com, show a range of eclectic styles. The Web becomes the primary route for researching and buying fonts. This reduces per font cost and, as a consequence, affects the income for typeface designers.

The Mystery of the
& Typographic Pro
Simplicity an
The evolution of han
earliest pictograms to
Cancellaresca F
Adobe Systems introdu
The Adobe Originals ty
Pro, a new font softwa
have been consistently
Adobe Systems introd
The Adobe Originals t
Pro, a new font softwa
have been consistentl

2003 Robert Slimbach *Brioso Pro*, an extensive family based on Italian Renaissance handwriting (*top*). Brioso is proportioned in four "opticals": Caption (6-8pt), Text (9-13pt), Subhead (14-24pt), and Display (25pt and up).

Twin
Cold
Twin
warm

2003 Erik van Blokland and Just van Rossum of LettError develop *Twin*, a morphing mutiple master typeface. "Formality" is adjusted with the addition of serifs (*top*), "informality" is adjusted with a character's roundedness, and "weirdness" can be adjusted by replacing letters with abstract symbols. Up to sixteen variations exist for each character, and user preferences determine which character is used.

Appendix: Twenty-six letters evolve

PRE-ALPHABETIC WRITING

| 3000BC EGYPTIAN HIEROGLYPHICS | 2900BC BABYLONIAN CUNEIFORM | 2500BC ETHIOPIC | 1500BC SAMARITAN | 1200BC PHOENICIAN | 1000BC EARLY GREEK | 800BC CLASSICAL GREEK | 700BC ETRUSCAN | 300BC ROMAN FORMAL | 114AD TRAJAN COLUMN | 400 RUSTIC CAPITALS | 600 UNCIALS |

> "We use the letters of our alphabet every day with the utmost ease and unconcern, taking them almost as much for granted as the air we breathe. We do not realize that each of these letters is at our service today only as the result of a laboriously slow process of evolution in the age-old art of writing." *Douglas C. McMurtie*

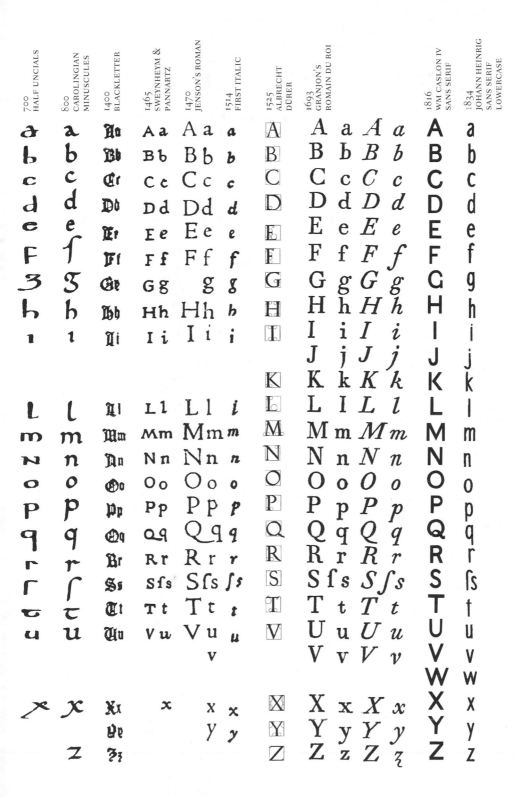

Glossary

Accented character A character with added mark that indicates a changed sound. See *Diacritic*.

AFM (Adobe Font Metrics) A file in which a font's character widths, kerning pairs, etc., are stored.

Agate Five-point type and "agate line" spacing (5¼ points, or 14 to the inch) used in newspaper advertising.

Aldine Typography that is derived from Venitian printer Aldus Manutius and his type cutter, Francesco Griffo, c1500.

Alignment Having elements' edge placement agree. Optical alignment is always more important than measurable alignment.

Alphabet The characters making up a language, arranged in their traditional order.

Alternate character A differently designed character that may replace the primary version.

Ampersand The sign (&), Latin *et*, meaning "and."

Analphabetic Characters that lack a place in the alphabetical order. Diacritics such as the umlaut, and characters such as the asterisk are examples.

Anti-aliasing Smoothing the jagged edges of on-screen digital images.

Antiqua or **Antikva** Early Roman type drawn by Niccoli and Poggio based on northern Italian manuscripts of the 11th and 12th centuries.

Antique A display type style from the late 1800s to the early 1900s.

Aperture The openings in letters like *C*, *S*, and *a*. See *Counter*.

Apex The part of a letterform where two lines meet as in *A, M, V, W*.

Apostrophe A mark that indicates missing letters or a possessive. Also used as a single close quote.

Arm A horizontal stroke that is unattached on one or both ends as in the uppercase *F, L, T*, and *X*.

Ascender The part of lowercase letters that extend above the median in *b, d, f, h, k, l, t*. See *Descender*.

Asterisk The sign (*) used to indicate a footnote.

@ The "at sign," used since 1536 to mean "each one for the price of," has been reborn in e-mail addresses. Known as "cat tail" in Finland, "cinnamon roll" in Norway, "elephant's ear" in Sweden, "little dog" in Russia, "monkey tail" in Holland, "small snail" in France and Italy, "spider monkey" in Germany, and "strudel" in Israel.

ATF (American Type Founders) The largest metal type foundry in the United States, founded in 1892, by merging several small foundries.

ATM (Adobe Type Manager) A program that accesses the outline version of a typeface for on-screen display.

Axis The primary angle of stress of a letterform.

Back slant Type posture that slants to the left. Compare to *Italic*, which slants to the right. Uncommon and difficult to read in any but extremely short segments.

Ball terminal A round shape at the end of an arm in characters like *c* and *y* in such typefaces as *Bodoni* (**cy**) and *Clarendon* (**cy**).

Banner A headline that extends across the full width of a page or spread.

Bar The horizontal stroke of a letterform like *F, H, T, Z*.

Baseline Implied line on which letterforms sit.

Bastard In metal type, a letter foreign to the font in which it is found.

Bastarda A cursive Gothic letter style with pointed descenders and looped ascenders used in Germany in the 15th century. William Caxton, England's first printer, introduced Bastarda to England in 1476. See *Blackletter*.

Batter Metal type that is damaged or worn and gives an imperfect impression.

BCP (Bézier Control Point) A handle that controls the curve described by mathematical equations in PostScript outline fonts. Named for French computer scientist Pierre Bézier.

Beardline Invisible line that indicates the bottom of descenders.

Bevel In metal type, the sloping surface rising from the shoulder to the face of the letterform.

Bicameral Two alphabets joined together, as in the Latin alphabet with both upper and lower case characters. *Unicameral* and *Tricameral* typefaces exist.

Bitmap A character image represented as a pattern of dots or pixels on a screen. See *Outline*.

Bitmap font A font made of pixels for on-screen viewing only. Also called *Screen font*.

Blackletter Heavy, angular types based on medieval script writing. The first metal type in Europe, and that used by Gutenberg. The five categories of blackletter are *Bastarda, Fraktur, Quadrata, Rotunda*, and *Textura*.

Body copy The primary text of a story. Usually identified by a medium weight and a body size of 8 to 12 points. As distinguished from headings, display type, captions, etc. Also called *Body matter*.

Body size The height of the type. This originally referred to the height of the metal block on which letters were cast. Digital type's body size is measured slightly beyond the highest and lowest points of the characters. See *Point size*.

Bold A typeface that is heavier and wider than the roman style of the same typeface. See *Light face*.

Bolding Using a computer's ability to synthetically create bolded typeforms. These are not the same, nor as good, as authentic bold fonts.

Bowl The round forms that create the body shape of letters like the uppercase *C, G, O,* and *Q,* and the lowercase *b, c, d, q,* and *o.* A large bowl indicates a large x-height. Also called the *eye* or *counter*.

Brackets 1) The curved joint between the stem and serif. 2) Squared characters [ ] used with numerals. See *Parentheses*.

Calligraphy Hand-drawn letters. From the Greek meaning "beautiful writing."

Cap height The height of capital letters, measured from baseline to top of the uppercase letterforms. Lowercase ascenders sometimes exceed cap height.

Capitals Uppercase letters, from inscriptional letters at the head, or capital, of Roman columns.

Cap line The implied line at the top of capital letters.

Caption Descriptive copy near an image. Intended as display copy, it is to be read before the text. Originally, a caption had to be positioned above its image. See *Legend*.

Caret The symbol (|) used to indicate an insertion. First used by 13th century scribes.

Carolingian script A 9th century script developed for Emperor Charlemagne.

Case In metal type, a shallow rectangular box for type divided into a compartment for each character. Capitals are placed in an "upper case" and all others are placed in a "lower case."

Centered Alignment in which the midpoints of each element are positioned on a central axis. The ragged edges of such a column are mirror images.

Chancery A handwritten typestyle with long, graceful, curved ascenders and descenders.

Character Any letter, numeral, or punctuation mark.

Character count The total number of characters and spaces in a manuscript.

Character map A table that assigns glyphs to specific keystrokes. Also called *Keyboard layout*.

Character set The letters, figures, punctuation marks, and symbols that make up a font.

Character width The horizontal dimension of a character, including the white space assigned to it on either side.

Chase A metal frame into which type and blocks are fitted in preparation to print a page. The type is held in place by *furniture* and *quoins*.

Cicero A European unit for measuring the width, or "measure" of a line of type, equal to 12 Didot points. The cicero is slightly larger than the Anglo/American pica.

Cold type Printing which is not produced by the hot-metal process. May use founders' type, a typewriter, phototypesetting, or digital setting. See *Hot metal*.

Colophon Information at the end of a book and sometimes on Web sites that describes its production.

Color, typographic The lightness or darkness of an area of type. Typographic color is affected by the type's size, posture, weight, and letter-, word-, and linespacing.

Column rule A vertical line between columns of type.

Compose In metal type, to set copy in type.

Composing stick In metal type, a portable L-shaped holder for hand setting letters.

Compositor In metal type, the person who prepares type for printing.

Condensed A narrow version of a typeface that fits more characters into a given space.

Contents In multi-page documents longer than eight pages, a listing of its sections, stories, or chapters.

Contrast, typographic The amount of variation between thick and thin strokes of a letter. Helvetica has little contrast, **Bodoni** has high contrast.

Copy Matter to be set in type.

Counter The space, either completely or only partially closed, in letterforms like *a, e, o, u,* and *A, B, C, S.*

Cross bar A horizontal stroke connecting two stems, as in *A* and *H*. Also called *Cross stroke*.

Cursive Typefaces with fluid strokes that look like handwriting. Similar to *Italic*, though looking more handwritten.

Dash A horizontal punctuation mark (–) used as a separator. A short dash is known as a *hyphen* (-).

Descender The part of a lowercase letter that extends below the baseline in *g, j, p, q, y*. See *Ascender*.

Descender line Implied line marking the lowest point of descenders in a font.

Diacritic A mark added to a character to indicate a changed sound, for example, acute (é), tilde (ñ), and umlaut (ü). See *Accented character*.

Didot point European unit of type measurement established by Frenchman Firmin Didot in 1775.

Dingbats Illustrative characters in a typeface. Also called *Picture font* and *Flowers*.

Diphthong A ligature made of two vowels, like œ and æ.

Display face A decorative typeface meant for larger sizes. Often illegible for long passages or at text sizes.

Display type Letterforms whose purpose is to be read first. Usually identified by a large body size, bold weight, and prominent position.

dpi (Dots per inch) A measure of screen or printer resolution.

Drop cap A large initial set into the top left corner of body copy. A drop cap's baseline must align with a text baseline. See *Stickup initial.*

Drop folio A page number placed at the bottom of a page when most page numbers are positioned at the tops of pages, as in the first page of a chapter.

Dry transfer lettering Rub-down characters invented in England in 1961. Their use precipitated a more playful approach to display typesetting.

Ear Small stroke attached to some lowercase letters like the **g** and **r**.

Egyptian A group of display types with slab serifs. So named because the types' popularity coincided with a mania for ancient Egyptian discoveries in the 1830s.

Ellipsis A single character of three dots indicating an omission. The spacing of an ellipsis (…) is generally distinct from three periods in a row (...).

Em Unit of measurement based on a square of the size of type being used. An em of 10-point type is 10 points wide by 10 points tall; an em of 14-point type is 14 points wide by 14 points tall. Usually used as a spacing definition for paragraph indents.

Em dash The longest dash in a typeface. An em dash is the same width as the type size being used: 10-point type, which is measured vertically, has a 10-point-wide em dash. The em dash separates thoughts within a sentence and should not have spaces added on either side (xx—xx). This rule can be bent by replacing the em dash with an en dash surrounded by two spaces (xx – xx); the em dash is simply too wide in many typefaces and draws attention to itself.

En Unit of measurement based on a vertical rectangle of the size of type being used. An en of 10-point type is 5 points wide by 10 points tall; an en of 14-point type is 7 points wide by 14 points tall.

En dash The width of an en, the second-longest dash in a typeface. The en dash separates numbers and should not have spaces added on either side (55–66). Also used in place of a hyphen for compound adjectives.

Enschedé The most famous Dutch printing company, founded in 1703 by Izaac Enschedé.

EPS (Encapsulated PostScript) Computer document file format used to transfer PostScript files between applications.

Erratum Latin term for an error discovered after the document has been printed. Its plural is *errata.*

Estienne A firm of Parisian scholar-printers, founded in 1501 by Henri Estienne.

Ethel A French ligature of the *o* and *e* letters (œ).

Expanded A wider version of a typeface. Also called *extended.*

Expert set An additional set of characters designed as a companion to a basic character set. Expert sets may include old style figures, small caps, ornaments, alternate characters, and swashes.

Eye See *Bowl.*

Face A type family or group, like News Gothic or Perpetua. Also, in metal type, the printing surface of a type character.

Family A group of typefaces derived from the same typeface design. Usually includes roman, italic, and bold versions. May include small caps, old style figures, expanded, condensed, and inline versions.

Figures Either Arabic numerals (*1, 2, 3, etc.*) or Roman numerals (*I, II, III, IV, etc.*).

Finial A flourish at the end of a main stroke in some typefaces. See *Terminal.*

Fleuron and **Flower** See *Ornaments.*

Flush A typographic term meaning *aligned* or *even.* Type can be set flush left (even on the left and ragged on the right); flush right (even on the right and ragged on the left); or flush left and right (more properly called *justified*).

Flush paragraphs Paragraphs in which the first word is not indented.

Folio A page number.

Font A set of characters, including capitals, small letters, numerals, and punctuation, that share common characteristics. In metal type, a font was a type of a particular size. Digital type uses scaleable outlines, so a font now merely means a complete set of characters. Also called *Face, Typeface,* and in England, *Fount (though pronounced 'font').*

Footnote Short explanatory text at the bottom of a page. Sometimes more useful than the main text.

Foreword Introductory copy not written by the author of a work.

Format The general appearance or style of a design or area of type.

Forme In metal type, type and blocks locked in a chase for printing.

Founders type In metal type, type cast for hand composition.

Foundry The place where type is manufactured. A foundry was originally a place for metalwork; modern typefoundries are digital.

Fount English term for *Font*. Pronounced "font."

Fraktur A style of German blackletter originating around 1510. See *Blackletter*.

Furniture In metal type, bars of metal or wood below type height placed around a form of type to fill the space in a *chase*.

Galleys In metal type, printed proofs.

Geometric A class of sans serif that developed in the Bauhaus. Examples are Futura and Avenir.

Gothic Another name for *Grotesque*.

Glyph A character in a font.

Grid A skeletal guide used to ensure design consistency. A grid should show type widths, image areas, margins and spaces to be left empty, and trim size.

Grotesque or **Grotesk** A class of sans serif. So called because it was considered ugly when it was introduced in the mid-1800s. URW Grotesque and Franklin Gothic are examples of grotesque faces.

Gutenberg, Johannes Inventor of movable type in 1450. His 42-line Bible of 1455 was the first book to be produced with his technology. It looked like the handwritten books of the time, but could be duplicated in quantities and speeds never before achieved.

Gutter Space between columns and on either side of the bound inside margins of multiple-page documents.

Hairline The thinnest strokes of a typeface. Also, the thinnest line which an output device can make, usually ¼ point.

Hair space In metal type, the thinnest space between type.

Hand set Type that has been composed one metal letter at a time in a *stick*.

Hanging indent A paragraphing style in which the first line stands out to the left. Sometimes called an *outdent* or *flush and hung*.

Hanging initial An initial letter placed in the margin next to body copy.

Hanging punctuation Allowing lines that begin or end with punctuation to extend a bit beyond the column width for optical alignment. An indicator of typographic sensitivity and craftsmanship.

Headline The title or primary type in a composition.

Hinting Mathematical formulas applied to outline fonts to improve the quality of their screen display and printing on low-resolution printers.

Hot metal Typesetting and the printing process that involves casting type from molten lead.

House style The style of spelling, punctuation, capitalization, and spacing used by a publisher.

Humanist A class of sans serif that looks a bit like handwriting, or at least don't look too mechanical or geometric. Identifiable by having a humanist axis, or angled emphasis related to handwriting. Examples include Formata and Syntax.

Imprimatur Latin meaning "Let it be printed." In early books, it indicated that permission to print the work had been given by an authority.

Imprint Required by law, the name of the printer and the place of printing.

Incunabula "Cradle," used to describe the first fifty years (1450-1500) of printing with movable type.

Indentation or **Indention** Any setting that is short of the full column measure, usually in the top left corner of text.

Inferior figures Small letters or numerals printed at the foot of ordinary characters (H_2O). Also known as *subscript*.

Initial A letterform or decorative element at the beginning of a paragraph for visual contrast and to designate the beginning of a section of text.

Inline A character in which part of the interior has been carved out for a highlight effect. Examples are Ramona and CASTELLAR.

Intertype Similar to *Linotype*.

Italic Types that slant to the right, based on 15th century Italian Renaissance script. The first italic was designed by Aldus Manutius in 1501. Italics must have letters that are distinctly different from the roman version of the typeface, like *a* and *a*, or it is an *oblique* version, like a and a.

Justification Aligning both the left and right sides of a column of type by distributing space evenly between words and, if necessary, letters.

Kern (noun) The part of the letter that extends into the space of another. In metal type, this had to be hand filed on each letter.

Kern (verb) Removing space between specific letter pairs in order to achieve optically consistent letterspacing. See *Tracking*.

Layout A sketch of a design indicating placement of type and imagery.

Leaders Pronounced "leeders." A line of dots that lead the eye across a wide space. Often found on contents listings.

Leading Pronounced "ledding." Space between lines of type that appears between the descenders of one line and the ascenders of the next. Digital leading is added *above* a given line of type. The name comes from metal days when strips of lead were inserted between lines of type.

Lead-in Pronounced 'leed-in.' The first few words of a paragraph set to attract attention.

Legend Stand-alone descriptive copy that relates to an image. See *Caption*.

Legibility The ability to distinguish between letterforms. See *Readability*.

Letterspacing Equivalent to *tracking*, *letterspacing* is used to describe general spacing between letterforms. See *Kern*.

Ligated A typeface with connected letters, usually a script face. Examples are *Cabarga* and *Linoscript*. Pairs of ligated letters are called *ligatures*.

Ligature Conjoined characters into a single one, as in fi and fi for consistent optical spacing.

Light or **Light face** A lighter variation in the density of a typeface. Opposite of *Boldface*.

Line spacing See *Leading*.

Lining figures Numerals that are equivalent to the cap height of the typeface (1234567890). To be used in charts and in all-caps settings. Also called *modern figures* and *ranging figures*. See *Old style figures*.

Linotype In hot metal type, the first machine composing type in slugs with matrices assembled by keyboard and automatically distributed back into the machine after casting. Invented in 1886, it dramatically speeded up the typesetting process. Similiar to *Intertype*.

Lockup In hot metal type, the preparation of a completed page, or *form*, of type and images by securing it in a chase with *furniture* and *quoins*.

Logo Greek for "word." Abbreviation for *logotype*, a corporate identifying mark.

Logotype In metal type, a word or several letters cast as one unit. Also, a company's identifying mark.

Lowercase Noncapital letters like *a*, *b*, *c*, etc. The term comes from the placement of the typecase relative to the uppercase (A, B, C, etc.) characters. Also called *minuscules*.

Ludlow In hot metal type, a machine composing display-size type in slugs with matrices assembled by keyboard and hand-distributed back into the machine after casting. Precurser to *Linotype* and *Intertype*.

Magazine In hot metal type, container for type matrices on a typesetting machine.

Majuscules See *Uppercase*.

Manuscript Literally "written by hand." It refers to books written before printing types and to original copy prepared by an author prior to publication.

Margin The space at the four edges of a page. There are four margins: *head margin*, *foot margin*, *side margin*, and *gutter margin*.

Mark up In all type prior to digital setting, specifying every detail necessary to have type set.

Matrix In hot metal type, brass or bronze "female" mold used in typesetting machines to cast "male" letters from molten metal. See *Punchcutting*.

Measure The width in picas of a line or column of type.

Median The implied line that defines the top of lowercase letters that have no ascender. The top extent of the *x-height*. Also called *mean line* and *waist line*.

Medium The weight of a typeface midway between light and bold. Also called *regular* and *normal*.

Metrics Digital font information that manages the spacing attributes of a font, including character widths, sidebearings, kerning pairs, and line spacing.

Minuscules See *Lowercase*.

Minus leading Removing space between lines of type to give it a more unified and darker look. Should always be used with all caps display type and with great care on U/lc display type to keep ascenders and descenders from overlapping. See *Leading*.

Misprint A typographical error. See *Typo*.

Modern A typeface with vertical stress, strong stroke contrast and unbracketed serifs. Examples include **Bodoni** and **Ellington**.

Modern figures See *Lining figures*.

Modified sans serif Sans serif faces with partial serifs to increase legibility. Examples are Optima and Rotis SemiSerif. Also called *Semiserif*.

Mold In hot metal type, the part of a typesetting machine in which molten lead hardens into printable *slugs*.

Monospaced type Typefaces in which each character occupies the same horizontal space. A remnant from typewriter technology. Figures in charts are more legible when monospaced. See *Variable spaced type*.

Monotype A trade name for a typesetting machine invented in 1887 by Tolbert Lanston of Ohio.

Multiple master Fonts with user-defined characteristics, called *instances*, like width and weight.

Neo-grotesque A class of sans serif faces designed since 1945, including Helvetica and Univers.

NFNT (New FoNT) Macintosh font numbering system which assigns numbers to screen fonts.

Oblique An angled typeface in which the roman characters have been slanted to the right, not redrawn. See *Italic*.

Octothorp The number or pound sign (#). So named because it indicates eight farms surrounding a town square.

Old Style Type originating in the 15th and 16th centuries. There are two classes of Old Style types: *Geralde* and *Venetian*, both characterized by diagonal stress and bracketed serifs. Examples are **Caslon** and **Garamond**.

Old style figures Numerals that vary in height so they blend into a paragraph of text (1234567890) Sometimes called "text figures," and mistakenly called "lowercase figures." See *Lining figures*.

OpenType Cross-platform type coding that allows a font to be used on both Macintosh and Window machines. It also allows for almost limitless number of characters in each font.

Optical alignment Adjusting elements or letterforms so they appear aligned, which is more important than actually being aligned.

Optical character recognition (OCR) Software that converts a scanned page into raw text without keyboard operation.

Orphan A word or word fragment at the top of a column. A sign of ultimate carelessness. See *Widow*.

Ornaments Decorative characters (✿✸◖) used to embellish typography.

Outline font The mathematical representation, or *vector*, of characters that can be scaled to any size and resolution. Also called *printer font*.

Outline type Letterforms whose edges are drawn but whose interiors are left empty.

Parentheses Rounded characters ( ) used with text. See *Brackets*.

Period A punctuation mark (.) that indicates a full stop.

Phototypesetting Setting type by means of light exposed through a film negative of characters onto light-sensitive paper. Introduced in the 1960s and replaced by digital typesetting in the mid-1980s.

Pica One-sixth of an inch, or 12 points. Because it is divisible by points, and thus perfectly accommodates type measurement, it is useful to use the pica as the default for planning all design space. Approximately equivalent to the European *cicero*. See *Point*.

Pi font A font made of mathematical symbols.

Pixel (PICture ELement) The basic unit of screen display. More pixels per inch results in improved resolution.

Point One-seventy-second of an inch, or one-twelfth of a pica. The basic unit of vertical measurement of type. Equivalent to the European *Didot point*. See *Pica*.

Point size The size of a typeface measured from just above the top of the ascenders to just beneath the bottom of the descenders. Invented in 1737 by Pierre Fournier le Jeune. Also called *Body size* and *Type size*.

PostScript Adobe Systems' page description software. Using a complex mathematical formula, characters and images are defined as outlines and printed as dots.

Posture The angle of stress of a typeface. There are three postures: roman, *italic* or *oblique*, and ʙackslant.

Printer font See *Outline font*.

Proofreading The exacting process of reading and checking set type against the manuscript for accuracy. Until the advent of digital typesetting, proofreading was done by specialists as a part of the typesetting process. Now done by the designer with the aid of spell-checking software.

Proportionally spaced type See *Variable spaced type*.

Punchcutting The process of cutting letters into steel, then punching the letters into softer brass matrices, from which lead type is cast. See *Matrix*.

Punctuation Non-alphanumeric characters used to clarify meaning by breaking text into phrases and sentences.

Quad In metal type, pieces of blank metal under type height which are used as spacers.

Quadrata A class of *Blackletter* type.

Quoins In metal type, wedges used to tighten spacing material around the type *form*.

Ragged Type that is set with one edge rough: flush left/ragged right or flush right/ragged left. There are two kinds of ragged: rough rag, in which hyphenation is either set to a wide measure or is not used; and smooth rag, in which the hyphenation zone is set to less than a pica. Ragged left type is difficult to read beyond three lines.

Raised cap See *Stickup initial*.

Readability The quality of reading, determined by letterspacing, linespacing, paper-and-ink contrast, among other factors. See *Legibility*.

Recto Any right-hand page in a bound document. Always odd numbered. See *Verso*.

Reference mark A symbol in text connecting related information.

Relative unit A fraction of an em space, and therefore proportional to the type size.

Resolution The number of dots per inch (dpi) displayed by a printer or pixels per inch on a screen, which determines how smooth the curves and angles of characters appear. Higher resolution yields smoother characters.

Reversed out White or light color dropped out of a dark background.

Rivers Accidental vertical strips of white visible when word spacing is greater than line spacing. A result to be avoided by the careful typographer.

Roman An upright, medium-weight typeface style, based on the classical lettering found on the Trajan Column in Rome and the later humanistic writing of Italian Renaissance scribes. There are two classes of roman type: *Old Style* and *Modern*.

Rotunda A class of *Blackletter*.

Rough rag Type set without hyphenation, causing a pronounced variation in line length. See *Tight rag*.

Round Hand Types with rounded letters.

Rubrication The insertion of handwritten initial letters in early printed books.

Rule A line.

Runaround Type set around an image or element. The ideal distance is one pica, or enough space to separate, but not enough to dissociate, the type and image from each other.

Run in Text set without paragraphs.

Running head A line of type that repeats on every page, usually near the page number.

Sans serif From the Latin "without serifs." Type without cross strokes at the ends of their limbs. Usually have consistent stroke weight. There are four classes of sans serif types: *Grotesque/Gothic*, *Geometric*, *Neo-Grotesque*, and *Humanist*.

Screen font See *Bitmap font*.

Script Type, typically joined, designed to imitate handwriting. The four classes of script type are *Blackletter/Lombardic*, *Calligraphic*, *Formal*, and *Casual*.

Serif A small terminal at the end of an stroke or arm of a letterform.

Serif, bracketed A serif where the area between the stroke and serif has been filled in with a curved triangle.

Serif type Type whose limbs end in cross strokes. Usually have variation in character stroke weight. There are four classes of serif types: *Old Style*, *Transitional*, *Modern/Didone*, and *Slab/Egyptian*.

Set width The width of a character and its side spaces.

Set solid Type set without additional linespacing.

Shoulder In metal type, the nonprinting surface of type or a slug.

Side bearing The space between the left-most (or right-most) edge of the letterform and the edge of the space in which the character exists. Each character has two side bearings: left and right. Side bearings ensure that letters don't bump into each other – unless you make them do so on purpose.

Slab serif Type with especially thick serifs. All *Egyptian* typefaces are slab serifs.

Slug In hot metal type, a line of cast type. When stacked with other slugs, it becomes a column. After printing, the slugs are melted for repeated use.

Small cap figures Numerals designed to to be used with a small caps alphabet.

Small caps Capital letters that are about the size of the x-height of lowercase letters of the same typeface. Unlike capital letters set a few points smaller, true small caps are proportionally drawn to appear the same weight as their full-size capitals and lowercase characters.

Solid Type set without additional linespacing.

Spaceband In hot metal type, device with moveable wedges which expand between words to bring the line to full measure in Linotype and Intertype machines.

Spacing The space and its arrangement between and around letters, words, and lines of type. It has been said that spacing is 90 percent of typograhic practice.

Stem The main straight stroke of a letter.

Stickup initial A large initial set at the top left corner of body copy. A stickup initial's baseline must align with the first text baseline. Also called *elevated cap*. See *Drop cap*.

Stress The general direction of a letter, whether vertical for romans, or diagonal for italics.

Style Variations of a typeface, including roman, *italic*, **bold**, light, condensed, and extended.

Subhead Secondary type that explains the headline and leads to the text.

Subtitle Explanatory type that follows the title of a book.

Superior letters The small letters ($X^AX^BX^C$) or figures ($X^1X^2X^3$) set next to normal characters. Also called superscript.

Swash characters Old Face italic types with calligraphic flourishes (*ABCDEGkntz*).

Swell The thicker parts of curved strokes.

Tabular figures Numerals designed to occupy the same width, for use in vertically aligning tabular data.

Tail A character's last stroke, usually diagonal and leading from left to right, as in *K*, *Q*, and *R*.

Teardrop Overhanging part of a swash letter.

Terminal The hanging stroke of letters like *a*, *c*, and *f*. There are five styles of terminal: ball, beak, finial, half-serif, and teardrop.

Text The main portion of a story. See *Copy*.

Text face Types designed for maximum legibility at 9-12 points reading size. Also called bookface.

Text figures See *Old style figures*.

Textura A class of *Blackletter*.

Texture The overall impression of an area of type. Determined by typeface, size, linespacing, color, and column structure.

Thick space A unit of measurement equal to one-third of an em.

Thin space A unit of measurement equal to one-fifth of an em.

Tight rag Type set with a small hyphenation zone, causing minimal variation in line length. See *Rough rag*.

Titling Type which is only available as capitals.

Tracking Adjusting overall letter and word space in a line or paragraph. See *Kern*.

Transitional Serif types developed in the late 18th century. They evolved between *Old Face* and *Modern* and share characteristics of both of these styles. Examples are **Baskerville** and **Ehrhardt**.

Tricameral Three related alphabets. A tricameral typeface could include, for example, UPPERCASE, lowercase, and SMALL CAPS. See *Bicameral*.

TrueType An outline font format that eliminates the need for a separate screen font.

Turnovers Type that continues on a subsequent line.

Type Letterforms for reproduction. In metal type, a rectangular block, having on its surface in relief a letter or other character to be printed.

Type case In metal type, a shallow tray of metal or wood divided into compartments to contain the characters of a font of type.

Typeface A set of characters of a certain design and bearing its own name, like BEN SHAHN, Eureka or Linolschnitt. A typeface usually includes alphanumeric figures (letters and numerals), punctuation, accents, and symbols. See *Font*.

Type family All styles and variations of a single typeface. May include italic, bold, small caps, etc.

Type foundry The place where type is made. In metal type, the place where type was designed, punches cut, matrices punched, and metal type cast. In digital type, as little as a single computer.

Type high In metal type, the height of the type block. In the United States, type high was .918", while in Europe, type high varied from .918" to .979".

Typescript A typed manuscript. Raw copy to be formatted into a design.

Type speccing In all predigital typesetting methods, estimating the space typeset copy will occupy.

Typo A typographical error. See *Misprint*.

Typographer Historically, one who sets type. In modern usage, one who practices the craft and art of designing with letterforms as well as designing letterforms themselves.

Typographic color See *Color*.

Typography The art and craft of designing with type.

Type size See *Point size*.

U&lc (Upper & lower case) Typesetting using upper and lowercase letters. The normal setting for the bicameral latin alphabet.

Uncial From the Latin *crooked*. A calligraphic typestyle with rounded letterforms that combines some upper and some lowercase letters in a unicameral style.

Unicameral An alphabet with only one case, including Hebrew and Roman titling faces. See *Bicameral*.

Uppercase Capital letters like *A, B, C*, etc. The term comes from the placement of the typecase relative to the lowercase (*a, b, c*, etc.) characters. Also called *Majuscules*. See *Lowercase*.

Upright A roman typeface or regular sans serif face that stands vertically.

Variable spaced type Type in which each character is assigned its own width as determined by the character's inherent width. See *Monospaced type*.

Verso Any left-hand page in a bound document. Always even numbered. See *Recto*.

Vertex The point where a character's stems meet at its lowest joint.

Waistline See *Median*.

Weight The lightness or darkness of a typeface.

Whiteletter In contrast to the darker *blackletter* used in northern Europe in the 15th and 16th centuries, whiteletter is the lighter types used in Italy.

White space The emptiness that exists behind and around printed matter. Essential to typographic clarity and legibility.

Widow A word or word fragment at the end of a paragraph. Whole words are okay, but word fragments are careless and must be corrected. See *Orphan*.

Word space Space between words. Proportional to letterspacing: if one is open, both must be open. "Correct" word spacing is invisible: just enough to separate words but not enough to break a line of type into chunks. The lowercase *i* can be used as a guide for approximate spacing.

"Wrong font" A substituted font replacing a font that the computer could not find.

X-height The distance from the baseline to the median in lowercase letters. So named because it is the height of a lowercase *x*, which has neither an ascender nor a descender.

Bibliography

I have selected the most important books on design and typography in the last 50 years. Some I have only seen; many I own and love.

The important thing about a bibliography is to have a road sign that points to further knowledge on a subject. Discovering books that help you understand and see a vast subject like design and visual communication in a new way is worth the effort.

You may note that the majority of these books are released by the same few publishers. Visiting these publishers' Web sites will lead you to many other worthwhile texts.

Some of these books are out of print. Of these, a few are being made available again every year. Many can be found as out of print selections at on-line auction sites.

The Type Directors Club Annual. New York: Harper-Collins Publishers, published annually.

Aldis, Harry G. *The Printed Book.* New York: Cambridge University Press, 1951.

Bartram, Alan. *Five Hundred Years of Book Design.* New Haven: Yale University Press, 2001.

Berry, W. Turner, A.F. Johnson, and W.P. Jaspert. *An Encyclopedia of Typefaces.* London: Blandford Press, 1970.

Blackwell, Lewis. *20th Century Type (remix).* Corte Madera CA: Gingko Press Inc., 1998.

Bringhurst, Robert. *The Elements of Typographic Style.* Point Roberts, WA: Hartley & Marks, 2004. 3rd ed.

Budliger, Hansjörg. *Jan Tschichold: Typograph und Schriftentwerfer.* Zürich: Kunstgewerbemuseum, 1976.

Burns, Aaron. *Typography.* New York: Reinhold Publishing Corp., 1961.

Carter, Rob, and Phillip B. Meggs. *Typographic Specimens: The Great Typefaces.* New York: John Wiley & Sons, 1993.

Carter, Harry. *A View of Early Typography Up to About 1600.* Oxford: Clarendon Press, 1968.

Carter, Sebastian. *Twentieth Century Type Designers.* New York: W.W. Norton, 1995.

Chappell, Warren. *A Short History of the Printed Word.* Boston: David R. Godine, 1980.

Dair, Carl. *Design With Type.* 1952. Reprint, Toronto: University of Toronto Press, 1982.

Dowding, Geoffrey. *Finer Points in the Spacing and Arrangement of Type.* 1957. Reprint, Point Roberts, WA: Hartley & Marks, 1995.

Dürer, Albrecht. *Of the Just Shaping of Letters.* New York: Dover, 1965.

Fertel, Dominique. *La Science Practique de l'Imprimerie.* 1723. Reprint: Farnborough, UK: Gregg International, 1971.

Firmage, Richard A. *Alphabet Abecedarium: Some Note on Letters.* London: Bloomsbury Publishing, 2001.

Friedl, F., N. Ott, & B. Stein. *Typography: An Encyclopedic Survey of Type Design and Techniques Throughout History.* New York: Black Dog & Leventhal Publishers, 1998.

Frutiger, Adrian. *Type Sign Symbol.* Zurich: ABC Edition, 1980.

Gill, Eric. *An Essay on Typography.* Boston: David R. Godine, 1993.

Ginger, E.M., S. Rögener, A-J. Pool, and U. Packhäuser. *Branding with Type: How Type Sells.* Mountain View, CA: Adobe Press, 1995.

Goudy, Frederic W. *The Alphabet and Elements of Lettering.* Berkeley & Los Angeles: The University of California Press, 1942.

Goudy, Frederic W. *Typologia: Studies in Type Design and Type Making, with Comments on the Invention of Typography, the First Types, Legibility and Fine Printing.* Berkeley & Los Angeles: The University of California Press, 1976.

Gray, Nicolette. *A History of Lettering: Creative Experiment and Letter Identity.* Boston: David R. Godine, 1986.

Haley, Allan. *Typographic Milestones.* New York: John Wiley & Sons, 1997.

Heller, Steven, and Philip B. Meggs, eds. *Texts on Type: Critical Writings on Typography.* New York: Allworth Press, 2001.

Hlavsa, Oldrich. *A Book of Type and Design.* New York: Tudor Publishing, 1960.

Hollis, Richard. *Graphic Design: A Concise History.* New York: Thames and Hudson, 1994.

Hutchinson, James. *Letters.* New York: Van Nostrand Reinhold Company, 1983.

Jean, Georges. *Writing: The Story of Alphabets and Scripts.* New York: Harry N. Abrams Inc., 1992.

Kelly, Rob Roy. *American Wood Type: 1828-1900, Notes on the Evolution of Decorated and Large Types.* New York: Da Capo, 1977.

Kinross, Robin. *Modern Typography: An Essay on Critical History.* London: Hyphen Press, 1992.

Lawson, Alexander. *Anatomy of a Typeface.* Boston: David R. Godine, 1990.

Lupton, Ellen, and J. Abbott Miller. *Design Writing Research.* New York: Kiosk Books, 1996.

McCloud, Scott. *Understanding Comics: The Invisible Art.* New York: HarperCollins, 1994.

McGrew, Mac. *American Metal Typefaces of the Twentieth Century*. New Castle, DE: Oak Knoll Press, 1993. 2nd Edition.

McLean, Rauri. *The Thames and Hudson Manual of Typography*. London & New York: Thames and Hudson, 1992. Reprint edition.

McLean, Rauri. *Typographers on Type*. New York & London: W.W. Norton & Company, 1995.

Merriman, Frank. *A.T.A. Type Comparison Book*. Advertising Typographers Association of America, 1965.

Miller, J. Abbott. *Dimensional Typography*. New York: Princeton Architectural Press, 1996.

Morison, Stanley. *A Tally of Types*. Jaffrey, NH: David R. Godine Publisher, Inc., 1999.

Morison, Stanley. *First Principles of Typography*. Cambridge University Press, 1967. *2nd Ed.*

Morison, Stanley. *On Type Designs Past and Present: A Brief Introduction*. London: Ernest Benn, 1962.

Morison, Stanley, and Kenneth Day. *The Typographic Book 1450-1935; A Study of Fine Typography Through Five Centuries*. Chicago: The University of Chicago Press, 1963.

Moye, Stephen. *Fontographer: Type by Design*. New York: MIS Press, 1995.

Müller-Brockmann, Joseph. *Grid Systems in Graphic Design: A Visual Communication Manual for Graphic Designers, Typographers and Three Dimensional Designers*. New York: Visual Communication Books, Hastings House Publishers, 1981.

Negroponte, Nicholas. *Being Digital*. New York: Basic Books, 1995.

Norton, Robert. *Types Best Remembered, Types Best Forgotten*. Kirkland, WA: Parsimony Press, 1993.

Ogg, Oscar. *Arrighi, Tagliente, Palatino – Three Classics of Italian Calligraphy*. New York: Dover Publications, 1953.

Pederson, B. Martin. *Graphis Typography I*. Zurich: Graphis Press Corp., 1994.

Prestianni, John (Ed.). *Calligraphic Type Design in the Digital Age: An Exhibition in Honor of the Contributions of Hermann and Gudrun Zapf*. Corte Madera, CA: Gingko Press, 2002.

Rand, Paul. *A Designer's Art*. New Haven: Yale University Press, 1985.

Reed, Talbot B. *A History of the Old English Letter Foundries*. London: Faber and Faber Ltd., 1952.

Remington, R. Roger, and Barbara J. Hodik. *Nine Pioneers in American Graphic Design*. Cambridge, MA: The MIT Press, 1989.

Rogers, Bruce. *Paragraphs on Printing*. New York: Dover Publications, 1979.

Rondthaler, Edward. *Life with Letters…As They Turned Photogenic*. New York: Visual Communication Books, Hastings House Publishers, 1981.

Rothschild, Deborah, Ellen Lupton, and Darra Goldstein. *Graphic Design in the Mechanical Age*. New Haven: Yale University Press, 1998.

Ruder, Emil. *Typography: A Manual of Design*. Adapted by Charles Bigelow. New York: Hastings House, 1981.

Smeijers, Fred. *Counterpunch: Making Type in the Sixteenth Century, Designing Typefaces Now*. London: Hyphen Press, 1996.

Spencer, Herbert, ed. *The Liberated Page*. San Francisco: Bedford Press, 1987.

Spencer, Herbert. *Pioneers of Modern Typography*. Cambridge, MA: The MIT Press, 1982. *2nd ed.*

Spencer, Herbert. *The Visible Word*. New York: Hastings House, 1969.

Spiekermann, Erik. *Rhyme & Reason: A Typographic Novel*. Berlin: H. Berthold AG, 1987.

Steinberg, S.H. *Five Hundred Years of Printing*. Harmondsworth, UK: Penguin Books, 1974.

Swann, Cal. *Language and Typography*. New York: Van Nostrand Reinhold, 1991.

Thompson, Bradbury. *The Art of Graphic Design*. New Haven: Yale University Press, 1988.

Tracy, Walter. *Letters of Credit: A View of Type Design*. Boston: David R. Godine, 1989.

Tschichold, Jan. *Asymmetric Typography*. Trans. by Rauri McLean. London: Faber and Faber, 1967.

Tschichold, Jan. *The Form of the Book: Essays on the Morality of Good Design*. Trans. by Hajo Hadeler. Point Roberts, WA: Hartley & Marks, 1991.

Tschichold, Jan. *The New Typography: A Handbook for Modern Designers 1928* Trans. by Rauri McLean. Berkeley: University of California Press, 1995.

Tschichold, Jan. *Treasury of Alphabets and Lettering*. New York: W.W. Norton, 1995.

White, Alex W. *The Elements of Graphic Design: Space, Unity, Page Architecture, and Type*. New York: Allworth Press, 2002.

White, Alex W. *Type in Use*. New York: W.W. Norton, 1999. *2nd Ed.*

White, Jan V. *Editing by Design*. New York: Allworth Press, 2004. *3rd Ed.*

White, Jan V. *Graphic Idea Notebook*. New York: Allworth Press, 2004. *2nd Ed.*

Wilson, Adrian. *The Design of Books*. San Francisco: Chronicle Books, 1993.

Index

Colophon

Credits

ABCDEFGH
ijklmnopqrstu
VWXYZ12345
67890abdcdef

Thinking in Type is set in *Fairfield* and *Egiziano Black. Fairfield* was designed by Rudolf Ruzicka as a metal face for Linotype in 1939. It was digitized and the family was increased from the original two to 20 members by Alex Kazcun in 1991.

Born in 1883 in Bohemia, now part of the Czech Republic, Ruzicka emigrated to Chicago in 1894. He immediately began a six-year apprenticeship with a wood engraver and moved to New York City in 1903. Ruzicka opened his own printing shop and illustrated books and developed improvements for wood engraved color printing. 1935 was a good year for Ruzicka: he had a one-man show at the American Institute of Graphic Arts; he received the AIGA's Gold Medal; and he was contracted by Chauncey W. Griffith, the director of typographic development at Mergenthaler Linotype Company, to design a new typeface that took advantage of the unique features of their typesetting equipment. Named for the Connecticut town in which Ruzicka lived, *Fairfield* took four years to complete.

Thinking in Type was designed and typeset by Alexander W. White.

1 SYMBOLS Henry Dreyfuss; **CHART** Visible Language Magazine **5** TAXONOMY Maxim Zhukov **13** LEAVES A Kinetic Design; **PIZZA, MORESCHI, CLOCK** Unknown **19** GH Chris Chapman; **CK** Marios Georgiou; **ZB** Michael Kwan; **FY** Xin Bai Wu; **AN** Terence Meng-Leong; **FX** Michael Jin; **HU** Melissa Medina; **SZ/SZECHUAN** Joy Scott **25** A, R Art Lofgreen; **B** Jack & Chris Hough; **C** Carl B Graf; **E** John Stoneham; **F** Kenneth Hollick; **G** Unknown; **H** Scott Ray & Arthur Eisenberg; **I** Rolf Harder; **J** Wolfgang Heuwinkel; **K** Cynthia Vaughan; **L** Walter Bernardini; **M** Bill Gardner; **N** Terry Jeavons; **O** John Stegmeijer; **P** John Massey; **S, Y** Stuart Ash; **T** Gary Templin; **U** Félix Beltrán; **W** DC Stipp; **Z** Michael Scanlan & Tom Cutter **27** MOUKA Czech for *flour* **37** LQSBTA Edward Catich **45** JE PARS DEMAIN French for *I'm leaving tomorrow*; **DANKE GLEICHFALLS** German for *The same to you*; **QUERÍA DESAYUNO** Spanish for *I'd like breakfast* **47** DUNHILL, NATURAL HISTORY Unknown **57** I Rosanna Gonzalez; **F** Scott LoPresti; **M** Carlos Oropeza **59** NYCSEX Pentagram; **PLATAANIT** Kosti Antikainen; **ABSTRACTIONS** Unknown, Unknown, Dalzell, Unknown; **HEWITT** Unknown **63** ADP, DELL, CIT Unknown; **FEDEX** Lindon Gray Leader **65** C'EST BON French for *That's good*; **TU´NCZYK** Polish for *tuna fish*; **AVELÃS** Portuguese for *hazelnuts*; **VASÁRNAP** Hungarian for *Sunday* **69** BIRTH ANNOUNCEMENT Crombie-Bourne & Kickshaws Press; **DJAVAN** Gualter Pupo & João Bonelli; **IL BARBIERI** Unknown **73** I.E. Kenneth To Po Keung; **65** Elliot Strunk & Kevin Pojman; **RECLAME, LA PARISIEN, PAPIR** Unknown; **MOBEL** Ernst Keller (1928); **JAZZ IN WILLISAU** Niklaus Troxler; **DIECUTS** Milton Glaser; **TYPE FUNNEL** Pentagram; **E** Olaf Leu; **ARCCA** Bob Aufuldish; **EXPO** Enzo Finger; **PAPERMANIA** Bob Gill; **T** Unknown; **JEG** Wictor Leonard Faanes; **NIL** Italo Moro; **PLEXIGLAS LOGO** Anton Staankowski in 1938 (!); **PAPIR** Svein Erik Larsen; **TRANSIT CHECK** Unknown **75** IRAN Michael Beirut; **VASTAANOTTO** Finnish for *reception*; **ALLES** Fons Hickmann; **LISTENING** Choy-Ha Liu; **TEQUILA** Wuquan Wu; **SPACE** Rosanna Gonzalez; **ASYMMETRY** Paul Terranova; **EMPTINESS** Ricky Li; **THE** Christopher Void; **SPACE IS** Ricky Li; **THE SEVEN** Gabriel Benitez **77** SEX, GOD & GREED Unknown **79** DOMINUS Unknown; **NEM BESZÉLEK MAGYARUL** Hungarian for *I Don't Speak Hungarian*; **BDV (BASLER DRUCK UND VERLAG)** Joos Hutter; **COX** F.H.K. Henrion (1963) **81** PARAPET STUDIES AND PROCESS PANELS Terrence Meng Leong Chong; **LOGO/CHICKEN/AMPERSAND CHART** Adapted from Visible Language magazine; **BULLPENS** Michael Jin; **HACKSAW** Wascar Santos; **ABACUS** Melissa Medina; **FLYWHEEL** Christopher Chapman; **GOSSAMER** Xin Bai Wu **83** TOP ROW Joel Mentor, Colette Waite, Wuquan Wu; **MIDDLE ROW** Rosanna Gonzalez; Joel Mentor; Danielle Roddey; **BOTTOM ROW** Vasheena Doughty; Joel Mentor; Carlos Oropeza **87** VIBE Anisa Suthayalai & Allison Williams; **COEXISTENCE** Fons Hickmann **91** LESS TALK Unknown; **MY OLD CHAIR** Albert Gomm; **HAVE I PEAKED?** Unknown; **BENICIO** Unknown; **LOST** Emil Weiss; **TWO FRIENDS** Emil Weiss; **DRUG DEALER** E. Steinberg **93** CLEAN CUT Steiner Oddløkken; **BRAIN DAMAGE** Unknown; **GLASS** Kit Hinrichs & Amy Chan; **BT** Unknown **95** LÍTÁ JAKO Czech for *He flies around like a rag on a broomstick, ie: He's a ragmop* **101** TEAR DROP Shuichi Nogami **107** METROPOLI Rodrigo Sánchez & María González **109** VEGAS MAP GRAYS Unknown; **VEGAS MAP LINE** Robert Venturi; **DESERTED** Herb Lubalin **113** EGYPT Unknown **115** IMAGINATION Matthew Beckerle; **BALE DE CIDADE** Guto Lacaz; **EVERYTHING IS** Jonathan Gray; **EYE-POPPING** Vince Frost **131** FORTUNE COOKIE Unknown; **BRAILLE** Unknown **133** CHEDDAR CHEESE British Government Printing Office, c1946; **AUSSTELLUNG** Andreas Uebele & Eicher Siebdruck, 2001; **AND JESUS** Eric Gill **135** ABCO Unknown; **MALTE LAURIDS** Daniel Pelavin; **THE ENEMY** Wyndham Lewis, 1927 **141** ULRICHI Johann Schöffer, 1519; **BODY MAP** Johannes de Forli, 1491; **BUILT CAPTION** Susan DeLuca; **POSTERS** Ivan Chermayeff; **ESPÍRITOS** La Shawn Wiggins; **CARDINAL** Wu Quan Wu; **MAP** Rymn Massand & Kai Zimmerman; **SCHLINK** Michael Glidden; **DANS TOUTES** Rob Gelb; **GRAFIK** Hermann Eidenbenz 1938; **GIANT** Erica Marks; **SIGHT** Unknown; **TUROPHILE** Herb Lubalin; **CALENDAR** Tina Kron & Georg Dejung; **SIRINELLA** Max Huber, 1946; **BICYCLE** A.M. Cassandre **143** CAROLINGIAN MINUSCULE Missal, Austria, 1170; **INITIALS** Juan de Yciar, 1550; **ABCS X4** Unknown; **TYPE/IMAGE ALPHABET** Alulema, Barria, Benitez, Brown, Doughty, Foronda, Godina, Gonzalez, Li, LoPresti, Oropeza, Perez, Roddey, Terranova; **DINING FOR FRIENDS** Hayes Henderson & Will Hackley; **OVERWHELMED INITIALS** Unknown; **GUGGENHEIM** Ivan Chermayeff; **PEOPLE** Murvyn Kurlansky; **PICTURE FONTS** Ladislav Sutnar, 1941; **DOUBLE PHILOSOPHIE** Unknown, 1760; **BROOM COVERS** El Lissitzky, 1922; **PAULA SCHER** Paula Scher; **MOZART** 40 Unknown; **WORD PLAY** John Langdon; **MAHLER** Unknown; **A/TH** Eric Gill; **PRODUCTION** Jean Carlu, 1942; **BIANCO** Unknown; **BIKINI** Fons Hickmann; **MARRIAGE** Herb Lubalin; **QUINTET** Pierre Vermeir; **MINIMAL** Igor Andjelic; **SPECIAL K** Unknown; **MADISON SQUARE GARDEN** Wuquan Wu; **EXPERIMENT** Bruno Marek & Sabine Berens **145** STUDENT TEXTURE 1 Chirag Bhakta; **STUDENT TEXTURE 2** Amy Putnicki; **LA PELLE** "To make way"; **DARSI** "To go underground"; **FAR ALA** "To make way"; **"A" LOGO** Unknown; **TRL LOGO** Unknown; **SAS LOGO** Rosanna Gonzalez; **HP LOGO** Lucy Li; **THE LAST CITY** Carlyle Aris; **ALOHA** Unknown; **FIRST CALL** Unknown **173** 1890s From the Collection of Maria Shkolnik **177** 1920 From the Collection of Maria Shkolnik **179** 1925 From the Collection of Maria Shkolnik **185** 1947 & 1954 From the Collection of Maria Shkolnik

F.H.K.**HENRION**   JONATHAN**HOEFLER**   ARMIN**HOFMANN**   GERARD**HUERTA**

TAKENOBU**IGARASHI**   OLAF**LEU**   ZUZANA**LICKO**   LEO**LIONNI**

HERB**LUBALIN**   ALVIN**LUSTIG**   LASZLO**MAHOLY-NAGY**   P.SCOTT**MAKELA**

ALDUS**MANUTIUS**   PIERRE**MENDELL**   OLDRICH**MENHART**   OTTMAR**MERGANTHALER**

ROBERT H.**MIDDLETON**   STANLEY**MORISON**   WILLIAM H.**PAGE**   JIM**PARKINSON**